The Secular Lyric in
Middle English

The Secular Lyric in Middle English

By

ARTHUR K. MOORE

GREENWOOD PRESS, PUBLISHERS
WESTPORT, CONNECTICUT

To My Wife

PREFACE

Numerous editions and articles bear witness to the continuing interest of students in the lyrical remains of medieval England. Few specimens of any importance whatsoever remain unedited, and the best of the Middle English lyrics have been reprinted many times. Yet the larger issues relating to origin and development have received only incidental consideration or none at all. The explanation of this neglect doubtless lies in the fact that the lyrics—the secular in particular—have survived in small batches not closely joined in time and place. As a consequence, fitting the extant material into an acceptable pattern involves the construction of hypotheses not soon to be confirmed, judging from the slow accumulation of really significant evidence in this century. Difficulties notwithstanding, I have attempted out of a keen and enduring interest to frame a comprehensive, though necessarily tentative, view of the secular lyrics written down in Middle English.

In limiting this survey to the secular lyric I am of course reflecting my own personal inclinations, although the separation of profane song from religious accurately represents the medieval attitude. Moreover, the typical questions raised by the religious lyric are more theological than literary and fall therefore on the fringes of criticism. But the need for study in this direction I do not for one moment deny. I do hazard the judgment, however, that on the basis of intrinsic merit the secular lyrics are more deserving of notice than the religious.

It has been my purpose throughout to avoid the appearance of sentimental antiquarianism, a fault which, I think, undermines many otherwise splendid studies of early literature. Uncritical appreciation can in no way enhance the value of medieval poetry, but it can diminish the authority of the critic. Though not asserting the existence of absolute standards of excellence, I do single out for serious attention those specimens which by sound and sense imply moderate achievement as tested by postmedieval criteria. Mediocre lyrics and metrical curiosities are represented only to illustrate deplorable tendencies or to achieve a measure of completeness. I mention this unexceptional point of view solely for the reason that too often close study and high praise have been lavished upon verse which appears to have little illustrative value and less literary virtue.

Some explanation of a few seeming deficiencies and distortions may be in order. The terms employed to designate the stages of lyric development, such as "embryo," "immature," and "perfected," have a validity limited to the context and should be so regarded. The emphasis which the notes place upon French relationships should not be taken as a denial of native traditions; one influence is obvious, the other less demonstrable. A bibliography assembled from the references has not been deemed advisable; the rather large number of titles might very well suggest a degree of completeness not in accord with actual fact. Bibliographies more or less exhaustive now cover nearly every segment of medieval literature and should be consulted directly by the student. Of prime importance are *A Critical Bibliography of French Literature: The Mediaeval Period*, comp. U. T. Holmes, Jr. (Syracuse, 1947); *The Index of Middle English Verse*, comp. Carleton Brown and R. H. Robbins (New York, 1943); and *A Manual of the Writings in Middle English (1050-1400)*, by J. E .Wells (New Haven, 1916), with supplements. Time has not permitted consideration of the verse of Humfrey Newton, which appeared in the March, 1950, number of *PMLA*. This addition to the *vers de société* of the fifteenth century, though interesting, does not materially alter the generally accepted view. As Professor R. H. Robbins, the editor, observes, "Newton . . . shows himself a typical product of the times."

The generous assistance which I have received in the preparation and publication of this book I wish to acknowledge with the deepest gratitude and in particular to express my thanks:

To the several editors who have granted me permission to reprint the following articles: "Chaucer's Lost Songs," *Journal of English and Germanic Philology*, XLVIII (1949), 196-208; "The Form and Content of the Notbrowne Mayde," *Modern Language Notes*, LXV (1950), 11-16; "Mixed Tradition in the Carols of Holly and Ivy," *MLN*, LXII (1947), 554-56; "Middle English Verse Epistles," *Modern Language Review*, XLIV (1949), 86-87; "Robene and Makyne," *MLR*, XLIII (1948), 400-03; and " 'Somer' and 'Lenten' As Terms for Spring," *Notes & Queries*, CXCIV (1949), 82-83.

To Professor F. N. Robinson and the Houghton Mifflin Company for permission to quote liberally from *The Complete Works of Geoffrey Chaucer*.

To the Carnegie Foundation for the Advancement of Teaching for two grants-in-aid awarded through Tulane University.

To Miss Marguerite D. Renshaw, reference librarian of the Howard-Tilton Memorial Library of Tulane University, for arranging a large number of interlibrary loans.

To Professors Graydon W. Regenos and William S. Woods who advised me in matters pertaining to their special interests, Medieval Latin and Old French literature, respectively.

To Professor Donald Davidson, by whom I was introduced to the study of medieval lyric and encouraged to bring the present study to completion, and to Professor Haldeen Braddy, who out of the fullness of his knowledge of Middle English made innumerable suggestions for the improvement of this book.

To the administrators of the Margaret Voorhies Haggin

Trust Fund (established by Mrs. Haggin in memory of her husband, the late James Ben Ali Haggin) for substantial assistance to this and similar publishing projects undertaken by the University of Kentucky Press.

To the Research Fund Committee of the University of Kentucky for a grant-in-aid, without which publication would have been impossible, and to Professor James Merton England, editor of the University of Kentucky Press, for careful attention to editorial requirements.

And finally to my colleagues Professors Herman E. Spivey and Thomas B. Stroup for wise counsel and substantial aid.

A. K. M.

Lexington, Ky.
April, 1950

CONTENTS

CHAPTER ONE

LYRIC DEVELOPMENT

ALTHOUGH INDICATIONS OF AN EXTENSIVE SECULAR lyric tradition in medieval England are relatively abundant, few specimens have survived of the light songs which enlivened baronial hall and village green from the accession of the first William to the coming of the musical Tudors. Without question, the accounts of literary activity contain a major error of emphasis because the materials of manuscripts were chosen as a rule according to utilitarian rather than esthetic standards. By the ethical and critical principles which governed the multiplication of literary works in religious houses, the secular lyric was pre-eminently ineligible for preservation, having for the purposes of the Church no obvious relevance. There was a further reason for the exclusion of the type in that popular song was associated with various time-honored observances of heathen origin. Although the strictest ecclesiastical view of literature ordinarily prevails in extant compilations, the clergy as a whole possibly did not regard secular singing as outrageously iniquitous. Many clerics, like Chaucer's Friar, doubtless retained in memory repertoires of worldly songs—songs of Midsummer revel, village dance, and Yuletide wassail, as well as more artistic lyrics of courtly love. That these were seldom recorded is not surprising, since monastic scribes were engaged for pious work—the duplication of homiletical treatises and poems of religious devotion; a copyist could hardly be expected to offend his abbot by entering on scarce vellum such lively songs as were in any event widely known. Whether with forethought or not, the preservers of medieval culture then exercised a form of censorship by means of the power of selection, as a poem not deposited in the library of a monastery had slight chance of surviving. It must be allowed therefore that the relative abundance of religious lyric reflects the taste not of the whole people but of a minority, a small though articulate group who created the rather artificial division of song into pious and profane, as if the two sorts were fundamentally different.

A more logical cleavage occurred in the last half of the fourteenth century with the introduction from France of a lyric mode utterly decorous and artificial. Cultivated by learned men, the ballades and other stanzaic patterns in the French fashion were intended for recitation and silent reading, rarely for singing. Since this poetry, stilted and diffuse, did not encourage memorization, copies were actually needed; as a consequence, art lyric from Chaucer to Dunbar survives in considerable quantity. That Lydgate, the tedious monk of Bury St. Edmunds, wrote in this style is some evidence that the Church considered it innocuous. Meanwhile, popular song undoubtedly continued to flourish in oral tradition, but neither clerics nor men of letters were disposed to leave circumstantial records of a form of expression which was, by the courtly conception of lyric, literature of a crude and elementary character. Because the literate stratum of the late Middle Ages was little concerned with oral art, verse in the artificial manner by sheer bulk demands attention as the main stream of lyric poetry; yet it accurately mirrors the taste only of the somewhat effete aristocracy, not of all classes of society. Knowledge of that song which was neither religious nor courtly must therefore come largely from semipopular remains and the scattered animadversions of joyless clergy.

Among the "synnes of the mowthe," wrote Richard Rolle of Hampole sometime after 1348, are "to syng seculere sanges & lufe tham . . . [and] to syng mare for louyng of men than of god."[1] The great mystic at his Richmond hermitage merely confirmed the historic opposition of the Church to secular lyric. By this, the orthodox ecclesiastical view, reiterated from the sixth to the sixteenth century, medieval song is unequivocally divided between pious and devotional and lewd and worldly sorts, the one kind calculated to remind man of Heaven, the other to increase his awareness of the flesh.

Such promulgations as Rolle's acknowledge the power of lyric song to release the elemental passions which the Church restrained and the continued popularity of those vernacular lyrics contemned anciently as *amatoria, diabolica,* and *turpia.*[2] Popular song was a conspicuous symbol of the unholy variety and joy of the world and a key to unlock primordial longings in the well of folk memory. Words and melody were an inevitable accompaniment of scintillating dances *en rond* and orgiastic perambulations in Maytime, indisputable manifestations of a native spirit unreconciled to the concept of a world utterly doomed by the machinations of Satan. Songs of Alysoun and Bele Aeliz reasserted love and frivolity and dissipated momentarily the ghastly vision of a vast and lurid gulf awaiting the souls of unregenerate sinners, who in their brief flourishing contemplated the mundane with perilous delight. Heaven here or hereafter— religion offered no compromise. A serious poet of the thirteenth century weighs the eternity of hell against the transitoriness of joy.[3] Where is now the laughter and the song, he asks? "Al that ioye is went away," and punishment begun for those who found paradise on earth:

> Hoere paradis they nomen here,
> And nou they lien in helle .I.-fere;
> The fuir hit brennes heuere:

Torn between desire for Heaven's bliss and love of material things, medieval man regarded popular song with an ambivalence well-nigh hypocritical by modern standards. He indulged his passion for sensuous melody, but suppressed the evidence of such transgression. As a consequence, the recorded history of secular lyric before Chaucer is a series of profound silences occasionally broken by a burst of song or a derogative observation from the pulpit. Meager though they be, these patches of worldly poetry, gleaming in a wasteland of metered profundities and expressions of divine longing, trace the early development of lyric art.

This study takes as its special province the secular lyric from the beginnings to about 1500, leaving to the musicologist and the theologian such related problems as appertain mainly to their disciplines. The limitation does not derogate against the religious sort, which alone constitutes an interesting chapter in the history of western culture; but the division of lyric by pious and profane is altogether significant of the medieval attitude.

No blame attaches to the Church, however, for a second division, which resulted from the destruction in the thirteenth or early fourteenth century of the happy alliance of words, music, and singer. The tangential flight of song as music and of sentiment as lyric unbalanced the complete art, and except for an interval during the Renaissance the parts have seldom been united satisfactorily in the main stream of literature. This development may be tentatively explained by the rise of the professional musician and the man of letters, neither of whom commanded a working knowledge of the other's craft. This statement is a half-truth and by no means accounts for all of the internal stresses which produced the fracture of lyric song, but it is useful as a scaffolding upon which the complex contributing causes may be assembled for examination. If the result is a more involved explanation of lyric growth, it may also be a truer one.

Partly as a consequence of fragmentation, medieval lyric

runs an eccentric course, never one thing or two, but always
a rapidly shifting concept. No definition, therefore, compre-
hends the diversity of its parts. The lyric in Middle English
ranges from naked ejaculation to extensive analysis of feel-
ing, from predominantly narrative song to wholly subjective
statement. It is religious and secular, sung and unsung. To
describe it in terms of length, content, point of view, form,
origin, or manner of presentation is to invite a multitude of
vitiating exceptions. Schelling insisted upon the "song-like
quality" and subjectivity of lyric,[4] which is the orthodox,
though not entirely adequate, view. Similarly, Bliss Reed
emphasized the dominance of emotion and melody: "All
songs; all poems following classic lyric forms; all short
poems expressing the writer's moods and feelings in a
rhythm that suggests music, are to be considered lyrics."[5]
Rhys propounded a longer though not essentially different
definition.[6] In 1903, Erskine recognized that poetry might
be lyrical in form or expression and constructed touchstones
which permit separate analyses of spirit and physical char-
acteristics: "The test, then, of lyrical quality is the twofold
historic standard of musical origin and of direct subjective
expression. The test of lyric form is first, the unity of the
emotion resulting from the lyric stimulus, and secondly, the
formative effect of the stimulus upon the development of
the emotion."[7]

Particularly in the medieval period, allowance has to be
made for songs with large narrative cores, songs which,
though recounting events, are nevertheless infused with the
sensibilities of the authors. Schelling, Rhys, and Reed by
implication exclude narrative song, which Romance phil-
ologists are bound to accept as lyric, or establish special
categories to accommodate *chansons de toile* and *pastour-
elles*.[8] Thus, the *pastourelle* is in France a lyric, but the
ballad, which develops in an analogous manner (that is,
dramatically), is in England *sui generis*. Reed specifically

excludes the genre from his definition. Palgrave admitted narrative, as well as descriptive and didactic poetry, provided that it was "accompanied by rapidity of movement, brevity, and the colouring of human passion." This amendment, taken with his notable criterion, "Lyrical has been here held essentially to imply that each Poem shall turn on some single thought, feeling, or situation,"[9] is unquestionably more useful than definitions which cease with melody and a self-conscious author. Since medieval lyric is a heterogeneous corpus not easily circumscribed by fixed external requirements, a definition which recognizes continuous diversification encounters a minimum of exceptions. It is convenient therefore to regard lyric as amplified exclamation in verse; that is, direct or indirect commentary on segments of experience, ideally marked by freedom of the emotions and liveliness of the imagination. And this definition, of course, includes the pious, as well as the worldly sorts obnoxious to the priesthood.

The *cantilenae* against which the Church railed were presumably of two general classes: the songs of the minstrels and the dance songs of folk festivals. The simple *chansons de carole* which have survived are not especially iniquitous and seem hardly deserving of the opprobrium of the clergy. As early as the sixth century, however, the Church recognized a strong connection between holiday songs and heathen rites surviving among the new converts of northern Europe and rightly or wrongly regarded these vestiges of paganism as hurtful to the cause of Christianity. In the May Day and Midsummer fetes, there was, besides the sympathetic magic of the perambulations of the "may" and the various oblatory and lustral rites, an element of licentiousness which religion could not condone.[10] Robert Mannyng of Brunne suggests as much in his homiletical *Handlyng Synne*, a loose translation of William of Wadington's *Manual des Pechiez:* "Daunces, karols, somour games, / Of many swych come many shames."[11] The Church managed to impart a religious coloring to some of the observances,[12] but was forced to condemn such flagrant manifestations of paganism as were persistently germinated in the hidden recesses of folk memory, where dogma scarcely reached. On occasion, the reversions took an especially unpleasant form, according to Mannyng's pronouncement against revelers who invaded the sacred precincts of the church:

> karolles, wrastlynges, or somour games,
> who-so euer haunteth any swyche shames
> Yn cherche, other yn chercheyerd,
> Of sacrylage he may be a-ferd.[13]

To illustrate the consequences of such sacrilege, this pious Lincolnshire monk relates the old story of the fabulous carolers of Kölbigk, of which the Latin source is the *Vita Sanctae Edithae virginis* (*ca.* 1300).[14] Cursed by the priest for refusing to stop their dancing in the churchyard during Christmas, they are compelled to go on dancing for twelve months, singing the *carole,*

> Equitabat Beuo per siluam frondosam,
> Ducebat secum Merswyndam formosam,
> Quid stamus, cur non imus?

Trans. Bevo (Bovo elsewhere) was riding through the leafy
forest. He was leading with him beautiful Merswynd.
Why do we stand; why do we not go?

Despite the dreadful *exempla* issued from the pulpit, the dances and songs continued; profanation of the temple by masqueraders was not unknown even as late as the sixteenth century. Alexander Scott's charming lyric *Of May*[15] attests the vigor of the ancient customs, which retained the distinctive form if not the full significance of the primitive rites. Though the Reformation put an end to the invasions of the churches, Protestants succeeded no better than Catholics against the folk festivals.

From an early date the Church understood that the direct prohibition, such as Mannyng's, was not alone sufficient to check dance song. The Franciscans undertook with some success to adapt secular lyric to the uses of religion, a project which doubtless accounts for the abundance of fifteenth-century carols. Another and exceedingly curious means of adaptation is demonstrated by two thirteenth-century sermons, in which snatches of popular song are invested with religious significance. One preacher, long thought to be Stephen Langton, archbishop of Canterbury at the time of his death in 1228, employed a *chanson de carole* of Bele Aeliz[16] to demonstrate that evil could be turned into good.[17] Thus, in the characteristic gestures of the dance—the melodious voice, the joining of arms, and the stamping of feet—the author discovered an incredible but nonetheless pious meaning; and to accomplish his purpose, "vanitatem ad veritatem reducere," he converted the prominent features of the *carole* into worthy Christian symbols. The wise English primate may have been incapable of a project so absurd as an attempt to mask the profane implications of the *carole* with a religious gloss, but the hierarchical authorities unquestionably sanctioned such methods of neutralizing the heathen flavor of popular song. The text of the piece attributed to Langton—"But I say unto you, That every idle word that men shall speak, they shall give account thereof in the day of judgment"[18]—was also used by a cleric whose Southern dialect sermon is preserved in MS. Trinity College, Cambridge, B.I.45.[19] The idle words in this instance are apparently from a *carole*: "Atte wrastlinge mi lemman i ches, / and atte stonkasting[20] i him for-les." The application is utterly ridiculous, though the medieval mind, accustomed to finding allegory under every stone, probably thought the far-fetched relations nothing unusual. Not every dance song was per se objectionable,[21] but the Church could hardly allow exceptions to the general condemnation of secular lyric. In any event, it could be proved syllogistically by the dialecticians of the cloth that whatever is not good is therefore evil, and a negative argument was under the circumstances as effective as a positive. What the medieval churchman, like Fra Lippo Lippi's prior, really wanted in the songs of the people was spirituality and "no more of body than shows soul." Hence, an ordinary chanson of Bele Aeliz, with its powerful assertion of primal joy, is understandably obnoxious:

> C'est la gieus, la gieus, q'en dit en ces prez.
> Vos ne vendrez mie, dames, caroler.
> La bele Aeliz i vet por joer,
> Souz la vert olive.
> Vos ne vendrez mie caroler es prez,
> Que vos n'amez mie.
> G'i doi bien aler et bien caroler,
> Car j'ai bele amie.[22]   ll. 5413-20

Trans. It is down there, down there, as one says in the meadows. You will not come, ladies, to dance. Lovely Aeliz goes there to play beneath the green olive. You will not come to dance in the meadows, for you do not love. Yet I ought to go there and dance, for I have a lovely lady.

The medieval minstrel was no less repulsive to the pulpit than Bovo and his sacrilegious carolers of Kölbigk; Latin and vernacular treatises are full of animadversions on his notorious kind. As might be expected, *Handlyng Synne* expresses an orthodox opinion of minstrelsy at the beginning of the fourteenth century:

> what seye ye by euery mynstral,
> That yn swyche thynges delyte hem alle?
> Here doyng ys ful perylous,
> Hyt loueth nother God ne goddys house;
> . . . .
> Yn foly ys alle that they gete,
> here cloth, here drynke, and here mete.[23]

This condemnation excludes none of the secular entertainers who wandered over northern Europe from the ninth to the end of the thirteenth century, delighting lords and ladies of great houses with *cantilenae* and *spectacula* and not infrequently relieving the pious monotony of monastic life with such performances as were unlikely to promote frenetic spirituality Scarcely less immune to the strictures of the hierarchy than the lowest *mimus* were the Goliards, those talented clerks who in the twelfth century wore their vows with utter insouciance and hymned the flesh in such remarkable lyrics as are now represented in the *Carmina Burana*. But this premature Renaissance was short lived, as the Church, despairing of reforming the profligate *ordo vagorum*, uttered degradation upon them in 1231 at Rouen. Deprived of the rights of clergy, they soon disintegrated.[24]

One of the first intimations of clerical waywardness in the Isles dates from 679, when a council at Rome, dealing with English affairs, prohibited the maintenance of *citharœdas* (probably gleemen) in religious institutions.[25] Despite periodic injunctions of this sort, minstrels continued to find occasional support from the clergy until the fourteenth century. There was, however, no slackening of the official attitude toward secular entertainers in England or France, as the large number of references gleaned by Faral and Chambers well attests.[26] In the thirteenth century, the heyday of minstrelsy, the traditional opposition was reaffirmed in councils, statutes, and ecclesiastical tracts, although Chambers has found evidence that one class of minstrels was privileged to perform before the Lord's anointed. Bishop Robert de Grosseteste kept a harper, who presumably sang religious songs. Thomas de Cabham, a thirteenth-century archbishop of Canterbury, writing on the classes of minstrels, mentioned those "qui cantant gesta principum et vitam sanctorum."[27] But in the face of the general disapprobation in which the minstrel was held, it cannot be allowed under any circumstances that *chansons de geste* and saints' legends constituted any significant fraction of the minstrel repertoire. The Middle Ages recognized various types of entertainers, of course, and religious tracts mention *histriones, scurrae, joculatores, mimi,* among others, all comprehended by the term *jongleur.*[28] That they ranged from mimics and tumblers to musicians of real talent was, however, unimportant to the Church. Their common secularity was quite enough to provoke a general condemnation from the pulpit.

Idlers and rogues so swelled the ranks of itinerant singers in the fourteenth century that Edward II restricted the movements of even respectable minstrels by defining the conditions under which they might visit the noble houses to which they had formerly resorted with much freedom. This proclamation unquestionably favored minstrels attached to wealthy households. Edward IV in 1469 reaffirmed and strengthened the earlier repressive policy by forming a guild headed by his own minstrels, with the purpose of eliminating the shiftless pretenders by denying them license.[29] The acts of the crown prove that minstrels, however degenerate, remained popular with the people; but the main stream of literature had nevertheless passed them by, and such singers as were left deserve hardly more attention in literary history than acrobats, tumblers, and jugglers, who have never ceased to attract the curious. Persecution by Church and State did not directly collapse minstrelsy; wayfaring folk fattened for a time. Nonetheless, the highly stratified social pattern taking shape in the fourteenth century made no provision for the minstrel as such.

However important *jongleurs* may have been for the dissemination of culture in eleventh- and twelfth-century Europe, they were by 1300 largely parasitic. Education came to free more and more individuals of the privileged classes from dependence upon wandering singers and raconteurs for their knowledge of literature. "From this time [1283] to the dissolution of colleges in 1548," Leach writes, "scarcely a year passed without witnessing the foundation of a college at the university, or a collegiate church with its grammar school attached."[30] Of course, a high degree of literacy was never achieved, but the quantity of literary remains in the vernacular suggests a considerably enlarged reading public. The demand for manuscript material was sufficient to keep scribes busy multiplying copies of poems and prose treatises until the beginning of printing. That other side of minstrelsy, the music, provided employment for increasing numbers at court. In 1290, 426 minstrels attended the marriage of Margaret of England and John of Brabant. The wedding of Isabella cost her father Edward III a hundred pounds for minstrels alone.[31] There is good reason for thinking that most of these were instrumentalists. If indeed music at this time was handed over to musicians and literature to men of letters, the versatile minstrel was a victim of specialization. The full effect of this likely development became apparent in the altered taste of the patrons of the arts. Support was withdrawn from the practitioners of lyric song and given to professional performers on *vieille,* lute, guitar, bagpipe, rebec, psaltery, and shalm; and, more importantly, to the Geoffrey Chaucers, men of letters whose primary sources were books, not oral literature. And unlike troubadours and trouvères of old, the new race of poets ordinarily did not compose lyric meant for singing. The common minstrel, who must always have been dependent for his repertoire upon talented poets, was thrown back on his own inadequate resources and had as a consequence little to offer a public increasingly better educated and somewhat more discriminating. The illiterate whom he had perforce to serve were commonly in no position to support him in the traditional style. The golden age of the Taillefers had gone forever.

References scattered through Chaucer's poetry suggest

that the majority of minstrels seated in or around the court, where they would be known to the poet, were musicians and that those who still cultivated the ancient lyric-song tradition were beneath the notice of a man of letters. Chaucer confesses absolutely no indebtedness to popular lyric, although for artistic purposes he intercalates several snatches in the *Canterbury Tales*. In the *Squire's Tale*, Chaucer wrote, "Whil that this kyng sit thus in his nobleye,/ Herknynge his mynstralles hir thynges pleye,"[32] and further in the same tale,

> Toforn hym gooth the loude mynstralcye,
> Til he cam to his chambre of parementz,
> Ther as they sownen diverse instrumentz,
> That it is lyk an hevene for to heere.[33]

These observations do not of course prove that the instruments were not used for accompanying lyric, but a detailed passage from the *House of Fame* strongly supports the suspicion that in courtly circles the minstrel had become chiefly a musician:

> Many thousand tymes twelve,
> That maden lowde mynstralcies
> In cornemuse and shalemyes,
> And many other maner pipe,
> That craftely begunne to pipe,
> Bothe in doucet and in rede,
> That ben at festes with the brede;
> And many flowte and liltyng horn,
> And pipes made of grene corn,
> As han thise lytel herde-gromes,
> That kepen bestis in the bromes.[34]

Chaucer may not have endorsed the Parson's narrow view that by "mynstralcie . . . a man is stired the moore to delices of luxurie,"[35] yet the collector of the customs of the port of London shares with the learned poets of his generation and the next a sedateness and modesty, by which they are distinguished from the less restrained trouvères and *clerici vagantes* of the twelfth century. This is not to say that Chaucer, Gower, and Lydgate are egregiously ascetic, although the religious strain in all three demands recognition. Not one of them is capable of the full-throated lyric cry, and in their ballades they manage to avoid the appearance of reality, maintaining a kind of detachment which lends no credibility to their exclamations of love-longing. This is less the decorum of *amour courtois* than a pious circumspection, perhaps the result of an ingrained suspicion that frank, emotional song was indeed Devil's work. This supposition need not be extended so far as to make a monk of Chaucer; after all, he wrote the *Miller's Tale*. One may nonetheless insist on the refined tone of literature after 1350; the learned poets dealt more confidently and happily with shadow than with substance.

Sometime between 1300 and the rise of Chaucer, the ancient lyric-song relationship dissolved in the main literary stream, the concept of song without music emerging as one of several results.[36] The Harleian lyrics may be in English the last flowers of a tradition stretching far beyond troubadours and trouvères to a period remote in the cultural history of western European peoples. Gaston Paris considered the Poitou-Limousin region as the incubator of those special lyrical forms which were cultivated first in Provence and later in northern France.[37] Indeed, some such theory of development is needed to explain the perfected art of the first troubadour, William, Count of Poitiers, who flourished at the beginning of the twelfth century. Scant remains of *caroles* in such longer works as *Guillaume de Dole* and *Le Roman de la Violette*, however, point the way back from sophisticated *pastourelles* and chansons to dance song at the primitive *fêtes de mai*. Until the end of the thirteenth century, French poets generally honored the ancient usage and kept words and music together.

Schooled in the old lyric-song tradition, troubadours and trouvères provided musical settings for their poems, achieving in a sense the Miltonic ideal of "soft *Lydian* Aires, married to immortal verse." These high-born artists were first of all poets, and the simple melodies which they composed were subordinate to the subtle statements of their chansons. Though the notation is not altogether clear, musicologists do not regard the music as technically advanced. To Wooldridge, the tunes sound like "jog-trot," but he concedes that a better understanding of the music may well vindicate the trouvères on this count.[38] Technical complexity of the sort appearing in learned music at the end of the thirteenth century is hardly to be expected from the like of Thibaut de Champagne and Conon de Béthune. Adam de la Halle attempted polyphony, but he was a poet of the decline and half a professional anyway. Troubadours and trouvères were ideally neither instrumentalists nor vocalists; instead, they entrusted their lyrics to *jongleurs* (Prov. *joglars*) who sang them far and wide. Thus was knowledge of the inspired verse of Bernart de Ventadour, Bertran de Born, Arnaut Daniel, and Guiraut Bornelh borne into Italy, Spain, and northern France.

Poetry of this kind, analytical and metaphorical, obviously could not tolerate prominent instrumental or vocal effects. Granted a high auditory receptiveness, the medieval ear was still incapable of attending simultaneously to intrusive musical accompaniment and the subtle turns of poetic thought. As long as melody remained a patient and discreet handmaiden of lyric, the partnership was ideal; but this unequal union could not endure on the learned level, where music was rapidly gaining independent excellence. Guillaume de Machaut, perhaps the best musician of France as early as 1324[39] and for several decades after, brought to poetry a knowledge of melody which his predecessors did not possess. It is no gain for literature that his music incorporates the most advanced techniques of the period,[40] since the sentiment is commonplace, the expression vague. Though the canon of Rheims doubtless considered himself a latter-day trouvère, the spirit of the old genres of unrestricted form largely escaped him. In the first half of the fourteenth century, moreover, the archetypes of most modern musical instruments were in use and, even when comparatively unrefined, were nevertheless suitable for ensembles.[41] This increased musical activity was matched by the emergence of the literary figure, who sought an audience through the medium of books. These developments were inevitably inimical to the tradition of lyric provided with simple melody and rather quickly drove it out of the main stream.

From the time of Chaucer until the Renaissance, extant secular lyric is generally of two sorts: the amorous complaint and compliment of courtiers and others, who, like Lydgate, affected the artificial manner; and the semipopular carol— the first designed for recitation, the second for singing. Saving a few indelicate carols and several miscellaneous songs, nothing can be claimed confidently for the minstrel from the imposing bulk of verse which has survived. The simplest explanation is that popular song was so lightly regarded that scribes were unwilling to give it space on precious parchment or that it was seldom thought necessary to write down a piece which everybody knew by heart. Now the verse of Lydgate and Hoccleve, for example, had a good chance to survive, because it was meant to be read, as well as recited. It was written down in the first place and frequently multiplied by copyists, as fifteenth-century manuscripts attest.[42] Too, courtly lyrics must often have been copied as they went the rounds of society. On the other hand, those who esteemed popular song undoubtedly memorized much of what they heard, but felt no compulsion to set down the words of a song. A song without notation would have had for the literate few no special significance. There is, moreover, no reason to think that wandering singers would often find occasion to commit their repertoires to writing, although the fragments of MS. Rawlinson D. 913 are a precious exception. Medieval minstrelsy is then poorly understood, neither repertoires nor circumstantial accounts of performances having got into the records. The names of minstrels survive in considerable numbers,[43] yet not one is to be identified with an extant song, unless it be Minot.

That there was an abundance of minstrel song to the end of the Middle Ages can hardly be doubted, though it may be questioned whether the lyrics were of high literary quality. No such talented group as the trouvères is known to have existed in England, and it is improbable that the learned composers to whom the Harleian lyrics are owing employed a *jongleur* class to disseminate their handiwork. These poets, possibly monastic ones, were themselves transitional, having reached a stage not far removed from the practice of letters as it has been understood since Chaucer. Still, such minstrels as remained would have appropriated songs from any source whatsoever, asking the leave of none, and failing that would have relied upon their own slender talents. It is impracticable to judge medieval minstrel song from the fragments which have come down, although such lively pieces as might be expected to divert a wayside audience are unimpressive as literature. Since the passing of the communal dogmatists and the folk-song authority Cecil Sharp, the inventive faculty of the fabulous folk has not been highly valued. A British folklorist has recently reaffirmed the view that traditional lyric—words and music—is popular by destination only. By his formula, medieval culture issued from manor house and church to find secure lodging among the illiterate. "The only poets and musicians from among the peasantry," Raglan remarks, "were clerics, and their culture was not of the folk, but of the monasteries and universities."[44] For a century or two after the Conquest a degree of homogeneity may be claimed for British communities; in the fifteenth century, stratification by education left the unlearned no conspicuous part in the making of literature, if they ever had any. Such lyric as time has preserved from the transition period (and there is an abundance) would be generally unpalatable to the folk, who are often discriminating if not creative. On any account, the character of popular lyric at the end of the Middle Ages remains largely undetermined.

Four hundred years of poetical and musical activity on English soil have left fewer than three hundred lyrics of all kinds—religious, didactic, and secular; and less than one third of the total number preserved between the *Canute Song,* composed after 1000, and the *Complaint of Chaucer to His Purse* (1399) may be reckoned in any way *amatoria, diabolica,* or *turpia.* Lyric song—particularly the secular kind—fared a great deal better in Provence, France, and Germany. Nearly five hundred troubadours are known at least by name, and more than twenty-five hundred lyrics have survived, many with music.[45] More than a hundred French poets are known to have lived before 1300, and the early lyric is represented in upwards of fifty *chansonniers.*[46] Indeed, the Latin and German lyrics of the *Carmina Burana* far exceed the Middle English total of secular lyrics from before 1400. One hundred and seventeen poets have been identified for the English period from 1050 to 1500,[47] but few of these wrote lyrics, and even fewer lived before 1300. Though England was a sparsely settled country until the Renaissance, it cannot be allowed that these figures are a true index to the production of lyric song in the island.

For example, a leaf from a minstrel's book, luckily bound up with the miscellaneous matter of MS. Rawlinson D.913, affords a brief view of the song esteemed by the populace about 1350.[48] Although disappointingly fragmentary, these remains are nevertheless the fullest and probably the most authentic record of popular song in Middle English. As ill fortune would have it, the two least corrupt of the eleven texts are French—one a variety of *chanson de mal mariée* and the other a dance song. The pieces in general lack the enriched texture of the Harleian lyrics, although *Maiden in the mor lay* by its exquisite diction recalls the perished wealth of the fourteenth century:

> Maiden in the mor lay, in the mor lay,
> seuenyst fulle, seuenist fulle,
> Maiden in the mor lay, in the mor lay,
> seuenistes fulle ant a day.
> Welle wat hire mete, wat was hire mete?
> the primerole ant the—, the primerole ant the—;
> Welle was hire mete, wat was hire mete?
> the primerole ant the violet.
> Welle wat was hire dryng?
> The chelde water of the welle spring.
> Welle was hire bour, wat was hire bour?
> The rede rose ante lilie flour.

A corrupt drinking song has some historical interest as the first of its kind in English, and two other lyrics represented only by opening lines begin with intriguing images: "al nist by the rose, rose;/ al nist bi the rose i lay" and "Al gold Ionet is thin her." Even less informative are the scraps from the *Red Book of Ossory*,[49] though these appear to be of a light-hearted kind with the Rawlinson.

That an abundance of song was cultivated on the popular level at the end of the Middle Ages is strongly argued by extensive lists of titles in *Colkelbie Sow*, a narrative poem of the Bannatyne Manuscript; and the *Complaynt of Scotland* (1549).[50] Several of the latter group have been identified with extant sixteenth-century songs, and the "hunttis of cheuet" and the "battel of the hayrlau" are possibly the well-known ballads.[51] The *Complaynt* list is demonstrably heterogeneous, and a number of the songs are hardly to be considered popular. Little courtliness is suggested, however, by the titles sung and played at the gathering of rustics in *Colkelbie Sow*. This passage of the homely narrative appears in every way to be an authentic slice of ancient Scottish social life:

> A maistir swynhird Swanky,
> And his cousing Copyn Cull,
> Fowll of bellis fulfull,
> Led the dance and began
> play us *Joly lemmane* . . .[52]

Was this a fiddle tune like *Guilderoy* or the accompaniment for reels on the order of the *Flowers of Edinburgh, Glasgow Lasses*, and the *Mountain Hornpipe?* At another point, ring dancing is clearly indicated: "Than all arrayit in a ring/ Dansit *My deir derling.*" One should certainly like to know the air *My deir derling*, as well as *Trolly lolly; Cok craw thow quhill day; Twysbank and Terway; Joly lemman, dawis it nocht day; Be yon wodsyd; Late, laite on evinnyngis;* and *Lulalow, lute cok*, to mention a few. Very likely knowledge of these fifty songs, besides furnishing information about the singing habits of the folk at the end of the Middle Ages, would throw light on popular lyric in vogue even a century earlier. Beyond a few songs which are examined elsewhere, there is little more direct indication of the oral literature to which the Church took violent exception.

There remains one other resource—popular balladry—demanding notice, even if the evidence is extremely difficult to interpret. The English ballad is in most instances later than the Middle Ages, and it is characteristically manipulated in an unlyrical way. Nevertheless, in their introductions numerous specimens acknowledge a kinship with medieval lyric that chance alone does not suffice to explain. A point of contact between 1200 and 1500 is a permissible assumption, although the circumstances surrounding the exchange of conventions are and will probably remain unknown. As a genre checked in its development by falling out of the main current, the ballad would be on any basis a jealous guardian of its conspicuous features. The fracture and subsequent tangential flight of the ballad as form came of necessity before song of the developing stream suppressed the details of its pre-Chaucerian history. Whatever the intermediate stages in the evolution of the so-called Child type, numerous ballad introductions confess relationship to the *pastourelle, chanson de toile,* and even the ubiquitous nature prelude, one of the most persistent conventions in medieval literature. Whether the relationship is actually indebtedness remains unclear. Certainly the nature settings, which occur in genres as diverse as *sirvente* and romance, need not be referred directly to lyric origins. The immediate value of the connection is to suggest the higher incidence of secular lyrical forms than the meager remains allow.

Thus, no fewer than three ballads—*Crow and Pie,* the *Baffled Knight,* and the *Knight and Shepherd's Daughter*—accord with the scheme of the normal *pastourelle,*[53] and a fourth, the *Broom of Cowdenknows,* recalls the French genre in many of its details. In France likewise, the old type survived in oral tradition,[54] although not in the ballad form; French *pastourelles* of the transition have a deal of tra-la-la and various other lyric frills. Yet other ballads with "riding out" introductions fall into classes designated as *chanson dramatique* and *chanson à personnages,*[55] which are both comprehended by Chambers' general term, *chanson d'aventure,*[56] applicable alike to songs in which the poet is merely an observer and those in which he acts a part.[57] It should be emphasized, however, that many of these speci-

mens are not *pastourelles* or *chansons de mal mariée* and
display a connection with the types only in the opening.
The portrait of a noble lady busied at needlework in her
chamber is the commonplace introduction of several *chansons de toile* and of nine ballads.[58] Were this the only
instance of marked similarity between French and English
song, the relation should be dismissed as a product of pure
chance; however, the demonstrated fondness of medieval
England for imported lyric urges consideration.   Sir Edmund K. Chambers, who favors a Scandinavian origin for
English balladry, intimates that the weaving song convention was transmitted to England by way of Denmark.[59] On
the other hand, the *carole*, not the lyrical romance, has
usually been regarded as the French form which migrated
to Denmark in the twelfth century and there acquired a
narrative framework.[60]   Sir Edmund's view requires acceptance, then, of an unlikely occurrence, that the *chanson
de toile*, along with the *carole*, was taken over by the Danes,
transformed into ballad, and exported to Scotland.   An
alternative explanation, which surely occurred to the great
English scholar, that the weaving song was brought in
directly by Normans, lacks substantial support.[61]   It is not
evident from medieval remains that the *chanson de toile*,
oldest of indigeneous genres of northern France, was ever
cultivated in England; moreover, it was long vanished in
France before the rise of English lyric.   The resemblances,
nevertheless, are stronger than the theories which seek to
explain them.
The *chansons de toile* commonly represent the woman's
point of view.   She is normally unhappy in love, though
for a variety of reasons—opposition of parents, separation,
misunderstanding.   Aside from the introduction, English
ballads do not closely resemble the French type; only *Burd
Ellen and Young Tamlane*, as far as it goes, vaguely recalls
the autochthonous weaving songs:

Burd Ellen sits in her bower windowe,
With a double laddy double, and for the
double dow
Twisting the red silk and the blue.
With the double rose and the May-hay.
Till once there by cam Young Tamlane:
'Come light, oh light, and rock your young son.'

Tamlane rejects the invitation and goes away to sea with
Ellen's curse upon him. Almost invariably, thé woman of
the ballad is "sewing at her silken seam," though her French
counterpart may be sewing on any garment:

Bele Yolanz en ses chambres seoit,
d'un boen samiz une robe cosoit,
a son ami tramettre la voloit.
en sospirant ceste chancon chantoit.
'dex, tant est douz li nons d'amors:
ja n'en cuidai sentir dolors.' etc.[62]

Trans. Lovely Yolanz sat in her chambers; of a good satin
a garment she sewed. She wished to send it to her
friend. Sighing, this song she sang: "God, how
sweet is the name of love; I never expected to feel
sadness from it."

The persistent "bele" of the chansons is matched in English
by "lady"—Lady Isabel, Lady Margaret, Lady Alice. Other
ballads use similar introductions, but do not strengthen
the connection between the twelfth-century French genre
and English balladry, which is at best tenuous.

These scattered traces merely confirm what everyone has
suspected: an unintentional alliance of the prejudiced and
the thoughtless has very nearly obliterated the lyric wealth
of medieval Britain.

As it is sketchily revealed, Middle English lyric acknowl-
edges the operation of two principles—amplification and
diversification—by which the unelaborated exclamation of
primitive song develops into art forms. The concept of a

simple, emotional statement as the germ of English—and indeed of western European—lyric proceeds of necessity from deduction and analogy, for the significant details of the history of early song in Britain have been suppressed by successive layers of tradition. English historiographers, moreover, have been utterly careless of oral literature: no song older than the thirteenth century survives with notation, and such fragments as antedate 1200 are of limited usefulness. Although the primitive sort may not now be recovered from the decayed memories of folk dead long ago, the evolutionary process can be plotted in three classes of lyrics—embryo, immature, and perfected—which, though remote in time from the dawn of art, fairly represent the significant stages of development.

The embryo stage in its early and hypothetical phase (that is, prehistoric) receives some confirmation from the practice of retarded cultures, where the emotional utterance, often bound to manual accompaniment, has not passed beyond exclamation. On this level, feeling is generally implied rather than stated, and the song proper is usually functional. Of course, all art is functional to a degree, but much primitive song has particular uses in ceremony and is probably not often regarded as a legitimate object of esthetic contemplation apart from ritualistic exercises. The temptation to vary and elaborate is checked by certain stable factors in the whole exhibition, whether dance, mimetic posturing, or propitiatory offering. Once ritual is fixed, it acquires validity in the conservative mind of the folk, and alteration is resisted. Some change is inevitable, but the principle nevertheless holds that ritual song, whether checked in print, like the *Doxology* and the *Te Deum*, or preserved only in memory, tends to hold its shape.

Besides the functional sort, there is a numerous class of personal songs, in which feeling is no more communal than composition. Many lyrics are intended, sometimes exclusively, for the use of those who composed them, as Miss Pound has remarked,[63] and others are solos, which, if the property of all, nevertheless express personal emotion. A more individualized statement could scarcely be imagined than a Pawnee woman's welcome to returning warriors, "Ah, now I have seen you." The sense of joyful surprise is borne by the exclamatory "Ah!" (Pawnee *hi-a*), a high, undulating cry, in length of utterance constituting half the song.[64] Hardly more elaborate is a song of love-longing from the Chippewa, which man or maid might sing hour on hour, changing the gender of the agglutinated compounds to suit his or her sex:

> Why should
> I, even I
> Be jealous
> Because of that bad boy?[65]

From the suggestion of the poem each singer creates his own experience. Still, one may properly ask why the composer did not amplify the rhetorical question. The answer is simply that the poet of the homogeneous community owns no obligation to analyze the emotion which accompanies his perception of significant events, such as the trials of love, the onset of spring or winter, the planting and gathering of the crops, the ravages of war and storm, death and disaster, and specialized religious activity. He furnishes the prominent features of a situation, but makes no attempt to direct individual response. Dilatation is a technique, which various isolated aboriginals of America, Australia, Africa, and Asia have not developed. Elaborated sentiment in lyric has unquestionably been among western Europeans the product of formal education and complex social relationships. The disciplined intellect requires symphonic restatement of a theme; the aboriginal is content with mechanical repetition. A ritualistic dance song of the Biak

Islanders of Netherlands New Guinea, for example, is re-
peated as many times as necessary to complete the exercise.
For the Papuan performers in the intricate file dance, in-
tonation probably varies from one phase of the exercise to
another, but the lyric is patently repetitive:

> Wo-ke-ke wa-ja-so
> Wa-ke-ke wai-ja-so (bis)
> To-bo po-om-fo-ri
> Wo-ke-ke wai-ja-so[66]

The hypothetical *fêtes de mai* of Poitou and Limousin,
out of which western European lyric may have grown, are
not necessarily approximated by the festivals of the Stone
Age culture of Biak, but some of the ancient danre songs
luckily saved from destruction in Europe are just such
rhythmical statements as one should expect to find culti-
vated by primitive peoples, whether of France or of the
land of the Chippewa. Several *chansons de carole* of the ro-
mance *Guillaume de Dole* are in structure and sentiment
as elementary as lyric may well be, and these presumably
retain conspicuous archetypal features. A lively *carole*
creates a spectacle of maidens dancing beneath the shade
of an olive tree at the edge of a fountain:

> La jus desouz l'olive,
> Ne vos repentez mie,
> Fontaine i sourt serie.
> Puceles, carolez,
> Ne vos repentez mie
> De loiaument aimer.[67]   ll.2360-5

Trans. Down there beneath the olive, do not repent; the
fountain runs softly there. Maidens, dance; do not
repent of loving loyally.

The combination of olive tree, fountain, dancing, and
maidens communicates what is for everyone in the environ-
ment a familiar, though nonetheless thrilling, experience.

The significance of the rudimentary symbols is known to all, and any enlargement of the particularized passion of the author would be superfluous, if not a flagrant exhibition of egotism. Although a more personal note is struck by a fourteenth-century invitation to the dance, possibly of Irish origin, the emotional impact comes from the prospect, not from what the poet feels about it:

> Icham of Irlaunde
> ant of the holy londe
> of irlande.
> "gode sir, pray ich the,
> for of saynte charite
> come ant daunce wyt me
> in irlaunde."[68]

With this lighthearted appeal may be compared the implicit passion of a dance song from the Chippewa of Minnesota:

> My sweetheart,
> A long time
> I have been waiting for you
> To come over
> Where I am.

Miss Densmore calls this the "favorite social dance" of the tribe, and adds, "Both men and women engage in it; an invitation to dance is accompanied by a gift, and the first invitation is usually given by a woman, the man returning it with a gift of equal value. The dancers form a circle, facing the drum and moving clockwise with a shuffling step."[69] Whether designed for accompanying dance,[70] work, or magical rites, embryo lyric is direct and brief. Emotion is implicit in the abrupt declarations. That is, the poet does not announce the existence of a passion; he asserts a condition instinct with it. In subjective art lyric, the poet uses the analytical faculty to discuss an emotional state; the less sophisticated artist calls attention to a particular situation, from which the audience creates its own special experience. Embryo lyric then suggests a reaction, but does not prescribe one. Learned poets are not barred from using this method, and many good objective lyrics have been written since the Middle Ages, usually in expanded form.

English lyric is so far sophisticated when it begins to appear in the thirteenth century that few specimens are useful illustrations of the archetypal pattern. Expanded statement is the norm, ejaculation the exception. By this time in England, the stratification of society had noticeably progressed, two nationalities were partially amalgamated, the benefits of education were more widely distributed than ever before, and powerful social ideals had come to condition conduct and thinking on all levels. As a consequence, the disciplined intellect, filled with social tensions, almost invariably amends simple impulse before emitting it as poetic statement. The complex arrangements of European lyric were of course accidental, but complications of one kind or another were inevitable. Involved social relationships could not be expressed simply as "I love you" by Bernart de Ventadour; indeed, his special case was not to be comprehended by an exclamation so naive. The forces which immediately created the form of the Provençal *canso* are now quite lost to sight, but the need for a polite and somewhat indirect manner arose with romantic love. This does not imply that social intercourse among aboriginals is not complicated by taboos, but simply that western Europe in the Middle Ages forced literature to express the breadth and depth of its artificial society. Unfortunately, the ideal purposes of lyric were ultimately smothered by a web of decorum, and the concreteness and frankness of the embryo disastrously vitiated toward the close of the medieval period.

Although English song does not begin with pure exclamation, neither does it commence at the perfected stage which troubadour lyric achieved in the twelfth century and trouvère in the thirteenth. A little more than a century divides Chaucerian ballades from an ejaculatory song of about 1225,

> Mirie it is while sumer ilast
> With fugheles song
> Oc nu necheth windes blast
> And weder strong
> Ei, ei, what this nicht is long
> And ich with wel michel wrong
> Soregh and murne and fast . . .[71]

Correlation of mood and season was an obvious but not unattractive means of accomplishing expansion. In this instance, the poet draws an effective contrast between the happiness of summer and the melancholy of winter, motifs employed singly in countless medieval poems. Hopelessly stereotyped by the thirteenth century, the nature preludes came to serve a decorative use, and often were not organically related to the main issues of the poetry which they introduced. Thus, the nature setting of a brief song of MS. Douce 139 is insufficiently articulated with the poet's love-longing:

> Foweles in the frith,
> The fisses in the flod:
> And I mon waxe wod,
> Mulch sorw I walke with
> For beste of bon and blod.[72]

A much more successful attempt is *Western Wind*, a lyric cry of exquisite beauty caught up in a Tudor songbook (MS. Royal Appendix 58):

> Western wind, when will thou blow?
> The small rain down can rain.
> Christ, if my love were in my arms
> And I in my bed again![73]

The implications are manifold. Likely enough the season is winter, the poet's condition miserable. He longs for the springtime "When Zephirus eek with his sweete breeth" blows over England in warm currents laden with moisture from the Gulf Stream. This is the "azure sister of the spring" which resuscitates dormant nature and sets the spirit of man aglow in the blessed revival. "Small"[74] is here the happiest epithet imaginable, exactly describing the sifting rainfall of the island. The idea of spring and rain suggests and supports the central statement, which for all its frankness is an immortal expression of primal longing. Even modern critics, who are usually unconcerned with early lyric, esteem the directness and particularity of this one. Beside the elemental passion of *Western Wind* may be set the reinforced statement of a hyperbolic Middle High German lyric, which further illustrates the possibilities of the embryo sort:

> Waere diu werlt alle min
> von deme mere unze an den Rin,
> des wolt ih mih darben,
> daz diu chünegin von Engellant
> laege an minen armen.[75]

Trans. Were the world all mine, from the sea to the Rhine, I should deprive myself of it, if the queen of England lay in my arms.

Although these full-throated exclamations strike directly to the heart of human affairs, they are not for that folk song. Theoretically, a learned poet could at any time slough off the complex of conditioning and qualifying factors which he brings to bear on simple impulse and then express such exquisite naïveté as early medieval lyric occasionally affords. Some have nearly succeeded, but most poets of modern times are devoted to the idea that society is complex and requires therefore ambiguous poetic representation. Yet measured by the number of taboos which they entertain, aboriginals who cultivate embryo lyric are as psychologically encumbered as western Europeans and their transatlantic kin.

On the second or immature level of lyric development, amplification is effected by mixed methods: narration, description, discussion, and occasionally rhetorical restatement. The burden of communication, however, rests mainly on graphic representation, with the result that the prime exemplars of this stage, the Harleian lyrics, are relatively objective. Normally, the sensibility of the poet is far less prominent than that of the trouvère, who pleads a special cause in the careful arguments of his *chansons d'amour*. Although the characteristic egoism of the conscious artist is plainly incipient, the focus of interest, when apparent, is external to the immediate attitude of the author. The uneven movement of the Harleian songs in general is an indication that the poets by no means had discovered satisfactory methods of imposing unity upon their experiences.

How much pre-Chaucerian poets knew about European lyric is difficult to determine. Numerous conventions presumably borrowed from French chansons were also nourished by romance, with which the English public was abundantly supplied during the thirteenth and fourteenth centuries. Anglo-Norman and French lyrics have been recovered from manuscripts in English libraries, but the quantity is possibly insufficient to suggest widespread influence. Moreover, these Romance songs are in many respects rather unlike the English. At all events, the Midland society, which fostered the Harleian sort, lacked the idealized lady-lover relationship with the concomitant concept of servitude. However artificial, this social circumstance afforded a unifying principle for love lyric and, what is equally important, a means to increased subjectivity. Thus, the trouvère could round out five, six, or seven stanzas by closely examining the numerous facets of his situation: the lover's debt to the lady, the physical distress of love, the lady's obligations to the servant in love, the proper manner of declaring devotion. Such analyses in a society which stood on far less ceremony would be merely tedious, if not dishonest. For example, the Harleian songs, which are strongly suspected of mirroring very real human relations, represent love as a fairly natural experience, without at the same time sacrificing romantic coloring.

The problem which the English poets faced was then how to enlarge upon the exclamation of devotion. They were already in possession of some of the equipment used by modern composers, and if they knew little of the advantages of expanded metaphor, allusion, and symbolism, the temptation to allegorize was spared them. Nevertheless, few seem to have acquired successful formulas of expansion, for the two prominent defects which the poetry evidences are lack of control and lack of a clear concept of unity. These limitations are fundamental and cannot be excused on the ground that the authors were essaying a form little understood. That they were experimenters is perfectly true, and much commendation is therefore due them, but the lyric must stand on its own merits. The tightest structures are those which, like *De Clerico et Puella* and *In a fryht as y con fere fremede,* have a large dramatic content. The former is an amorous *estrif* of marked liveliness and candor, while the latter, if not distinguished, is a fairly normal *pastourelle.* Without the steadying effect of dialogue these poets generally manage the parts of lyric with a careless hand. The *Fairy of Ribbesdale,* for example, is three-fourths description—a catalogue of feminine charms punctuated sporadically by the poet's exclamations. Similarly, *Annot and Johon* is a series of floral, jewel, and herbal images, all calculated to objectify the spiritual virtues of a "burde in a bour ase beryl so bryht." This dilatation accomplishes only synthetic unity and advances the art of the lyric not at all, and this notwithstanding brief passages of considerable charm. Excepting *When the nyhtegale singes the wodes waxen grene* and *Alysoun,* both love songs of rare excellence, no Harleian complaint of secular love fully develops a unified experience; and the perfection of these merely emphasizes the structural deficiences of most of the others.

Still, the esthetic integrity of a majority' of the Harleian lyrics can possibly be sustained on the likely assumption that they were subjected normally to auditory rather than to visual examination. If sung, as seems not improbable, their success depended not so much upon the structural unity and balance demanded by modern criticism as upon the happy articulation of sentiment, voice, and melody, which in combination doubtless corrected some of the deficiencies apparent to the eye. It is reasonable to believe that for the ear each of these lyrics consisted of patches of eloquence strung in a series having some unity of emotion. What the patches were, there is now no way of determining, although clichés, judged to be execrable in modern poetry, must often have been the segments possessing the greatest evocative power. Since the criteria which guided the Harleian poets cannot be recovered, their creations must be judged, albeit unfairly, by principles of later conception. Even so, the old songs possess an enduring charm. Few would value the perfected lyric developed at the end of the fourteenth century at a higher rate than the uncut gems of the immature stage, which yet recall "Dance, and Provençal song, and sunburnt mirth!"

With the solution of formal problems, the perfected state (that is, art lyric) was finally achieved and the fracture of the traditional words-and-melody relationship confirmed. Chaucer, the first conspicuous exemplar of the new style, turned for models to France, where the crucial transition had already been accomplished; the immature Harleian lyrics were a blocked tradition, exerting no known influence on later English poetry. Songs continued to be written, but few of those which survive are worthy of study as literature. Three interrelated consequences of the altered concept of lyric are immediately apparent: the reduction of concreteness, the destruction of the tridimensional basis of presentation, and the removal of the unsophisticated but nonetheless critical audience.

When singer and song dropped out of the combination, the composer lost two aids to communication—the power of the voice to interpret, the power of the melody to reinforce mood. At this distance, it is difficult to calculate the total effect of the three parts, but the rhythmical phrasing and gay abandon of such a lyric as *Alysoun* suggest that presentation by a competent artist would be extraordinarily moving. The richness and meaningfulness of the language virtually prove what otherwise should be suspected, that the audience demanded intelligible recitals of the poetic thought, unobscured by intrusive musical effects. Even today, ballad singers abide by this condition, without which words become merely vehicles for melody. The usually inane sentiments of Tin-Pan Alley songs demonstrate the ultimate result of the altered emphasis; nonsense syllables would often serve as well as meaningful words, for the music counts for everything. The carols of the fifteenth century—tediously devotional, commonplace, or scabrous in all but a few instances—clearly indicate the direction of song after the fracture. The thinness of the sentiment is presumptive evidence of the transfer of interest from words to· music. What importance can criticism attach to a refined song of the first half of the fifteenth century?

> Love wolle I withoute eny variaunce
> Trewly to serve with alle lovelynesse
> For yn hit is triste ande gentilnesse
> And that may manne honour and avaunce.[76]

Or to a madrigal from the same period?

> Go hert hurt with adversite
> And let my lady thi woundis see
> And sey hire this as y say the
> Farewel my joy and welcome peyne
> Til y se my lady agayne.[77]

The answer is of course that such songs have slight value as literature and properly interest only the musicologist. The songs of Wyatt, Campion, Shakespeare, and Burns, among others, claim exception from these invidious distinctions, and a number of estimable lyrics from 1500 to 1900 are eligible for musical setting. Much of the verse of Keats and Tennyson, for example, exhibits a verbal melody which invites musical utterance, and Byron's anapestic *Destruction of Sennacherib* compels recitative; but the main stream of lyric poetry flows along, often turgidly, without benefit of a great deal of melody. The cleavage has become so pronounced that literary criticism as a rule disclaims all responsibility for song, whether provided with meaningful lyric or not. Obviously, lyric meant for musical accompaniment poorly manages ambiguity and tortured sensibility, without which poetry in modern times fares rather shabbily.

Art lyric normally expands a sentiment, a thin narrative core, or a situation by means of restatement, the accumulation of ideas around a central point. The real focus and the apparent focus may or may not be the same, depending upon the purposes of the poet, but a unifying principle ordinarily appears on the plain surface. On this same level, development is sharply restricted, however much precedent and subsequent action may be inferred; and by this restriction, modern lyric holds aloof from narrative. This distinction was not fully acknowledged prior to the thirteenth century in France, and it was not wholly confirmed by the Harleian circle, although these poets obviously felt some compulsion to reduce surface action.

The catalogue of metaphors in *Annot and Johon* is some evidence that poets recognized a need for convenient formulas of non-narrative dilatation. The principle in this instance is defective, but the treatises of Geoffroi de Vinsauf and Matthieu de Vendôme sanctioned the method. Even Chaucer, it may be recalled, filled out the ballade addressed to Alceste in the *Legend of Good Women* with a list of noble women of antiquity. Medieval poets had a notorious predilection for catalogues, and Deschamps in particular esteemed the artifice. Much medieval art lyric, whether directly influenced by the textbooks or not, uses *interpretatio* (accumulation), periphrasis, apostrophe, prosopopœia, digression, and description. The ornaments (figures of words and of thoughts) appear singly and together in verse of all kinds.[78] Much of this is quite effective, as rhetoricians codified good practice as well as poor. The tropes, moreover, are among the best parts of language and have been used by poets who never heard of the trivium. Whether ornamentation is offensive as a principle remains in doubt; it is contrary at least to the theory of the organic, which demands that meaning shall proceed from all parts of a work of art. At the close of the Middle Ages, in any event, rhetorical amplification was more often than not a means of concealing the poverty of ideas. Poets callously substituted verbal ingenuity for inspiration. An appalling instance is the *reversaris,* translated to the vernacular as early as the thirteenth century, to judge from a specimen of MS. Digby 86. The author proposed to define love by the accumulation of attributives. For twenty-three tedious lines he maintained an antithetical balance, as the passage below illustrates:

> Love is sofft, love is swet, love is goed sware;
> Love is muche tene, love is muchel kare;
> Love is blissene mest, love is bot yare;
> Love is wondred and wo, with for to fare.[79]

This is by no means an isolated example; the method has numerous exemplars.[80]

Particularized passion requires for its proper expression a vocabulary of affective language. The Harleian poets for the lack of such terms were not well equipped to manage complex emotional situations and had therefore to depend to a great extent upon objective methods. Nevertheless, under the influence of social and intellectual forces, lyric tended inevitably toward subjectivity, and Middle English borrowed from French and Latin a veritable dictionary of abstract language. With such equipment, Chaucer and the ingenious versifiers who came after were able to shift communication from narration and description to exposition and thus give their own special attitudes adequate expression. But the fifteenth century brought little enthusiasm and less sincerity to the composition of conventional lyric, with the result that the book is filled with trite pleasantries, personified abstractions, and stereotyped sympathies. General and diffuse, this polite verse ranks with the worst ever caught up in the record of English literature. It marks the furthest development conceivable in the direction of abstractness—abstractness as applied to language, not to ideas. The ideas as a matter of fact are hopelessly threadbare. That the vaporings of the courtiers of the transition period were admired seems incredible nowadays, but the quantity of driveling complaints confesses the tendency of society. A proper technique for objectifying emotion was the obvious need of these fifteenth-century poets, yet, even if the means of restoring concreteness to lyric had been obvious to all, decorum would have been a formidable deterrent.

Courtly love, as obsolete at the end of the fourteenth century as knight-errantry, still claimed lip service from the English peerage and from poets whom they patronized. By the testimony of the verse (though not of history), manners

were well-nigh as refined as those of Hampton Court two
centuries later. Under the circumstances, poets cherished
the ancient statute of secrecy in amorous relationships and
rarely considered the artistic advantages of particularity in
lyric. To "number the streaks of the tulip" would be to
delineate the lineaments of the lady and so to identify her,
an intolerable proposition for poets who sought idealized
portraits, applicable to all lovely ladies and to none. In a
sense, the *chansons d'amour* of the earliest and best French
period (1180-1200) tended in this direction, but the inspired
lyric poets immediately following Chrétien de Troyes by
sincerity, well-managed figures, and soaring eloquence sur-
mounted the obstacles. The chanson, as the *canso* before,
admirably suited the uses of a class of aristocratic poets who
needed a complex form for the expression of delicate social
relationships, acute sensibilities, and controlled passions.
If constrained by synthetic barriers, the Thibauts de Cham-
pagne yet acted a sincere part. So much may not be said
of the English poets. No one imagines that the seasoned
diplomatist of Kent and London took much stock in the
concept of *li duz mal de amer*, even though he permitted
Troilus a prolonged and painful knowledge of this paradox.

Besides the decay of faith in the old ideal of servitude,
the acknowledged taste of the times for generalizations
fostered an unreal lyric atmosphere. In denying the virtue
of the variety of the material world, religion of necessity
interested itself in universals and used allegory more or
less ineffectually to objectify the abstract. The difficulty is
that allegory obviously does not mean what it says, and the
cavorting personifications make no sense in the surface
drama which they play out. A division of literature which
depends as strongly as lyric upon an exclamatory core can-
not do without solid referents to compel immediate compre-
hension. The communication of experience is disastrously
retarded by the abstractions, which must first be translated

into concrete terms. Ideas may be leisurely recovered from
behind the disguise of allegory, but not the emotion which
lyric has to offer. Yet allegory was a convenience to mask
the insincerity of transition poetry. By means of it, a poet
could achieve superficially the close metaphysical analyses
of chansons and *cansos* without greatly exercising his own
passions. The personifications were pawns which might be
manipulated with a feeling of detachment. Allegory and
decorum, both products of conservative religious tendencies,
acted to fix patterns of expansion and to formalize lyric.
Form was thus achieved at the expense of the vivid por-
traiture and frank human relationships which distinguish
pre-Chaucerian song. Yet, there is no alternative to the
view that literary circles were fairly well satisfied with this
state of poetry, however deplorable by later standards.

A step beyond this lyric filled with abstractions lay rich
new fields awaiting discovery and exploitation, but the
poetic imagination was as yet unprepared in the interest of
total effect to sacrifice quasi-logical development, which
indeed the medieval mind demanded. Symbolism had to
wait the accumulation of techniques—expanded metaphor,
ambiguous statement, oblique comparisons, and most im-
portantly the further reduction of the audience. Rudimen-
tary symbolism does crop out here and there in medieval
verse, as in the *Corpus Christi* carol. In the ballad *Sir
Patrick Spens*, which is possibly not medieval, "the newe
moone,/ Wi the auld moone in hir arme" is a symbol of
extraordinary power and beauty. Nevertheless, the poet
who wrote for a wide audience then as now labored under
the necessity of assigning such meanings to his symbols as
would meet with intelligent response from virtually all
within the culture area. Such clear-cut symbols as the
totemic "rose and briar" manifestation of *Lord Thomas and
Fair Annet* are necessarily limited in number and soon wear
thin with repetition; yet the public at large is not equipped

by education and capacity to assimilate symbols extracted from literature and science and assembled entirely in the interest of poetic effect. Though subtlety may emerge as a gross effect, the details must be readily intelligible.

Even at the perfected level in Middle English, the author could not narrowly restrict the range of comprehensibility of a poem; the audience, though reduced, would not tolerate local subtlety. *Vers de société*, like the immature lyric before, was meant for the ear, and recitation was usually more rapid than song. Hence, there was not time for incidental reflection; communication had to be clear and prompt. Even so, the stuff of this courtly verse—simulated devotion, moral philosophy, exaggerated piety—is fundamentally obnoxious to the spirit of lyric poetry and cause enough for failure. In history, these effusions signify the intellectual decay of the privileged at the close of the Middle Ages; in literature, the verse illustrates the perfection of form in the wrong direction.

CHAPTER TWO

THE HARLEIAN LOVE
LYRICS

THE FEBRILE STRAINS OF LYRIC LOVE SELDOM CAUGHT the utilitarian ears of copyists during the first two hundred years after Hastings; even Anglo-Norman chansons are rare. Until the appearance of the miraculous Harleian collection, amatory song in Middle English is without significant exemplars, although the somber plaint *Mirie it is while sumer ilast* and the Harleian political poem, the *Song of Lewes* (1264-65), compel attention as evidence of a secular tradition established by the middle of the thirteenth century. No date can be assigned to the bulk of the love lyrics in MS. Harley 2253 on any save linguistic grounds, which indicate a date around 1300. The special circumstances which nurtured these rare specimens, however, existed from about 1250 to 1325.[1] The songs could not have been written long before English displaced Anglo-Norman as the prevailing literary medium in courtly circles, and not long after the tradition exemplified by French lyric before Machaut succumbed to the genres of fixed form. In all likelihood, the circle of bilingual composers who wrote *Alysoun* and *In a fryht as y con fere fremede* were intimately acquainted with chansons and *pastourelles* of the sort in vogue before 1280, the lyric of Arras if not that of Thibaut de Champagne and Gace Brulé.[2] The assumption of strong French influence, however, does not exclude the operation of a native lyric tradition: the transfer of convention does not necessarily imply the transfer of spirit.

This freakish renaissance of Continental lyric was destined to be short lived. By the time the Harleian collector lodged the miscellaneous poems in manuscript at his Herefordshire priory, the unrestricted lyrics of the trouvères were collectors' items in France,[3] and form had come to dominate and thereby to suffocate the spirit of contemporary lyric. Meanwhile, the gifted poets who had grafted the quaint artifices of imported song onto the sturdy accentual stock of English verse perished without issue. Only a stray convention or cliché in the Vernon and other collections of religious lyrics discloses in the second half of the fourteenth century a residuum of the older poetry. The direction of art lyric thereafter until the end of the next century was largely determined by French genres of fixed form, notably the ballade, which Chaucer naturalized.

Idle as it is to speculate on the means by which the Herefordshire religious, if that he was, came into possession of the Harleian lyrics, knowledge of this matter could throw a great deal of light on the character of the authors. Brown supposed that they were minstrels or *vagantes* who performed at Leominster Priory from time to time,[4] and the dialectal diversity of the English songs is presumptive evidence of the participation of many hands. Collecting the pieces was probably the work of years, as the arrangement of the varied items in English, French, and Latin is haphazard. If the manuscript were made up as Brown surmised, one naturally would expect to find represented the dialect of London and the southeast Midland; instead, the language is predominantly that of the southwest Midland, the center of the alliterative revival during the middle of the fourteenth century. This generalization is even truer of the love poems than of the English pieces as a whole, for the political and satirical songs are usually Southern or Southwestern. The love songs exhibit numerous common traits, some of which doubtless may be referred to a hypothetical Anglo-French lyric tradition, but others of which require the supposition that the Harleian collector drew heavily upon the work of a circle of Midland poets, who were influenced by French patterns fallen into disuse sometime before 1300. *Fin de siècle* lyric seems not to have been the inspiration of the Harleian love songs. The relationships, often noted, of both secular and religious pieces in the manuscript show a community of interests, though by no means common authorship. Heider thought that not only the collector but also the individual authors were to be sought in the ranks of the clergy, *vagantes* as well as cloistered.[5] Notwithstanding the substitution of a clerk for the conventional *chevalier* in *De Clerico et Puella,* or the religious adaptation of *Lutel wot hit anymon,* the causes are insufficient to hand over the entire collection to the Church. Indeed, the part of seculars in the making of medieval poetry has been minimized for too little reason.[6]

Trouvère lyric underwent an inevitable sea change in the process of translation to the west of England. In metrics and spirit, the French mode was unsuited to the special conditions obtaining in England during the thirteenth century. For syllabic scansion, the English adapters wisely substituted the accentual line; for *amour courtois,* a more normal relationship of the sexes. Social modes beyond the confines of London were so obviously incompatible with the artificial situation projected in the late *chanson d'amour* that it is little wonder that English poets altered the relation of lover to lady, though at the cost of a convenient formula of dilatation. As Heider has observed,[7] the worship of the characteristically reluctant fair provided substantial content for a lyric; the French poet could analyze at great length his condition as a servant of love. To the lack of this course, the relative objectivity of the Harleian lyrics is partly owing. However conventional much of the apparatus may be, the particularizing tendency is clear enough; the "eye blake" of Alysoun may not prove her "bon and blod," but the intimate style of the poet suggests as much. On this point, at least, the English lyrics may properly be differentiated from most French and Anglo-Norman chansons of the second half of the thirteenth century. Moreover, for lack of techniques of expansion the English poets of necessity mixed considerable quantities of narrative and descriptive matter with their arguments. As a consequence, feeling is not described so much as it is expressed in scattered exclamations. If not entirely implicit, emotion is seldom elaborated to the point of diminishing objectivity to any important extent. Feeling swirls and eddies in the wake of the action, and the poet's attitude counts on the surface for less than the object of his passion. This may be described technically as objective lyric. It depends for success on the proper fusion of exclamation with frame and is more difficult to manage in expanded form than the subjective sort filled out by formulas of amplification. The objective method was not always successfully used, but even the failures are noteworthy as tapestries. Certain lyrics, like *Annot and Johon* and *Ichot a burde in boure bryht,* presume some knowledge of rhetorical elaboration and, though still concrete, are too obviously ingenious. Fortunately, the trend toward generalization and artificiality is not here advanced ruinously far, and these poets may be said to have their eyes focused clearly on real women.

Such Anglo-French chansons[8] as English manuscripts afford do not appear to stem from the same level of lyric development as that which produced the Harleian specimens. Six diffuse chansons of a late thirteenth-century manuscript of Cambridge,[9] by a single author, are for the most part learned and analytical. The clearest and best of them is the last, *Quant le tens se renovele,* a not unpleasant catalogue of feminine charms mingled with the conventional lamentations of the humble lover; it is analogous to the Harleian *Fairy of Ribbesdale.* But the vague, diffuse sort unquestionably prevails, harking back to the productive circle of Arras in the middle of the century. *Li grans desirs de deservir amie*[10] of Jehan Bretel, the most prolific poet of Arras, is precisely such an exhibition of profuseness and unreal humility as first Machaut[11] and later the Chaucerians came to esteem. Once artificiality and insincerity were taken for granted, deterioration became certain. A chanson of Adam de la Halle—*Il ne muet pas de sans celui qui plaint*[12]—is instinct with didacticism, a further defect of thirteenth-century French lyric. Affirming the traditional relationship of the humble lover to his lady—"de bien amer veil maintenir l'usage"—he sermonizes briefly on the proper attitude of the lover. Adam's lady, who emerges obscurely in the last two stanzas of the chanson, is never more than an adumbrated figure. Even a French love epistle of the Harleian manuscript—*Ferroy chaunsoun que bien doit estre oye*[13]—accords poorly with the English complaints. A lover's lament over the defection of an unidentified lady, it is devoid of particularization and has nothing to communicate besides a commonplace sentiment. The excellence of the English songs is not readily explicable in terms of the French matter floating in the literary milieu of the late thirteenth century, and perhaps ultimately the merit of the work must be referred to the genius of a group of poets whose names have not survived in a single instance. The very lack of a vocabulary of the affections and a *douce dame* who required masking worked for greater objectivity, and the fact that their subjects were real women—a plausible conjecture—fostered sincerity.

The possibility that Provençal lyric influenced English poets has been explored by Chaytor and Miss Rees; neither was willing, however, to declare for direct borrowing.[14] Though troubadours visited England and English kings demonstrated a fondness for Provençal queens, the Albigensian Crusade had disrupted literary activity in the south of France sometime before Middle English became a cus-

tomary vehicle for love lyric. Had English song flourished
soon after the marriage in 1153 of Henry II and Eleanor of
Aquitaine, daughter of William, duke of Aquitaine, and
granddaughter of the troubadour William IX, a case for
indebtedness might be made on external grounds alone; but
a century elapsed before the appearance of native lyric.
The striking parallels between English and Provençal song
were indeed significant did not trouvère poetry afford iden-
tical conventions. Chaytor concedes that northern France
was probably the transmitting agent. Identical rhyme
schemes are not important evidence,[15] because variety was
a requirement of the lyric art, in the trouvère country as
well as in Le Midi. Whatever the ultimate truth, the hypo-
thesis that the lyric of Provence directly influenced English
is unnecessary.

Not all of the lyric forms of northern France seem to have
rooted in English soil; such as did were often modified.
The meagerness of the remains checks a sweeping generali-
zation, though it is altogether probable that the English
poets were skillful adapters rather than slavish imitators,
and this notwithstanding numerous formulas and clichés
obviously plucked directly out of French. Several poems
in one way or another recall special French types—*sirven-
tois, jeu parti, chanson de mal mariée*—but English poets
seem reluctant to follow the patterns strictly, with the re-
sult that pure specimens are relatively rare. Though traces
of the *chanson de toile, pastourelle,* and *aube* appear in
popular ballad, the relations are far from clear. Indigenous
types there surely were, but no one, it seems, will ever know
for certain what they were. It is only by the greatest good
fortune that examples of this early lyric have survived; if
no longer popular, it happily retains some reminders of that
less artificial state whence it came.

If Gaston Paris has reasoned correctly, the study of love
lyric begins properly with the *reverdie,* originally a primi-

tive response to the spring.[16] From the persistence of the
nature introduction in *chansons d'amour,* Paris concluded
that the spring element was an essential feature of the dance
songs of the *fêtes de mai,* the basic type from which courtly
poetry developed.[17] Some trace of the ancient celebrations
has survived in scattered lyric fragments. Jehan Renart[18]
gives an account in the romance *Guillaume de Dole* (1200)
of a group of town folk bearing "lor mai" from the wood;
as the Maytime procession moves along, maidens sing an
accompaniment, which the poet has thoughtfully inter-
calated:

> Tout la gieus sor rive mer,
> Compaignon, or dou chanter.
> Dames i ont bauz levez:
> Mout en ai le cuer gai.
> Compaignon, or dou chanter
> En l'onor de mai.[19]   ll. 4154-9

Trans. Down there on the seashore, companion, now to
sing. The ladies there have joyfully commenced;
for that I have a very gay heart. Companion, now to
sing in honor of May.

The pagan May observances persisted in one form or an-
other. A lyric of the fifteenth century discloses the inten-
tion of a youth to seek the permission of his lady to bring
to her the "may"; that is, to deposit a young tree beneath
her window:

> Vecy la doulce nuyt de may
> Que l'on se doibt aller jouer,
> Et point ne se doibt on coucher:
> La nuyt bien courte trouveray.

> Devers ma dame m'en yray,
> Si sera pour la saluer
> Et par congié luy demander
> Si je luy porteray le may.[20]

Trans. Here is the lovely night of May, when one ought to
go to play, and one should not lie in bed. I shall
find the night quite short. Before my lady I shall go.
So it will be to address her, and for permission ask
her, if I shall bring to her the "may."

According to the theory advanced by Paris[21] and widely
accepted (with some qualifications),[22] the *reverdie,* along
with other forms of dance-song origin *(rotrouenges, chan-
sons de mal mariée),* migrated to northern France from the
borderland of Poitou and Limousin. This dissemination
of lyric genres was presumably anterior to and independent
of the Provençal impact on the North. Though originally
the purely unsophisticated folk-song accompaniment of the
May festivities, the *reverdie* apparently underwent prelimi-
nary development at the source and then advanced north-
ward through aristocratic channels. In *Guillaume de Dole*
it is the nobility who yet know the ancient snatches. The
type emerges in the late twelfth century as a stereotyped
introduction to chansons which are the product of conscious
artistry, and the folk origin is by no means obvious without
reference to the valuable scraps of song which forge the link
between the prototype and the contaminated trouvère
adaptation. The collective response has given way to the
individual cry of exultation, the elemental passion of the
dancing, singing throng to the detached appreciation of the
mature artist. As the *reverdie* becomes more and more con-
ventionalized, and as it is made to subserve the uses of
courtly love, the pattering feet and the chanting voices of
the throng are the less audible.

Yet something of the pristine beauty of the Maytime
chant remains in a few early examples which have come
down, something of the spirit which animated the mythical
folk, for whom the spring celebrations held a deep and
powerful significance before Christian influences entirely
dissipated pagan ritual. One such lyric, grouped by Bartsch

with the lyrical romances, expresses a sweet and sincere enthusiasm in the new season:

> En mai au douz tens nouvel,
> que raverdissent prael
> oi soz un arbroisel
> chanter le rosignolet.[23] st. 1

Trans. In May in the pleasant new season, when the meadows turn green, I hear beneath a bush the nightingale to sing.

And then a refrain which dances and sings itself:

> saderala don!
> tant fet bon
> dormir les le buissonet.

Trans. Saderala don! How pleasant it is to sleep beneath the little bush.

But before the twelfth century was out, courtly elements had diminished the native vigor of the *reverdie,* and trouvères usually employed it loosely as a correlative of their feelings. Thus, a nature introduction of Gace Brulé is recognizable as a wholly dispassionate and conventional prelude to a lyrical disquisition on the complications of *amour courtois:*

> Au renoviau de la douçor d'esté,
> Que resclarcist la doiz en la fontaine
> Et que sont vert bois et vergier et pré
> Et li rosiers en mai florist et graine,
> Lors chanterai, car trop m'avra grevé
> Ire et esmai ki m'est al cuer prochaine.[24]

Trans. Upon the return of the pleasantness of summer, when the water in the fountain sparkles, and when wood and garden and meadow are green, and the rose bush in May blossoms and reddens, then I shall sing; for too much has grieved me sadness and discouragement which are next to my heart.

The connection of the numerous spring songs in the
Carmina Burana with folk song is indeed tenuous, though
P. S. Allen has argued with uncommon persuasiveness for
the view that some of the lyrics were the work of nonclerical
poets who derived their inspiration in part from the coun-
tryside. The dance song *Ver redit optatum* in particular
struck Allen as a direct outgrowth of folk song.[25] English
affords nothing which may be closely associated either with
primitive recreation or with the lush milieu of the *Carmina
Burana*, although such specimens as have survived, like the
Cuckoo Song, are not lacking in the naive wonderment and
rapture with which man has always greeted the springtime.

The celebrated *Cuckoo Song* has usually been exhibited
in surveys and discussions of medieval lyric as a superb
example of early thirteenth-century poetical and musical
art, having been composed, it was supposed, before 1240.[26]
Though the excellence of the so-called *Reading Rota* re-
mains undiminished, recent investigation indicates for the
music, at least, a much later date than the one traditionally
accepted. Bukofzer has shown that the *Summer-canon*
could not have been composed prior to 1280, as "duple
rhythm," a demonstrated characteristic of the music, was
previously unknown in England.[27] On this and other
grounds,[28] he dates the accompaniment *ca.* 1310.[29] Consid-
ered unaccountably advanced as thirteenth-century song,
the *rota* is entirely explicable in terms of the musical prac-
tice of the following century. Bukofzer declares that the
composer's gift is all the better understood and appreciated
by the musicologist as it is examined within the limits of a
known tradition. The new dating of the notation proves
nothing about the age of the text, though the phonological
evidence by no means precludes a date later than 1240.[30]

Sumer is icumen in is the only English song among sev-
eral French and Latin specimens entered in a common-
place book (now MS. Harley 978) which was kept over a

period of many years by monks of Reading Abbey. There are no clues as to the identity of poet or composer or indications of the occasion for which the lyric was written.[31] It belongs to the general class of spring songs cultivated extensively on the Continent. The *Cuckoo Song*, however, is apparently not an imitation, as it lacks the gaudy description and love interest of the songs of greeting to the spring in the *Carmina Burana*[32] and the nature introductions of Old French poetry. The deceptive naïveté of the lyric has led some readers to the conclusion that it was popular in character, notwithstanding the altogether learned environment in which it has come down. A recent editor of the text, Carleton Brown, considered it "easier to believe that it was an imitation of Welsh folk-song than it was the invention of a learned composer"[33]—and this on Gerald's statement in the *Descriptio Kambriae* that the Welsh cultivated counterpoint in the twelfth century.[34] The music, it is hardly necessary to remark, shows no exceptional features by Bukofzer's dating, though it remains the first English composition for six voices. The text, moreover, exhibits a good many notable characteristics besides the "freshness and simplicity" which struck R. M. Wilson as the marks of folk song.[35] Whatever its ultimate origin, the *Cuckoo Song* is immediately the product of a finished poetic talent.[36]

One morning on the southern countryside, the poet becomes suddenly aware of the arrival of joyous "sumer" (probably April).[37] Realization comes in a moment so brief that he cannot hope by ordinary means to give concrete representation to the complex of impulses which unite almost as a single sense-impression to inform him of the happy fact. Nor can he by conventional methods animate the symbols which have flashed "sumer" upon his conscious mind. The composer properly takes rapid movement as the common factor of all that he sees or imagines, and this characteristic of the season he manages to introduce into the song. By mechanical means—the short line and the racing musical score—the poet creates an illusion of speed; but by a far subtler method, he co-ordinates the motion of the prominent objects with the meter.

The choice of onomatopœic *cuccu* (both note and bird) was a fortunate one. The bird suggests not only "sumer" but motion as well, and, as a consequence, "sing, cuccu" laces the parts together. Two kinds of movement are represented in the lyric—the slow, deliberate growth of plant life and the fast, erratic capering of animal life. These diverse sorts of activity are reconciled by verbs of motion. Thus "groweth sed and bloweth med" become for the moment discernible and imaginatively no less rapid than,

> awe bleteth after lomb,[38]
> lhouth after calue cu;
> Bulluc sterteth, bucke uerteth.[39]

And the persistent *cuccu*, the eternal note of spring, sounds a merry accompaniment to the animals frisking in the flowering meadow. Yet all is objectivity, all realism. The language is homely, the situation probable. In the fourteenth century, as now in isolated regions, the dun deer must have consorted with domesticated bovines. There is nothing essentially "poetic" about the elements which make up the song, and the composer has made no effort to elevate his subject. This is nevertheless art of a high order and an exceptional fusion of sense and melody.

Elsewhere in the fourteenth-century lyric there are suggestions of the *reverdie*. Several Harleian songs have nature settings much like the introductions of the courtly chansons. Perhaps a dozen brief *reverdies* are intercalated in the romance *King Alisaundre*,[40] where they are used as section headings. Though not without a faint charm, these pieces, unlike the lyrics of *Guillaume de Dole*, have but slight poetic merit or historical importance. Ornamentation is the author's very clear purpose,

> In tyme of May, the nyghtyngale
> In wode, makith miry gale;
> So doth the foules grete and smale,
> Some on hulle, som on dale.   ll. 2547-50

The loveliest of all the lyrics incorporated in romances is perhaps one from *Richard Coer de Lion:*

> Merye is, in the tyme off May,
> Whenne foulis synge in her lay;
> Floures on appyl trees, and perye;
> Smale foules synge merye.
> Ladyes strowe here boures
> With rede roses and lylye flowres.
> Gret joye is in frith and lake;
> Best and byrd playes with his make . . .[41]   ll. 3731-8

The *reverdie* in Middle English reaches its fullest and in some respects most artistic development in *Lenten ys come with loue to toune,*[42] which is perhaps the richest tapestry that the period affords. The most obvious flaw is the intrusive love motif which seriously disturbs the unity of the nature study. It is not until line 24 that the unidentified lady is suggested and then in a vague reference to "loue that likes ille." Though the conclusion (11. 34-36) reveals the poet's unsuspected desperation for lack of the lady's favor, the foregoing matter in no way leads to this new interest. The opening couplet may be borrowed from a poem of slightly different movement, for

> Lenten ys come with loue to toune,[43]
> with blosmen & with briddes roune,

is obviously of a looser fabric than the following lines or the corresponding couplets in the second and third stanzas. Lines 3 and 4 clearly show the difference:

> that al this blisse bryngeth;
> dayes eyes in this dales . . .

The passage is substantially the same as the introduction of *The Thrush and the Nightingale* (Digby 86),[44] the only significant difference being the substitution of *somer* for *lenten*. Significantly enough, a text of the debate in the Auchinleck MS. has "Le-" followed by several illegible letters; Brown takes the word to be *lenten*.[45] *Somer* is obviously the better form, for *lenten* (which the *NED* understands here as *spring*) had become confused with the Church fast beginning on Ash Wednesday and is certainly rare in the traditional sense from the thirteenth century on. Since the nightingale, mentioned in both poems, does not appear before April 15 (April 3 by the Julian reckoning),[46] *somer* here, as in the *Cuckoo Song*, suits the occasion. Stanza one remarks the gaiety of nightingale and thrush after "huere wynter woo." Stanza two is a series of lovely springtime phenomena:

> the rose rayleth hire rode,
> the leues on the lyhte wode
> waxen al with wille.
> the mone mandeth hire bleo,
> the lilie is lossom to seo,
> the fenyl & the fille;
> wowes this wilde drakes,
> Miles murgeth huere makes
> ase strem that striketh stille.

All nature is happily about its business:

> deawes donketh the dounes,
> deores with huere derne rounes,
> domes forte deme;
> wormes woweth vnder cloude . . .

While the dews moisten the earth, animals converse with their kind, and worms make love beneath the heavens, the poet seems by contrast to stand in doubt of the one he adores. If he fails to achieve her, he will become a fugitive—"wyht in wode be fleme."

The nature setting is vestigial in the few Middle English *pastourelles* which have survived, though numerous French specimens leave no doubt that the *reverdie* prelude was traditionally regarded as an integral part of this the most courtly variety of *chanson populaire*.[47] Everywhere the influence of the *chanson d'aventure* is manifest in the stereotype, "as I went riding the other day," which is without doubt the commonest introductory formula in Middle English. But English poets have so far modified the pattern as to leave little trace of the sweet springtime, the Gallic irony, and the easy-going morality, with which the Continental poets invested their songs of love adventure. Beyond the conventional "riding out" the fourteenth-century composers are unlikely to go, and most lyrics turn didactic or religious after a few verses. Only three pieces are properly to be regarded as *pastourelles*, and all were lodged in manuscript early in the century: *Als i me rod this ender dai* (Lincoln's Inn MS. Hale 135),[48] *In a fryht as y con fere fremede* (MS. Harl. 2253),[49] and *As I stod on a day me self under a tre* (MS. Lond. Coll. of Arms E.D.N. 27).[50] The reason for the relative scarcity of this popular French type in the Harleian manuscript is not now apparent; perhaps the collector, generally thought a religious, regarded the fundamental licentiousness of the motif a disqualification. Certainly, the tone of the one genuine *pastourelle* in the collection is moral.

One would like to infer from the surviving specimens and the large number of *chanson d'aventure* introductions that the *pastourelle* unluckily perished in large numbers, and this may have been the case; but the somber coloring of the Harleian and College of Arms examples raises the possibility that the English social climate was not friendly to the genre. Conditions were vastly altered from the heyday of the form in the twelfth and thirteenth centuries. Chivalry was less a fact than a literary convention. Church and State had vitiated the prestige of those happy purveyors of secular song, the minstrels. The fountain of lyric poetry in France, from which Britain was supplied, dried up with the decline of the trouvères. The circumstances described in the *pastourelle* were by the fourteenth century utterly detached from reality. Friars and "clerks of Oxenford" might wander out in search of love, but hardly errant knighthood. Moreover, the religious strain, seldom entirely absent from medieval English poetry, was confirmed to a suffocating degree, as the craft of literature came more and more to be practiced by the learned.[51]

However strong the religious strain, the Middle English poets were by no means the first to transfer the conventions of secular to pious song. Gautier de Coinci, the prior of Vic-sur-Aisne, who was born in 1177 or 1178,[52] developed the *chanson pieuse* at least a century before English amorous song began to appear. One of the lyrics associated with his name is a strange medley of sensuous imagery and lofty sentiment dedicated to the Queen of Heaven. The beginning is for all the world like a twelfth-century *pastourelle:*

> Hui matin, a l'ajournee,
> Toute m'ambleüre
> Chevauchai par une pree
> Par bone aventure.
> Une florete ai trouvee
> Gente de faiture . . .[53]

Trans. This morning at sunrise, ambling along, I rode through a meadow for pleasant adventure. A little flower I found, lovely of shape . . .

The refrain ends with an imprecation on those who desert the Virgin for women of the world: "Qui laist Marie pour Marot." For Marie (the Virgin) he will make a *reverdie.* After a spring passage, Gautier calls on clerks to lay aside secular song and apply themselves to "chançons nouv-

eles . . . de la flour dont . . . Chantent angle nuit et
jour":

> Mais tu clers qui chantes d'eles,
> Certes, tu rasotes,
> Laissons ces viez pastoureles,
> Ces vielles riotes . . .

Trans. But you, clerk, who sing of them, certainly, you act
foolishly. Let us leave these old *pastourelles,* these
old quarrels . . .

And so Gautier does, but his Blessed Virgin, "la bele, la sage,
la douce, la coie," is mighty like a secular fair.

In Harley *Blessed be thou, leuedy, ful of heouene blisse,*
the Virgin Mary is "bryhte & shene," "so fair & so briht,"
"so fayr & so hende."[54] She resembles the portrait of the
Virgin at the outset of another serious poem of the same
manuscript:

> Ase y me rod this ender day
> by grene wode to seche play,
> mid herte y thohte al on a may,
> Suetest of alle thinge . . .[55]

When y se blosmes springe opens with a *reverdie* and de-
velops the idea of Christ as the "lemman" of mankind.[56]
And even more remarkably, *Lutel wot hit anymon,* a song
of secular love, has a religious counterpart, Christ taking the
place of the worldly beauty.[57] The practice continued
during the fifteenth century. A supplication to the Virgin
in Bodley 939 employs the language of courtly complaints.[58]
Numerous carols, mostly of the fifteenth century, address
the Mother of Christ in the manner long before affected by
Gautier; and several preserve the *chanson d'aventure* intro-
duction.[59] Propriety aside, these songs are not without
value in tracing the decay of the traditional lyrics. Scat-
tered remains in the religious pieces and the ballads sug-
gest that chansons and *pastourelles* in the early style sur-
vived considerably longer than the written record reveals.

This circumstance may be taken as further proof that the manuscript collections, normally the work of monastic copyists, are by no means representative of popular taste in the Middle Ages.

The immediate origin of the English *chanson dramatique* is not a problem, as the French influences are all too evident; but the source of the *pastourelle* has evoked a great deal of speculation in France. Gaston Paris, of course, found in the dance songs of the *fêtes de mai* the source of this[60] and other lyric forms. In his opinion, the northern *pastourelle* developed quite independently of the Provençal *pastorela*, though from the same Poitou-Limousin region.[61] Jeanroy suggested that the type first rose in Le Midi on an aristocratic level and migrated to the North,[62] as the oldest specimen of the class is attributed to Marcabrun[63] and is dated anterior to the earliest French example. Faral has shown that the eclogues of Virgil furnished some suggestions for the method followed in these poems, though he does not suppose that the *pastourelle* sprang from classical sources.[64] The resemblance of the rejection motif in many French pieces to the theme of the "baffled knight" of popular literature has been examined by Jones.[65] Whatever the origin, the *pastourelle* as it exists in more than 150 specimens[66] is *poésie populaire* at the very point of becoming *courtoise*. In point of fact, some composers of *pastourelles* worked also with the *chanson courtois*. The conventional introduction—the springtime and the riding out—has earned for the *pastourelle* the reputation of a stereotype, which Jeanroy says it is not.[67] The best of the *chansons d'aventure* achieve a rich texture, beside which the English specimens seem bare. Nor can the misty English spirit of the fourteenth century often attain the gaiety, the bright if conventional springtime tapestry, or the sprightly and frequently realistic dialogue of the French.

Als i me rod this ender dai, the liveliest example in the

period, stands in the most intimate relationship to the French.[68] Since the conclusion is unfortunately lost, the rapprochement of poet and "litel mai" must be sought in a French parallel, which Miss Sandison first pointed out,[69] without implying, however, that it was the source of the Hale *pastourelle*. Skeat's reconstruction clears up the textual difficulties, and the situation becomes plain. The poet heard the maid singing a lament for the loss of a faithless lover, who had falsely her "bi-hot/ of loue trewe." He turned aside to the "herber swot" where she sat "under a bogh" and expressed the usual concern over her distress. Though the outcome of this pleasant encounter may be inferred, it is impossible to recapture the idiom and thus complete the fragment. The lovely refrain,

> Now springes the sprai—
> Al for loue i am so seke
> That slepen i ne mai,

and the smooth-flowing rhythm declare for a musical setting, although notation has not survived.

Böddeker detected the influence of the *estrif* on *In a fryht as y con fere fremede*,[70] and it is true that the argumentation is prolonged, perhaps excessively. In any case, the characteristic reluctance of the shepherdess to yield to the knight produces sharp repartee, and the Harleian piece represents no marked divergence from the type. The poet dispenses with much of the introductory machinery, and in the third line he states that "heo glystnede ase gold when hit glemede." "This burde bryht" quickly rejects the suit. The poet promises, "comeliche y wol the nou clethe," but does not enumerate the articles of clothing. This is a clumsy handling of the conventional proffer of gay dress. A French poet is much more effective:

> si vous donrai riche don,
> escarlate et pelicon,

la cainture de deus tors:
s'irons cueillir la violete
et si serons riches d'amors,
et si serez plus joliete
que l'aloete au point du jor.[71]

Trans. So I will give you a rich gift, scarlet and pelisse, a girdle of two windings. So we shall go to pick the violet, and so we shall be rich of love, and so you will be prettier than the lark at break of day.

As expected, the offer is rejected. The girl prefers to go poorly arrayed than to have fine "robes, ant synke in to synne." Thus the debate draws out without particular advantage to either. The end is obscure and inconclusive, but the poet is possibly rejected. The French *pastourell?* affords the conclusion with the simple rejection, though it is the least striking of the several possibilities. Sometimes the *chevalier* compels the *bergère* by force, which she may make only a show of resisting. Often she escapes by a clever ruse, or her friends arrive in the nick of time and beat the intruder. Occasionally the maiden appraises the situation shrewdly and comments on the turn of affairs with uncommon acumen.[72] *In a fryht* is clumsy beside the really good *pastourelles*, in both conception and execution. Moreover, the composer has carried metrical effects much too far: besides the expected complicated rhyme and alliteration, stanza-linking occurs at a number of points. The alliterated sound of the concluding verse of one stanza is carried over into the first line of the following, and the concluding syllable of the last line is repeated in the new stanza:[73]

. . . .
ne kepte heo non hethyng here,
"yhere thou me nou, hendest in helde . . ."

Intermittent alliteration also marks *As I stod on a day me self under a tre*, which is metrically the roughest lyric of the three under consideration. Yet, the College of Arms *pastourelle* achieves some particularity in the description of the maid's costume, and the language, though rough, is idiomatic and muscular. The poet finds the girl one morning in a meadow dressed perhaps too handsomely for pastoral pursuits:

> Of a blak bornet al wos hir wede,
> Purfiled with pellour doun to the teon;
> A red hod on hir heved, shragid al of shredis,
> With a riche riban gold-begon.

No simpleton, she reads a book as she rides along "hir selve al on." The man, announcing his intentions, asks Christ's blessing on her, but is quickly informed, "Thu findis hir nout hire the sot that thu seche."[74] The worldly wise *bergère*, if that she be, is not to be deceived. She advises him, "It is non ned to mak hit so tow . . . wend fort ther ye wenin better for to spede." Presumably, this *chanson d'aventure* is complete, as was the Harleian which also closed on the rejection note.

These *pastourelles* are not brilliant examples of English lyrical genius, and there is a possibility that they are less than representative of the body of such song written in the island at the end of the thirteenth century. French verve and éclat are nowhere to be observed; there are no dancing youth or maidens singing *dorenlots;* no sheep in a picturesque setting. The genre has perhaps come into the keeping of poets with little appreciation or understanding of the milieu from which it sprang, probably religious, too imbued with the sense of earth's wickedness to enter enthusiastically into the spirit of earth's *renouveau.* One must look to the *Baffled Knight*[75] for *l'esprit gaulois* in English. But the *pastourelle* has displayed amazing stamina and yet persists in oral tradition, as the researches of Cecil Sharp in this century have disclosed.[76]

If none of the English love songs translates precisely the spirit of the dainty *chanson d'amour*, all preserve some characteristic features and faintly echo the desperate plaint of the trouvère. Of the Harleian love lyrics sufficiently subjective to be regarded as complaints the most polished omits few conspicuous features of the stylized chansons. The familiar *reverdie*, constant overture of chanson as well as of *pastourelle*, is here commendably phrased: "When the nyhtegale singes, the wodes waxen grene,/ Lef & gras & blosme springes in aueryl, y wene." The nightingale crosses the Channel sometime after the middle of April[77] and settles as far north as Yorkshire on the eastern coast. Even then, as later, the nightingale was less a bird than a symbol of romantic associations, reaching back ultimately to the fertile soil of troubadour invention.[78] It is hardly surprising that in the next breath the poet would announce that the fabulous "dart of love" had pierced his heart, as it had wounded many a singer of Le Midi: "ant loue is to myn herte gon with one spere so kene,/ nyht & day my blod hit drynkes, myn herte deth to tene."[79] From the image of the bleeding heart, the poet goes on in the second, third, and fourth stanzas to describe his passion with undoubted sincerity. It is English love, intimately related to the object, and not French *amour*, which can survive in a rarefied state with less reference to the lady. Abstract love was not at this time congenial to the temper of English poets, partly on account of a lack of sophistication, partly for the reason that the chivalric ideal had lost its vitality. In the late thirteenth-century milieu, the rapturous analyses of the trouvères were impracticable. Yet, the advantage is not entirely with the ecstatic Chrétiens; this Harleian poet, for example, seldom takes his eye from the proper object, the "suete lemmon" for whom he has "siked moni syk." His sustained personal reflection on love, rare in the period, carries such conviction as a less particularized flight could not.

When the nyhtegale singes approaches in point of artistry
the carefully managed statements of French poetry, with-
out sacrificing the concreteness typical of pre-Chaucerian
lyrics. The more liberal English social mode permitted,
moreover, such frankness of expression and intimacy of
style as lend conviction to the poet's exclamations. The
egotistical trouvère bound by strict rules of conduct invites
attention to himself as a long-suffering servant of love,
whereas the unrestrained English poet can concentrate upon
a real situation instinct with thrilling possibilities. The
skillful French poet may achieve excitement, despite the
fundamental difficulty in the amorphous and static charac-
ter of the relationship which he acknowledges. On the
other hand, real love in a state of mounting tension is ob-
viously a more moving experience than a parlor game of
glances and blushes. Doubtless Chrétien de Troyes owned
a deep and abiding passion, but he was constrained by the
code set forth in the *De Amore* from coming to grips with
his beloved foe. Since he could only lament in *D'Amors,
qui m'a tolu a moi*[80] the condition to which service of *Amors*
had reduced him, generalizing was the only suitable means
of amplification. Not so the English poet! Little inhibited
by the rules of *amour courtois,* he has no hesitation in ask-
ing for what will relieve his pain:

> Suete lemmon, y preye the of loue one speche:
> whil y lyue in world so wyde other nulle y seche;
> with thy loue, my suete leof, mi blis thou mihtes eche,
> a suete cos of thy mouth mihte be my leche.

Ovidian and courtly love had long since fallen together,[81]
and the rules for the nice conduct of a lover were blurred.
This is not even "derne" love, since the poet incidentally
reveals that others know of the relation: "yef thou me louest,
ase men says . . . thou loke that hit be sene." Though
there is little reason to doubt that the poet wrote from per-

sonal experience, the geographical reference in the last
stanza is no clue as to the dwelling of the maiden, but
rather a conventional device, such as Jehan Froissart often
used to introduce his pseudo-*pastourelles*. Compare "Entre
Arbrecicourt et Mauni,"[82] with the English, "bituene lyn-
colne & lyndeseye, norhamptoun ant lounde,/ ne wot y non
so fayr a may, as y go fore ybounde." For unified expres-
sion, excellence of construction, and rhythmic grace, *When
the nyhtegale singes* ranks high among medieval English
lyrics, whatever it may lack of the spontaneity of *Alysoun*.

With longyng y am lad deserves mention here, as the poet
has made a painful attempt to write a sustained analysis of
the pangs of love. The first three stanzas are an imageless
profusion of commonplace declarations, loosely united by
the theme of unrequited love. Oddly enough, the poem
takes a turn toward particularity in the concluding stanza;
here the poet reveals not only that the maiden "woneth by
west," but that "heuene y tolde al his that o nyht were
hire gest." Sir Edmund was perhaps unduly titillated by
this disclosure,[83] as the desperate humility of the foregoing
complaint militates against a literal interpretation. Some
historical interest attaches to the poet's use of iambic tri-
meter, although it is in no sense an improvement over the
long-line.

Attention has centered on the stanzaic peculiarities[84] of
A wayle whyt ase whalles bon rather than on what for the
history of English lyric is more important: the curious blend
of courtly convention and conceit, innuendo, and blunt
realism. It is "derne" love of necessity, but this poet, unlike
the chivalric type, has not been satisfied to admire at a dis-
tance this "tortle that min herte is on." No veil of pretense
conceals the fundamental immorality of this clandestine
association, to which the woman's husband is an obvious
impediment. The poet, who appears himself to be married
("y wolde chaunge myn for his that is here fere"), states

his problem with commendable frankness, the sordidness of the relation notwithstanding. This "swete thing with eyenen gray" seems to be unhappy in the wedded state— "marred in mournyng," as the lover asserts. Wounded by her eyes, he rages inwardly at circumstances which will not permit him to reveal openly his love:

> Herkneth me, y ou telle,
> in such wondryng for wo y welle,
> nys no fur so hot in helle
>   al to mon,
> that loueth derne ant darnout telle
> whet him ys on.

The impression is strong that the lyric is autobiographical, the spasmodic unreeling of a wholly credible love affair. The concluding stanza,

> Ich wolde ich were a threstelcok,
> a bountyng other a lauerok.
>   swete bryd!
> bi tuene hire curtel ant hire smok
> y wolde ben hyd.

is delightfully naive and in fact one of the most surprising declarations in the language.

Ichot a burde in boure bryht is notable for a lovely, though irrelevant refrain,

> Blow, northerne wynd,
> sent thou me my suetyng!
> blow, northerne wynd,
> blou! blou! blou!

This fragment and two comparable snatches—*Western Wind* and the refrain of the *Unquiet Grave*[85]—have been associated by Chambers with folk song,[86] whatever the term may now signify. The poem proper is a *mélange* of catalogues and clichés; it has no unity, little meaning, however beautiful individual stanzas may be. Böddeker and Brown have remarked the resemblance of *Ichot a burde in boure bryht* to *Ichot a burde in a bour ase beryl so bryht, With longyng y am lad,* and *Mosti ryden by rybbesdale,*[87] which are hardly the best secular lyrics in the manuscript. The author or authors of these four (numerous parallel phrases argue for common authorship) appear to have had access to a variety of conventional thirteenth-century songs—French, or English imitations. To these hypothetical models are no doubt due the conceited style and wooden formulas, of which the catalogue of feminine charms is perhaps the most abominable. These four Harleian lyrics usually begin nowhere and go nowhere: excepting *With longyng y am lad,* they are almost entirely descriptive. The stanzas are strung together without much regard for logical arrangement, and the lineaments of the fair remain as ill-defined as those of the lady of courtly fifteenth-century lyric, despite a superabundance of metaphor. Since *Ichot a burde in boure bryht* reveals most of the author's lyric propensities, it will serve to illustrate the method.

This lyric is a patchwork of redundant images and hackneyed phrases. The first six stanzas are devoted to altogether conventional praise of the lady's beauty; the opening stanza, for example, is literally packed with alliterative formulas, several of which were patently threadbare in the fourteenth century:

> Ichot a burde in boure bryht,[88]
> that fully semly is on syht,[89]
> menskful maiden of myht,
>   feir ant fre to fonde;
> In al this wurhliche won,
> a burde of blod & of bon:[90]
> neuer yete y nuste non
>   Lussomore in londe.

The second stanza introduces a deplorable tendency toward *repetitio:*

> with lokkes lefliche & longe,
> with frount & face feir to fonde . . .

and this rhetorical artifice is given free rein in the sixth stanza, where no less than eight metaphors are strung together:[91]

> Heo is coral of godnesse,
> heo is rubie of ryhtfulnesse,
> heo is cristal of clannesse,
> ant baner of bealte,
> heo is lilie of largesse,
> heo is paruenke of prouesse,
> heo is selsecle of suetnesse,
> ant ledy of lealte.

The resemblance of this stanza to *Ichot a burde in a bour as beryl so bryht* is striking; coral, ruby, lily, periwinkle *(paruenke)*, and marigold *(selsecle)* are all terms of comparison in the latter poem, which is a series of metaphors and similes.

The poet introduces in the seventh stanza a curious allegory: to Love he complains that the knights of the lady— Sighing, Sorrowing, and Thought—have him "in bale broht." After hearing him through, Love recommends that he take the hoard of his "huerte hele" to the "swete ant swote," in the hope that she "with the wolle of bote derewortheliche dele." Whether this supplicatory maneuver succeeds is not apparent; the concluding stanza is an accumulation of hardships suffered by the poet on behalf of the lady:

> for hire loue y carke ant care,
> for hire loue y droupne ant dare . . .

The greatest importance attaches to the poem for the employment of allegory, which is certainly uncommon in lyric before Chaucer, although such petitions to the God of

Love[92] later became trite, when allegory had thoroughly permeated polite literature.

Romance convention and English spirit and rhythm are consummately wedded in *Alysoun,* one of the most satisfying of all medieval lyrics; despite its used furniture, the poem exhibits a pleasing naïveté and a racy movement unexampled in French song.[93]   Unlike the trouvère, in love with love and without hope of achieving more than acceptance of his service, the Midland poet thrills with the prospect of a union which has apparently been sealed with promises.   The melancholy of the third and fourth stanzas reflects the normal apprehension of a high-spirited suitor, not that of a hopeless lover.   Though he may worry "lest eny reue me my make," the throbbing refrain best agrees with his mood,

> An hendy hap ichabbe yhent,
> ichot, from heuene it is me sent,
> from alle wymmen mi loue is lent
> & lyht on alysoun.

The *reverdie* opening, faintly reminiscent of the refrain of *Als i me rod this ender dai,* is obviously conventional, but the poet in his ingenuous way has freshened the formula. The parallel between the song of the lover and the song of the bird is probably intentional:

> Bytuene mersh & aueril,
>   when spray beginneth to springe,
> the lutel foul hath hire wyl
>   on hyre lud to synge.

In the last four lines of the first stanza, the poet declares his "louelonginge"; only the "semlokest of alle thinge" can bring him bliss.   After a description of her person, he expresses the depth of his passion for lovely Alysoun with "eye blake" and "swyre . . . whittore then the swon."   Unless she will take him for "hire owen make," he will forsake

life and fated "fallen adoun." The sincerity of this an-
nouncement is implicit not only in the simple phrasing, but
in the very character of the relationship the lover desires,
for "make" implies marriage, a result intolerable to the
social order which spawned the *chanson d'amour*. Never-
theless, the song expresses the same physical distress of the
courtly lover: the poet's insomnia ("Nihtes when y wende
& wake") and pallor ("myn wonges waxeth won") are the
usual symptoms of *li duz mal de amer*. He is "wery so water
in wore" for fear of losing Alysoun; he will forbear to act
indiscreetly toward this "geynest vnder gore," who might
easily be alienated. The characteristic humility of the lover
and idealization of the lady are nonetheless modified, and
the artificial standards of courtly love appear to count for
little. If the emotion is counterfeited, no one suspects the
deception. Without benefit of rhetorical flourishes, the poet
has explicitly stated his feeling for black-eyed Alysoun,
representing himself as a sensitive person moved intermit-
tently by hopes and fears. The effect of the unified sen-
sibility is then to divert attention to the poet as a lover
whose experience is universal. He preserves the unity of
the song by carefully controlling subordinate descriptive
elements and amplifies the exclamatory core by such honest
disclosures as win an audience to enthusiastic support of
his suit.

The *Fairy of Ribbesdale*, possibly by the author of *Annot
and Johon*, is a not wholly unsuccessful expansion of the con-
ventional physical description.[94] It is not, as Miss Sandison
thought,[95] an undeveloped *pastourelle*. There is absolutely
no development; the poet has simply amplified every feature
of the medieval beauty, as portrayed in romance and lyric.[96]
It has nevertheless a richness of texture that clichés cannot
entirely dissipate and a romantic charm, associated however
sentimentally with "charm'd magic casements, opening on
the foam of perilous seas, in fairy lands forlorn."

In actuality, the lyric is a disguised catalogue. The fairy
of Ribbesdale is the apogee of medieval pulchritude, an
ideal compounded of the portraits of all the lovely ladies
of romance. With the stock images of courtly lyric, the
poet has pieced her together: "ase sonnebem hire bleo ys
briht"; "the lylie lossum is ant long"; "hyre eyen aren grete
ant gray ynoh"; "Heo hath browes bend an heh"; "hire lockes
lefly aren & longe"; "eyther cheke whit ynoh & rode on eke,
ase rose when hit redes"; "lefly rede lippes lele"; "teht aren
white ase bon of whal, euene set ant atled al"; "swannes
swyre swythe wel y sette"; "eyther arm an elne long"; "hyre
tyttes aren an vnder bis as apples tuo of parays"; "Heo hath
a mete myddel smal"; and "eyther side soft ase sylk." With
this composite many portraits in Old French and Middle
English might be compared, but a perfectly conventional
one from a chanson of Colin Muset serves to indicate the
author's indebtedness to the tradition:

> Ele ot brun poil, s'est plus blanche que fee,
> Droit nés, blans danz con est la flors en pree,
> Vairs euz rianz, boichette encoloree,
> Front blanc et cler, tendre come rosee;
> Gente de cors, de membres acemee,
> Ainz plus bele ne fu de mere nee.[97]

Trans. She had brown hair; she is whiter than a fairy,
straight nose, teeth white as flower in the meadow,
laughing gray eyes, small reddened mouth, forehead
white and clear, tender as the dew, lovely of body,
of limbs provided. A more beautiful one was never
of mother born.

Inexplicably, the English poet brings this apparent idealiza-
tion of the maid to a close with the laconic and wholly un-
courtly observation that one who "myhte nyhtes neh hyre
leye,/ heuene he heuede here."

De Clerico et Puella escapes the conventions of French

lyric as do few others of the period.[98] It is not properly to
be referred to any well-defined genre, though clearly shar-
ing features with the debate and the *chanson dramatique,*
and suggesting relationship with French lyric at several
points. This is a lyrico-dramatic poem on the order of those
inimitable and unclassifiable late fifteenth-century pieces,
the *Notbrowne Mayde* and *Robene and Makyne.* The dic-
tion is unadorned, almost rough; the phrasing idiomatic and
sharply redolent of the English countryside. Yet, it is the
work of an artist, perhaps a religious who broke loose from
conventional forms and compounded a dialogue of uncom-
mon merit. The situation is readily deduced from the
exchanges. It is a clandestine meeting, perhaps in the home
of the girl. The clerk[99] importunes; the girl resists. In the
first two stanzas, he speaks the part of the suffering lover:

> My deth y loue, my lyf ich hate, for a leuedy shene,
> heo is briht so daies liht, that is on me wel sene;
> al y falewe so doth the lef in somer when hit is grene;
> yef mi thoht helpeth me noht, to wham shal y me mene?
>
> st. 1

The Puella denies any interest in the clerk and furthermore
warns him of the danger of being found out. But he per-
sists and declares it were a "mykel sham" if he should die.
How much better it would be for both, the amorous scholar
continues, if "thou lete me lyue, & be thi luef, & thou my
suete lemman." He ignores her reiterated warning of a
menacing father and other kin and reminds the girl of the
bliss he felt when on one occasion, standing at a window,
they kissed fifty times. The Puella succumbs: "fader, moder,
& al my kun" notwithstanding, she grants her love to the
clerk that he may not on her account "woundes thole grylle."
   This dramatic lyric is a successful blend of courtly and
popular elements: the language of polite supplication and
the tough idiom of the countryside, the appearance of decor-

ous courtship beside red-blooded actuality. The clerk's calculated confession to the country wench, "sorewe, & syke, & drery mod byndeth me so faste,/ that y wene to walke wod, yef hit me lengore laste," is amusingly incongruous in a situation which mirrors social relationships at the *Reeve's Tale* level. But the clerk's nice behavior succeeds well with the girl, who, despite her stout demurral, is taken with the address of the ministerial student. Indeed, she is in the end won over by his learned speech, beside which her own is somewhat rude. If the same poet also wrote *When the nyhtegale singes*, he had the happy faculty of disengaging himself at will from his literary background, for this vigorous dialogue denies strong French influence. The very ease and rapidity of execution may be owing to the author's sense of freedom from formal restrictions. In such dramatic frames, which fill out naturally with action, the English lyric gift at this stage of development shows to advantage. The poorest exhibitions in the Harleian manuscript and in later collections as well are those which use rhetorical artifices and synthetic attitudes.

The exact purpose of another lyric of the Harleian manuscript is not apparent. Though two thirds of the piece are given over to advising women to beware of treacherous men, the first stanza is a perfectly commonplace nature setting such as one finds in numerous love songs:[100]

> In may hit murgeth when hit dawes
> In dounes with this dueres plawes,
>   Ant lef is lyht on lynde;
> blosmes bredeth on the bowes,
> al this wylde wyhtes wowes,
>   so wel ych vnder fynde.
>   . . . .
> so worly wymmen are by west;
> one of hem ich herie best
>   from Irlond in to ynde.

The personal reference provides the setting for a complaint
or a eulogy; neither is forthcoming. Instead, the poet gen-
eralizes about the instability of men in their relations with
women until the last three lines, where he declares that
Lily-face, presumably the lady mentioned in the first stanza,
should be reconciled to him if she would only take his ad-
vice. This disjointed structure is particularly characteristic
of Harleian songs and is with several other specimens ade-
quate proof that their authors were uncertain of the best
means of achieving unity.

Lutel wot hit anymon,[101] previously mentioned in connec-
tion with religious lyric, proceeds a bit more coherently,
though even in this instance the circumstances are far from
clear. An estrangement is implied by the statement, "Heo
haueth me plyht, & wyteth me wyth wronge," but it is the
poet's obvious intention to conceal the real situation. The
offense implied in the supplicatory third stanza, for example,
is deliberately unspecified:

> Adoun y fel to hire anon
>   ant crie, "ledy, thyn ore!
> ledy, ha mercy of thy mon!
>   lef thou no false lore!
>   yef thou dost, hit wol me reowe sore,
>   Loue dreccheth me that y ne may lyue namore."

And then the curious "O and I" refrain: "Euer & oo for my
leof icham in grete thohte,/ y thenche on hire that y ne seo
nout ofte."[102] Elsewhere in the poem striking passages in-
vite attention, though little is to be made of them in relation
to the whole. More than likely the lyric was written to
plead a special case before the poet's lady. The last stanza,
which is in the form of a salutation, suggests as much.

It is now generally agreed that *Weping haueth myn
wonges wet* is a perfectly sincere apology by a poet who
regrets having written satires of women;[103] the allusion to

the Virgin Mary is incompatible with an ironic intention. The mere mention of the Mother of Christ was enough, it should be recalled, to convert the misogynous bird of *The Thrush and the Nightingale* to praise of women. As lyric, the poem is diffuse and obscure, the reference to an unknown poet Richard creating ostensibly insoluble difficulties, notwithstanding Böddeker's tentative identification of him with the author of an Anglo-Norman poem in Digby 86.[104] But the worst of it is the poet's insistence on complex form. Alliteration is regularly overdone, and line- and stanza-linking are carried to an extreme. The first two verses, with loose fabric, go well enough, but the tighter lines following are gritty with heaped-up consonants:

> Weping haueth myn wonges wet
> for wikked werk and wone of wyt;
> vnblithe y be, til y ha bet
> bruches broken, ase bok byt . . .

The first eight lines of the stanza are four-stress, and a concluding batch of four lines is three-stress. These parts are linked by repetition,[105] and the last line is in turn linked to the following stanza:

> . . . .
> that is vnsemly ther hit syt.
> Hit syt & semeth noht
> ther hit ys seid in song;
> that y haue of hem wroht,
> ywis, hit is al wrong.

However rueful the poet may be, he does little to communicate his contrition. It is obvious that his time is taken up with the search for rhyme words and alliterative formulas, with the result that the poem says very little. Alliteration in Harley 2253 is not a metrical principle, and there is not the slightest excuse for the constant use of it. Such lines as "a stythye stunte hire sturne stryf" and "Hap that hathel hath hent" are metrical geese, which do the author of the insignificant palinode no credit.

Whether the sacrifice of spirit and coherence to form was a confirmed tendency among English poets at the beginning of the fourteenth century cannot be determined for the lack of an adequate sampling from the several decades immediately preceding Chaucer's appearance. Unmistakable evidence of artificiality and formalism does crop out in the Harleian collection, and several of the lyrics were inspired less by a desire to communicate experience than to display verbal ingenuity. In view of the emphasis placed on formal lyric features in France, contamination was probably inevitable. That the Harleian lyrics are relatively free of artificiality is partially owing to a cultural lag; for the free lyric spirit most brilliantly exemplified in late twelfth-century song had been disciplined, and religious and didactic verse had come into favor, notably with the memberships of the stuffy *puys*.

As for the influence of the trouvères on pre-Chaucerian poets, clichés and formulas generously acknowledge a substantial debt. The French lyric, however, was suggestive rather than prescriptive, and English poets seldom felt bound to follow the patterns strictly, although frequently using effective locutions translated from the polished chansons. The spirit and decorum of trouvère song, needless to say, were not translated, and the realistic love adventures and frank exclamations of *Alysoun, When the nyhtegale singes,* and *De Clerico et Puella* confess no external obligations.

CHAPTER THREE

SONGS OF SATIRE AND PROTEST

THE THEME OF RELIGIOUS OR SECULAR LOVE—LOVE
of Mary or love of Marot—engaged the attention of early
lyric poets almost exclusively, with the result that the bur-
geoning nationalism and incipient class struggle of the last
two centuries of the Middle Ages are seldom mirrored in
song. Most of the worthwhile Middle English lyrics de-
voted to political and social arguments were written between
1250 and 1350—between the *Song of Lewes* and the battle
songs of Laurence Minot. Before the reign of the third
Henry (1216-72), complaint, satire, and eulogy were in-
variably committed to parchment in Latin or French for
the edification of cloister or court. Both languages declined
in importance during the Edwardian era[1] as Middle English
became widely acceptable for literary purposes; but the
restoration of the spoken tongue was not accompanied by
lyric which adequately represented the impatience of the
folk with baronial and ecclesiastical injustice. Besides the
Harleian pieces, only Minot's command close attention be-
fore 1400, and in the transition non-amatory secular lyric
is no better than the insipid love poetry.

   For the dearth of lyric of this kind, there are several pos-
sible causes. The minstrels, who might have fashioned a
weapon as effective as the Provençal *sirvente*,[2] were in a
late stage of decline, the victims not only of the enmity of
Church and State but also of their own fading talents. Even
had they been productive, history would in all probability
reveal little of their work, because such extant lyric as suited
the needs of wayfaring entertainers, like the *Song of the*

Husbandman and the *Satire of the Consistory Courts,* would not often have created enthusiasm in monastic *scriptoria.* Neither clergy nor royalty was disposed to encourage criticism of its conduct from members of lower classes. Of course, by the fifteenth century, minstrelsy was inarticulate, and poets of learning were firmly bound to noble patrons. Moreover, dissident clerks, who in the thirteenth and fourteenth centuries wrote satirical poetry reflective of the attitudes of commoners, no longer felt free to write provocative verse in the face of repressive Church policies. That little meritorious political and social lyric was written after 1350 may be attributed perhaps to the menace which a poet dared in handling controversial issues as well as to the weakened creative impulse.

Then as now, fundamental difficulties troubled the author of occasional verse. It was no easy task to wax rhapsodic over affairs of the government and of the military. The issues were often too complex, too remote from human interests. Wine and women, life and death, these were ever subjects more amenable to emotional treatment than the dull processes of judiciaries and the dispassionate gestures of public servants. In most of the Middle English examples, interest is borne by narrative segments. The authors normally express a tedious didacticism or splenetic prejudice, which eschews intimate articulation with the framework. Hence, the emotion of the poet, however intense, merely punctuates the recital. Granted that political lyric tends to be polemical or simply assertive, it is still possible for a poet to infuse an incident of a battle or an arbitrary edict of the crown with his own glowing passion and thereby force the prosaic matter to express a particular emotion. The medieval poet, however, was often at a loss for a means of subordinating physical circumstances to feeling, because the unsophisticated audience unquestionably demanded a substantial narrative core, uttered with rele-

vance of detail and fidelity to literal truth. As a conse-
quence, some of the pieces are merely narratives studded
with unintegrated commentary, and few actually transform
the perishable stuff of medieval life into intense statements
of universal truth. For all its excellence, the *Song of Lewes*
does not mold the accidental circumstances of the Barons'
War into a clear and powerful statement of the political
awakening reflected in England by the advance of repre-
sentative government.

When Simon de Montfort overwhelmed Henry III at
Lewes in 1264, the movement toward the democratic pro-
cess gained for the moment a long stride forward; and
commoners throughout England had cause to cheer. The
Song of Lewes—popular and partisan in tone—celebrates
the capture of the king's brother Richard, earl of Cornwall,
who had taken refuge in a mill at the conclusion of the
battle. The lyric was probably composed shortly after
May 14, certainly before the death of the Earl of Leicester
at Evesham the next year.[3] The poet's use of English (this
is the oldest surviving political lyric) is explained by the
character of the audience for which the song was designed.
As a matter of fact, Latin and Anglo-Norman in the mid-
thirteenth century were still flourishing; poems in both
languages were written on the battle.[4] The author—min-
strel, gleeman, or *vagus*—shrewdly appraised the tastes of
his plebeian auditors and selected for vigorous and direct
literary treatment an incident no doubt relished by the
Montfort party. Though there is no proof that the lyric
was sung, melody is suggested by the swinging movement
of the monorhymed quatrains, embroidered with bob and
refrain. The quatrain has lines of four stresses, with an
indeterminate number of unstressed syllables, and sporadic
alliteration. The beginning—"Sitteth alle stille & herkneth
to me"—is a conventional minstrel introduction, a request
for attention not infrequently associated with popular song.[5]

Simon de Montfort was a Norman, son of that Simon who figured conspicuously in the Albigensian Crusade; yet he fired the imagination and captured the affection of much of England by his courageous opposition to Henry III. Henry had evaded the principles of the Magna Carta until brought abruptly into line by the Provisions of Oxford, enacted in 1258 by the so-called Mad Parliament. For the next six years, Henry was either repudiating the Provisions or reaffirming them under duress.[6] The political skirmishing of the Barons' War culminated in the battle of Lewes, which came as a direct result of Henry's refusal to abide by the Provisions. Though weakened by the defection of many nobles to the royalist party, Simon employed superior strategy in seizing the South Downs, dominating the position at Lewes held by Henry's forces, and by a ruse induced Prince Edward to attack his poorly trained recruits from London. With his main force, Simon swept over the left side of the royalist line, capturing the king, his brother Richard, and Edward.

Perhaps in deference to the crown, the poet forbears mentioning Henry and instead deals with a situation mainly involving Richard. The other members of the king's party noticed by the author—Earl Warenne, Hugh Bigod,[7] and Prince Edward—were, with Richard, at one time or another friendly to Simon and the cause of the barons. The poet's malice is, on account of their change of heart, not without justification. The song opens with a reference to an offer made by the barons to Richard in the interest of peace— "thritti thousent pound askede he/ fforte make the pees in the countre," but the proffer was declined. After retailing a bit of gossip in the second stanza about the earl's private life, the poet in the third rehearses the incident of the mill:[8]

> the kyng of alemaigne wende do ful wel,
> he saisede the mulne for a castel;
> with hare sharpe swerdes he grounde the stel,

he wende that the sayles were mangonel
     to helpe wyndesore.
Richard, thah thou be euer trichard,
     tricchen shalt thou neuer more!

Notwithstanding the effective mockery of Richard's vain attempt to stand off Simon, Cornwall appears to have had nothing for which to apologize at Lewes.[9] The allusion to Windsor in the "bob" is to be explained by Richard's efforts in the preceding February to organize resistance to the barons at Windsor and Oxford, a project in which Edward assisted. In the fifth, sixth, and seventh stanzas, the poet casts appropriate aspersions on Earl Warenne and Hugh Bigod, at the same time regretting that they were permitted to escape to France after the battle. In conclusion, he predicts that Edward, for acting the part of a scoundrel, willy-nilly must "ride sporeles o thy lyard al the ryhte way to douere ward"—that is, into exile.[10]

Satiric and mocking, the product of an emotion expended in a partisan cause long forgotten, the *Song of Lewes* has not now the power to re-create the fervor of the Barons' War; yet six centuries have not diminished the poet's deep earnestness or muffled the exultant throb of a hymn on a victory the people could claim altogether as their own. Nor is the song mainly of metrical and linguistic interest, for the poet displayed moderate skill in forcing loosely connected military and political circumstances into a clear and vigorous expression of the Montfort point of view. The lyric is assuredly marred by the author's self-righteousness, which was no uncommon fault of the times; but this attitude was an integral part of the experience which he intended to communicate. The threatening refrain, "Richard, thah thou be euer trichard,/ tricchen shalt thou neuer more," focuses attention on an individual who could be hated with unmixed feelings, as he was more closely identified with the Continent than with England. Cornwall's defeat at the mill signified the triumph of Montfort and of the people's cause, and the author's exultation over this minor incident points up the popular reaction to the greater victory. The *Song of Lewes* is, nevertheless, merely evidence of the democratic impulse, not a clear poetic expression of it. Although the complex stanza may be a French loan, the accentual scansion and rustic idiom stem from native resources. Whatever this vigorous poem may lack of lyric grace, it is indisputably English in spirit.

English animus during the reigns of the three Edwards was reserved in particular for Scot and Frenchman. In the *Song of the Flemish Insurrection,* an English minstrel chortles over the disgraceful defeat of French knighthood at Courtrai and incidentally furnishes a fairly circumstantial account of the uprising. England had a considerable interest in the Flemings during this period, as Edward had recruited allies along the northern border of France with the expectation of warring on Philip. Little came of the coalition inasmuch as a truce was struck in 1298. Since the Flemings were left without support, Guy of Dampierre, count of Flanders, went to Philip to make peace, but was imprisoned for his pains. Philip made a triumphal tour of the fief and concluded that the contention was settled. But on May 18, 1302, Flemish burghers brought off the "Matins of Bruges," in which every Frenchman in reach was slaughtered. A tremendous force of French armor, dispatched in the same year to avenge the massacre,

> Seuene eorles ant fourti barouns y tolde,
> fiftene hundred knyhtes, proude & swythe bolde,
> Sixti thousent swyers, among yunge ant olde,

was decisively defeated at Courtrai by the poorly equipped Flemings, ably led by the head of the craft of wool weavers, Peter Conig.[11]

Minor linguistic eccentricities and topical allusions have

doubtless impeded full appreciation of the artistry which goes into the construction of the *Song of the Flemish Insurrection*. It is perhaps to be regretted that the author expended his craft on a series of episodes which have nowadays no more than passing interest, but he had no way of judging the relative importance of the insurrection, which at the beginning of the fourteenth century was an event of some magnitude in European affairs. Considerations like these clearly should not enter into the evaluation of this lyric any more than into judgments on Tennyson's *Charge of the Light Brigade* or the *Revenge*.

The minstrel-author,[12] it may be presumed, wrote for an audience which required primarily a rousing narrative, instinct with all the animosity which the English in this period reserved for their hereditary enemies. The poet has unquestionably catered to the national prejudice and has emphasized that added source of gratification which the middle class took in the triumph of a guildsman army over French chivalry:

> Alas, thou seli fraunce! for the may thunche shome,
> that ane fewe ffullaris maketh ou so tome;
> Sixti thousent on a day hue maden fot lome,
>   with eorl & with knyht.

Though the framework of the song is narrative—as indeed are most pieces of a political kind in Middle English—it is no mere rehearsal of the cold facts of the Franco-Flemish contention. Cursory reading discloses the tension and suspense with which the episodes are invested.

Rhythm, represented in the *Song of Lewes* by a series of triphammer stresses, unrolls in a rippling succession of iambs and anapests in the looser fabric of the verse of the *Song of the Flemish Insurrection*. The meter is not of course deliberately measured; for this poet, like his contemporaries, composed with ear cocked for alliterated stresses. The tendency is nevertheless apparent:

in the lond of flaundres, among false ant trewe.
that the commun of bruges ful sore con arewe.

These lines demonstrate moreover the undulating move-
ment—the rise to the caesura, and the slight fading off—
by which this lyric stands rather apart from other specimens
of the Harleian manuscript. The stanza is complex, as ex-
pected at this time, with two four-stress triplets, each fol-
lowed by a three-stress *cauda*. The effect of the tail rhyme
is to vary the swinging motion of the monorhymed batches
of three long lines.

Internal evidence is quite enough to prove the poet's
familiarity with French, as the verse is larded with apt
French phrases—"pas pur pas," "dousse pers," "flour de lis,"
"par la goule de," and "nus ne lerrum en vie chanoun ne
moyne." As if to assure the audience of his command of
English idiom, the poet employs a group of images which
use has honored so frequently in the past five centuries that
they are now quite threadbare—"bohten hem ant solde,"
"ystyked ase swyn," "so liht so the hare," and "bittrere then
the galle." Figures of this kind served in the early four-
teenth century a perfectly legitimate function, having not
then a disgusting triteness. The expression is here occas-
ionally sharp and altogether effective. The ominous under-
statement of *Sir Patrick Spens* comes to mind when the poet
observes that "huere ledies huem [French nobles killed at
Courtrai] mowe abide in boure & in halle wel longe." When
the dismal news of the French rout comes to Paris, the king,

he smot doun is heued, is honden gon he wrynge,
thourhout al fraunce the word by gon to springe;
wo wes huem tho!

The poet is of course an English partisan and takes with his
contemporaries unpleasant delight in the slaughter of
French nobility; at the same time, he avoids the flaming

jingoism of Minot and the monitory smugness of the author of the *Execution of Sir Simon Fraser.*

The *Song of the Execution of Sir Simon Fraser* is an ugly reflection of political hatred, but nevertheless a true expression of the English attitude toward the Scots. Sir Simon was captured at the battle of Kirkencliff and executed in the autumn of 1306 after the conventional medieval manner. This event is the central matter of the piece, but the author incidentally discusses the campaign of Edward I to bring the northern territory under English suzerainty. The poem is colored by sententiousness and self-righteousness, by gratuitous advice mingled with childish threats. The poet probably addressed a nationalist audience, who relished the particularization of the execution—drawing, quartering, hanging, beheading, and burning of the bowels. Features of the song may now seem grimly humorous, such as the comparison of the reign of Robert Bruce with the short-lived career of the king of summer in the folk festivals,[13] although humor was probably no part of the poet's main intention. The last stanza but one is an oversimplification of the politico-military situation in 1306:

> the traytours of Scotlond token hem to rede,
> the barouns of engelond to brynge to dede,
> Charles of fraunce, so moni mon tolde,
> With myht & with streynthe hem helpe wolde,
>   his thonkes.
> Tprot, scot, for thi strif!
> hang up thyn hachet ant thi knyf,
> whil him lasteth the lyf
>   with the longe shonkes.

Like Minot, this partisan of Edward I envisages no justice save that of the English crown; unlike Minot, he cannot achieve and hold a high lyric pitch. Though obviously inferior to the two preceding lyrics, this Southern dialect poem retains minor historical interest.

The death of Edward I inspired an Anglo-Norman elegy of some depth, which was translated into English,[14] doubtless to satisfy popular demand. The English verse has the usual four stresses, though the tendency is toward an iambic foot, under the influence of the French line. The rhyme scheme is ababcbc, an early occurrence of the *Monk's Tale* scheme. Like other Harleian lyrics, this one may have been sung, though the command "herkneth to my song" is in the second line of the minstrel introduction merely a translation of "oiez . . . chançonete" of the original. Böddeker considers the French to be the work of a learned author.[15] The tendency toward iambic rhythm in the octosyllabic lines of the *Elegy on the Death of Edward I* is further confirmed in a comparable lament *On the Death of Edward III* of about 1377.[16] The poem is notable for a comparison of Edward to a ship, extended through most of the fourteen eight-line stanzas.[17] The rhyme scheme is like that of the preceding elegy. Edward II's evil reign brought forth a number of political complaints important as historical documents but of little lyric quality.[18]

Social protest is no doubt symptomatic of a healthy body politic. In England, the beginnings of vernacular complaint are coeval with the rise of a vigorous and intelligent laboring class—tenant farmer and skilled craftsman, sturdy types jealous of their liberties and increasingly aware of their importance to the realm. The poet who wrote the melancholic *Song of the Husbandman* expressed the sentiments of a new agrarian element which came in the Peasants' Revolt of 1381 to disclose the fearsome power latent in its numbers. If the social revolution, well under way during the reign of Edward I, was retarded by the Hundred Years' War, the movement was never actually brought to a halt in the rural areas of the kingdom.

The speaker of the lyric seems to be one of that class of relatively prosperous tenant farmers coming into promi-

nence during this period. Whether by origin a villein or a
freeman does not appear; but it matters little, for the yeoman
class which derived from villeinage came to have in the
fourteenth century as much importance as freeholders and
held considerable acreages directly from the landlord.[19]
The source of the husbandman's complaint is that his in-
come is insufficient to pay taxes, rent, and wages of those
day laborers he himself employs on the manor. The repre-
sentatives of the landlord exercise supervisory powers; they
earn as a consequence the bitter enmity of those from whom
they must exact the owner's part. The bailiff, who, in the
words of the poet, "bockneth vs bale, & weneth wel do" was
the general overseer of the manor. The hayward (or
messor) looked after the lord's grain,[20] and if zealous in
the performance of his duties would doubtless gain such
regard as the poet expresses, "the hayward heteth vs harm
to habben of his." Earlier, reeves and haywards were some-
times elected by their fellow-villeins to act as superinten-
dents under the bailiff, but, according to W. J. Corbett,
individual peasants often made strong efforts to escape the
responsibility of these positions.[21] It was originally the
special job of the beadle (or bydel) to collect the gafol from
the so-called gafol-gelders, who were freeholders of a
kind.[22] Collecting tax seems to have been the duty of the
"maister budel" of the poem, come pompously ("brust ase
a bore") to the holdings of those entered in his record.
Periodically in the fourteenth century, wood ran short, and
the woodwards had much to do keeping the tenants from
cutting the owner's timber or looking "vnder rys," as the
poet euphemistically expresses it. The tenant had more-
over to satisfy the "monie hynen that hopieth ther to," that
is, those laborers who expected a share of the harvest.[23] If
the king exacted every "furthe peni," as the poet avers,
taxation was unquestionably oppressive; and the practices
of the beadles in compelling quick sales of immature grain

("other sulle mi corn on gras that is grene") and work stock
("ich at the set dey [when tax due] sulle mi mare") were
likely to decrease the nation's wealth at the source. If some
exaggeration entered into the author's lament, "mai ich no
lengore lyue with mi lesinge," the sincerity of the brooding
complaint bespeaks a pressing grievance.

Largely on the evidence of the introduction—"Ich herde
men vpo mold make muche mon"—Böddeker concluded
that the *Song of the Husbandman* was the work of a wan-
dering scholar rather than of a farmer,[24] though more re-
cently he has been described as a "simple peasant" crying
in despair.[25] The poet implies that he had not always been
a farmer, "sethe y tok to the lond such tene me wes taht,"
and the complex rhyme and meter prove this singer no un-
lettered rustic. His intimate acquaintance with the manor
argues, on the other hand, an extensive knowledge of agri-
culture. There can be no question of the poet's sense of
oppression, which utters in every line a dismal view of con-
temporary conditions, "that maketh beggares go with bordon
& bagges." The expression is entirely personal, the emotion
explicit; this is not merely a running commentary or satire
on the evil state of the "lesse," but a poignant revelation of
the poet's own "cares ful colde." Subjectivity is here main-
tained, as it is not in most poetry of this kind. Whatever
deficiencies appear, the sustained mood imposes gratifying
unity on the song.

Chaucer's portrait of the evil Summoner confirms to a
large extent the description of an ecclesiastical tribunal
drawn in detail in the early years of the fourteenth century
by a victim of the "archdeacon's hook."[26] By this period,
the Church courts had acquired jurisdiction over far more
offenses than William I, in separating the religious and civil
judiciaries, had intended, and few activities, regardless of
their innocence, escaped the searching eye of canon law.
Henry II had tried unsuccessfully to wrest control over

various serious criminal offenses from the Church, but was stoutly opposed by Becket. No clerk—and clerks were all those with even the most tenuous connection with the Church—could be tried by civil authority, even though the charge were murder.[27] Yet, the bishops and their legalist representatives, the archdeacons, seem to have been interested mainly in moral infractions, which the spying summoners reported. Such causes the Consistory punished by the only means it had—penance, excommunication, and the like.[28] Yet money could work miracles in these courts; it could forestall even such investigations as might reveal a priest's concubine. Outright punishment fell on the poor, because the well-to-do usually preferred to pay a small tribute to avoid the embarrassment of a trial.[29]

Though the judgment imposed in the case set forth in the *Satire on the Consistory Courts* seems reasonably just, one cannot feel that justice flourished in the oppressive atmosphere of Consistory, with an "old cherl in a blake hure" presiding, while evil-speaking summoners crowd around to give evidence and venal clerks take down testimony—"heo pynkes with heore penne on heore parchemyn."[30] The defendant has been hailed to court to answer a familiar charge by one who shrieks that he must marry her. The court finds for the plaintiff and orders the customary redress:

> a pruest proud ase a po
> sethe weddeth vs bo;
> wyde heo worcheth vs wo
> for wymmene ware.

The conviction is lacking that the author was himself the victim; instead, the poem is probably an imaginative reconstruction of a commonplace drama by a poet who worked in the northern alliterative tradition. A strong personal note colors the narrative framework, and no little emotional tension comes out of the poor yeoman's recital of the evils of Consistory.

Two excellent satires against the friars are contained in MS. Cotton Cleopatra B.ii., *On the Minorite Friars* and *Song Against the Friars*.[31] Though written in the second half of the fourteenth century, these pieces use the loose measure of the Harleian complaints. The former poem has some claim to lyrical quality, since a variable refrain accompanies the monorhymed quatrains. The *Song Against the Friars* has fifteen complex stanzas, rhymed aaabcccbdede. Both, however, are rather more polemical than lyrical. The first is directed against the allegedly sacrilegious mystery plays, and the second exposes the condition of corrupt secularity into which the orders of mendicants had fallen.[32] These satires are apparently the work of clerics.

The Satire on the Retinues of the Great is one of the least attractive Harleian lyrics, though it has some value as social commentary on the life of grooms and attendants employed by the nobility. Perhaps for the reason that stressed syllables are in some verses alliterated in pairs, Wright and Böddeker afterwards arranged the stanzas in eight lines (xaxaxaxa), though the rhyme clearly calls for quatrains. By either arrangement, the result is jingling verse, hardly a shade better than doggerel. The first stanza shows how little the lyric art is advanced by this choleric exhibition:

> Of rybaudz y ryme ant rede o my rolle,
> of gedelynges, gromes, of colyn & of colle,
> harlotes, horsknaues—bi pate & by polle
> To deuel ich hem to lyure ant take to tolle!

Such expressions of feeling as thread most political and social songs of the thirteenth and fourteenth centuries show but dimly in a fabric woven largely of descriptive and narrative elements. Since the opinions of the minstrel-author harmonize rather perfectly with those for whom he performs, his personality counts for little; his attitudes are more communal than individual. The popular poet is rarely more than the shaping agent through which the mass mind expresses its inclinations. Emotion is commonly implicit, as there is not the slightest need for the singer to speak an individual part; the narrative, familiar to all, requires no interpretation. A minstrel, moreover, could not safely diverge from the majority mind; the very conditions of his employment precluded dissent from the opinions of those who maintained him. Under such circumstances, the personal utterance is muffled, the subjective pose rendered difficult. Nevertheless, a poet could by passionate devotion to a popular cause project his own burning enthusiasm into the conventional narrative framework and so inform the matter as to force it to yield to explicit emotion. With a shrill and inharmonious voice, Laurence Minot translates the military campaigns of Edward III into spirited national songs, exulting and fawning by turns, yet wholly expressive of the author's own fervor.

The fact that eleven battle poems copied into a Cottonian manuscript (Galba E. ix) in the early fifteenth century were composed by Laurence Minot is information isolated and therefore relatively useless, for nothing of the life of this man can be found outside of the verse, and internal evidence advances knowledge of him hardly a short step.[33] That he was a partisan of Edward is self-evident. That he wrote between 1333 and 1352 is likely. But there is not the slightest indication of his relations to the court,[34] of his family affairs, of his literary and political associations, in short, of those intimate details without which the poet cannot be fully accounted for. Even if available, life records would probably not explain the relation of Minot's work to contemporary lyric or reveal the patterns from which he drew suggestions. Minot admits little knowledge of the tradition embodied in Harley 2253, and he is associated with the alliterative revival only in a general way. In tone and texture the eleven poems stand quite out of the main stream of medieval lyric.

Minot, then, was a northern man, perhaps from the northeast Midlands, a gleeman or minstrel devoted to the cause of English unity and in particular to Edward III. Two metrical traditions appear in his work, the alliterative and the accentual, of which the latter is imperfectly managed. He seems to have been familiar with romances popular in his day, or so the abundant parallels indicate. The seventh song is prefaced by an allusion to romance, "Men may rede in romance right/ Of a grete clerk that Merlin hight,"[35] which, however, Hall considers a conventional introduction.[36] Minot has been described as the "father of the Border ballad,"[37] though his connection with that body of song is highly conjectural. Similarity of themes constitutes no significant likeness, and the spirit and form of his lyrics are not paralleled in ballad literature.

Brooding, sententious, mirthless, and even vindictive, Minot possesses little personal attraction. Utterly loyal to the English throne, he can conceive of no justice on the side of Frenchman or Scot, no virtue whatsoever in the adversary. The political world is divided between Edward's friends and enemies; for the latter the poet has unmitigated scorn. His chief weapon is a puerile metaphor, then as now associated with rustic speech; yet the audience which gloated with him over the victims of the king's wrath understood and unquestionably esteemed the euphemistic "kend him his crede" and "teched him to daunce," by which the poet emphasized the triumph of English justice.

War to Minot was a severe but inevitable product of French and Scottish intrigue, which one might regret but hardly avoid. The wish expressed at the close of the song on the battle of Halidon Hill, "Ihesu, for thi woundes fiue,/ In Ingland help vs to haue pese," has nothing of the spirit of compromise. He might ask for the Normans fallen in the Swyn that "God assoyle thaire sawls," but their fate is well deserved, since they oppose the king's "reght in France to win and haue." No trace of compassion shows in Minot as he contemplates the French and Genoese slain in the sack of Southampton in 1338:

> Sum was knokked on the heuyd
> That the body thare bileuid;
> Sum lay stareand on the sternes,
> And sum lay knoked out thaire hernes:

This is stark realism, the poet at his best. The passage takes its strength from the bald, unvarnished statement of a fact, a fact so hideous as to require, by the standards of art poetry, language appropriate to the sensational display of mangled flesh. Minot's comment—"than with tham was none other gle"—calls to mind the crafty understatement of Anglo-Saxon poets, with whom litotes was a treasured artifice. The sorry plight of the besieged burgesses of Calais Minot describes with the same cruel economy and disguised exultation:

> Oure horses that war faire and fat
> Er etin vp ilkone bidene;
> Haue we nother conig ne cat
> That thai ne er etin and hundes kene.

Here and there in his verse a striking image or well-turned phrase appears, although the tapestry of his 923 lines is usually thin. Occasionally he thickens the texture and sharpens the lines of his vignettes, and for these flashes his songs deserve some esteem. Such a one is the fifth stanza of the poem on the naval battle of Sluys. The night before the engagement, Edward III arrived with his fleet off Blanckenberghe. As if indifferent to the presence of the enemy, the French spent the night in revelry. The waning moon (here an evil sign)[38] contrasts ominously with the dancing on St. John's Eve, a night traditionally devoted to frivolity:

> Thai come byfor Blankebergh on Saint Ions night;
> That was to the Normondes a well sary sight.

Yit trumped thai and daunced with torches ful bright,
In the wilde waniand was thaire hertes light.

The victory went finally to the English, perhaps from the effectiveness of their archery, which Minot describes with a notable simile, "It semid with thaire schoting als it war snaw."

This northern poet was unquestionably more at home with the alliterated long-line, in his hands a rough but effective instrument. The lyrics on the battles of the Swyn and Bannockburn, whatever their literary worth, are fervent and intense recitals, short tirades punctuated by refrains linked to the monorhymed quatrains by the familiar device of repeated phrases. Despite a large admixture of jingoism and wounded pride, the Bannockburn song is in many ways the best of the eleven. Granted that the theme is unworthy, Minot goes straightaway about the business of demonstrating that the defeat at Bannockburn has been "wroken" by Edward. He establishes at the outset a contrast between the happy condition of the Scots nearly twenty years earlier and their present state:

Skottes out of Berwik and of Abirdene,
At the Bannok burn war ye to kene;
Thare slogh ye many sakles, als it was sene,
And now has king Edward wroken it, I wene,
It is wrokin, I wene, wele wurth the while;
War yit with the Skottes for thai er ful of gile.

Considering the downfallen state of Scotland at the time this was written, Minot's strenuous vindictiveness is in poor taste, but it is typical of the fanatical hatred and hysterical dread with which the English in the Middle Ages regarded the wild Scots peering ominously, as it was thought, over the marches of Northumbria. Hall thinks the poem was written soon after the battle of Halidon Hill, July 19, 1333.[39] When the English garrisoned the strong points of the Lowlands, Scots fled overseas, many going to Bruges, Flanders, as Minot observes. The successful military action of Edward III and Edward Balliol between 1332 and 1335 forms, rather than Bannockburn, the narrative framework. Narration, however, serves a minor purpose, because Minot's reason for alluding to the military events is to prove his thesis that Edward has avenged the earlier defeat. By this means, the lyric is unified. Tension comes out of the drumming refrain, varied from stanza to stanza but retaining the rhyme pair "while" and "gile." Chanted or sung,[40] it was calculated to arouse an audience to a frenzy of patriotism.

As a poet, Minot partially deserves the neglect which literary historians have accorded him. His eleven poems are rough and usually colorless animadversions on the enemies of Edward, the king whom he regarded with chauvinistic reverence. He is a mean-spirited man of narrow sympathies and cankered prejudices, giving vent to his passionate hatred of France and Scotland in short, compressed flights, often inane and irrelevant. His strong religious sentiments, which stud the verse like so many homilies, have nothing of the larger life of humanity—no compassion, no forgiveness. And yet he is a poet, capable of forcing into the bulk of heavy, unwieldy narrative his own surging emotions, of informing an unvarnished account of military action with the passionate nationalism which animated his entire being. Minot achieves subjectivity, if frenzied and shrill, and on this account stands a step closer than contemporary composers of political song to the poets of a later day who completely subjected narration and description to the play of personal feeling in those brief poems judged by all as lyrics.

Between *Widsith* and *Piers Plowman*, English literature is heroic, pious, didactic, and occasionally erotic, but consciously humorous almost never. Few rays of levity shine through the mists of Anglo-Saxon verse, and it were a creative imagination indeed which could detect many risible situations in Middle English poetry before 1300. For two and a half centuries after the Conquest, comic overtones are sporadic and probably unintentional in most of the places where they occur in prolix chronicles, homiletical treatises, and romances; lyric poetry is invariably serious, if not religious, during this period. Yet no one supposes that the Saxon or twice-transplanted Norseman was denied the gift of laughter. The practice of literature, was largely the prerogative of the clergy, a segment of the population least likely to commit to parchment the drolleries which enlivened the long winter nights in Heorot and the baronial establishments of the retainers of William of Normandy. As a consequence, fabliaux and beast fables, the humorous tales of oral tradition, have left little impression on the records.[41] Nevertheless, the employment of conscious humor as a literary device had perhaps to await the rise of an articulate bourgeoisie, whose prominence is foreshadowed in the late thirteenth century by the formal admission of burgesses to Parliament. This sardonic, vulgar intruder in the social scheme was a constant irritant, despising the condition of the "lesse," ridiculing the ideals of the "moore," yet a class which could feel, analyze, and express the fundamental contradictions in medieval life. From such social elements spring satire and its less baneful accompaniment, humor.

If humor were slow developing as literary convention in England (the record presents no alternative view), its first appearance in lyric poetry discloses a curious, Thurberesque whimsy, of which the language is all the poorer for affording so little. The *Man in the Moon* is a welcome antidote to the derivative saints' legends, penitential songs, and other religious effusions, which have been regarded, perhaps mistakenly, as the characteristic productions of a period noted rather more for piety than for levity. It was indeed a mature fancy, disciplined by extensive practice of the poetic craft, which overflowed into the consummate nonsense of this poem. The management of the five stanzas of alliterated verses, rhyming ababbab, is exceptionally orderly for the Harleian collection. The measure of the poet's success, however, is the tone of subdued whimsicality, perfectly sustained from beginning to end. For this consistency, and for the singular concept, the unknown author is alone responsible, and indeed it is his amiable personality which gives the nonsense permanent interest.

Some antiquarian importance attaches to the pseudo-dramatic framework of the *Man in the Moon*, which is based on a legend widespread in the Middle Ages. According to the version known in England, a thief was banished to the moon for stealing a bundle of thorns. The legend is related to the Biblical story of the man stoned to death by God's command for gathering sticks on the Sabbath.[42] In some accounts, the man in the moon is identified with Cain, though not in the English tradition.[43] But the real importance of the lyric rests on the sensibility behind the humorous comments and speculations.

The ridiculousness of the poet's address to the moon-dweller is the obvious source of humor in the poem. The wretch stands and strides, bearing on his hayfork the burden of thorns. The author imagines him fearful of falling and abiding therefore "muche chele" in the frosty climate of the moon. After considerable speculation, the poet concludes that some hedgekeeper has found the man in the moon illegally cutting from another's thicket the twigs required to protect the cuttings which he has just set out to close a gap in his own hedge, and has exacted from him security for his appearance to answer the charge.[44] If this be the case, the poet advises, "bring hom the trous,"

> We shule preye the haywart hom to vr hous,
>   ant maken hym at heyse for the maystry,
> Drynke to hym deorly of fol god bous,
>   ant oure dame douse shal sitten hym by.

Then, when the hedgekeeper is "dronke as a dreynt mous," the pledge may be redeemed from the bailiff. This kind, if facetious proposal goes unanswered by the man in the moon. Not only will he not come down as that other who "burnt his mouth with eating cold pease porridge" in the familiar nursery rhyme, but this one will not vouchsafe a reply. This humor of situation is all very pleasant and leaves the reader with a warm regard for the whimsical author. Beneath the easy grace of the nonsense, a more serious matter doubtless engaged the attention of the audience for which the poem was written. Comparing the man in the moon to a poor peasant found cutting wood reminds of the vexatious problem of protecting the manorial hedges from the ravages of a peasantry often in need of fuel. The "chele" of the moon suggests the cold of the long winter nights; the sorry plight of the man in the moon recalls the privations of landless folk. But social criticism is merely a by-product; the poet intended no more than a broad sympathy for humanity. Then, as now, the chief interest of the lyric sprang from the singular intellect pleasantly revealed in the sprightly fantasy. Even to the end, the poet maintains his disguise in a gaily inane observation on the recalcitrance of the man in the moon: "thah me teone with hym that myn teh mye,/ the cherl nul nout adoun er the day dawe."

A *Satire on the People of Kildare* is interesting chiefly as social commentary and hardly requires mentioning with the secular lyric. Seymour regards the poem as the work of a Goliard;[45] if so, a silly Goliard. That the author was a clerk appears from one of the idiotic refrains: "Sickirlich he was a clerk,/ That wrothete this craftilich werk."[46] The title, according to Seymour, is unjustified, as Dublin, rather than Kildare, afforded the religious houses to which reference is made. The impudent author addresses the saints with un-common familiarity[47] and vilifies orders and crafts,[48] though much less effectively than Dunbar in the *Devillis Inquest*. Despite the obscurities resulting from innuendo, some light is thrown on the corrupt practices of monk and friar, tailor and skinner. The first stanza as well as another illustrates the manner:

> Hail, seint Michel with the lange sper,
> Fair beth thi winges up thi scholder,
> Thou hast a rede kirtil anon to thi fote,
> Thou ert best angle that ever God makid.
> This vers is ful well i-wroght,
> Hit is of well furre y-broght.

One of the more interesting short alliterative pieces in Middle English is the *Satire Against the Blacksmiths*,[49] which is a scintillating expression of distaste for the noise and confusion created in the smithies at night. Residents of the vicinity of a forge were doubtless outraged by the nuisance, and the indignation which the poet felt could hardly be exceptional. Perhaps in anticipation of legal restraints, certain blacksmiths of London petitioned the lord mayor in 1394 to close the smithies at night because of the great inconvenience to the sleeping citizenry.[50] Though hardly as vituperative as Wells supposed,[51] the *Satire* achieves through vivid description an eloquent protest against the noisy smiths. The staccato of the heavily alliterated long line is peculiarly suited to translate the clanging interior of a smithy.

This is probably the first example of sustained onomatopœia in the language, and it is a tribute to the poet's artistry that the begrimed smiths come alive, straining in the stupefying heat of the forge. The acrid fumes of a smouldering fire, the confused pounding in the night, and the muffled cries for "coal, coal" are sharply conveyed by sound and sense:

> Swarte smekyd smethes smateryd with smoke
> Dryve me to deth wyth den of here dyntes;
> Swech noys on nyghtes ne herd men nevere,
> What knavene cry and clateryng of knockes,
> The cammede kongons cryen after col! col!

The hard-muscled smiths in leathern skirts sprawl and spit and tell yarns; gnaw and gnash and groan together at their work. The bellows goes "Lus! bus! las! das!," pouring a column of air into the bed of coals. At his anvil the master smith lengthens and joins fragments of glowing iron. As the pieces cool, he cuts them in two. Rapidly shaping a section, he beats out higher and higher tones on the hardening metal and finally "towcheth a treble." The poet then expresses the process onomatopoetically: "Tik! tak! hic! hac! tiket! taket! tyk! tak!"—first the hard, deliberate strokes, then the quick "tiket! taket!" of the shapening process, and finally the conclusive "tyk! tak!" For these "clothe merys" and "brenwaterys,"[52] who will let no one sleep, the poet wishes that "Cryst hem gyve sorwe." The roughness of the measure notwithstanding, this is conscious artistry, the like of which is not again devoted to the smithy before Dekker's *London's Tempe* (1629), but the "thwick-a-thwack" and "pit-a-pat" of the blacksmith's song in the play sound a false and anemic note, as compared with the virile clanging of the Middle English poem.

A comprehensive summing up of the political and social lyric of the period is utterly impossible, so numerous are the lacunae. Time and the diligence of antiquaries have unhappily failed to establish the identities or professions of most of the authors, the relation of the extant lyric to native and foreign traditions, the quantity of lost material, the manner of presentation, or even the audience for which the songs were written. Judgments of any kind are perforce laid over a foundation of hypotheses which seem in no hurry to become facts. The Harleian poets, if not Minot, are indebted to French models—so much is certain; but the glossy surfaces and carefully wrought designs of Continental lyric are poorly translated to the English songs, which are usually rough and deficient in unity. Few of these unknown poets—minstrels or clerks—adequately control their materials. The normal political lyric is a narrative frame studded with unintegrated commentary. The perfected organism, like the *Man in the Moon,* is perhaps not often possible for poets who in their brief flourishing seem not to have settled on form. Not having learned to use a vocabulary of the affections or rhetorical artifices, they had necessarily to piece out their recitals with narrative and descriptive materials, which generally constitute the major interest. Though it is hardly fair to compare the English poets with artists of the caliber of Bertran de Born, his fiery invectives disclose the possibilities of molding the commonplace episodes of political history to the uses of poetic statement, and at the same time fix a standard of excellence, measured by which the non-amatory song of Britain is aimless and loose-jointed. Defects conceded, these spontaneous and vigorous relics of political and social strife, though uncontrolled, frequently achieve a rough eloquence and occasionally a passage of real power and beauty.

CHAPTER FOUR

ART LYRIC:
A PRELIMINARY

COEVAL WITH THE EMERGENCE OF CHAUCER A NEW chapter opens in the history of English lyric, taking its main impulse from artificial and restricted French forms and depending for its cultivation upon men of settled habits. The break with the singing past was hardly as abrupt as the meager remains suggest, although the naturalization of foreign techniques proceeded rapidly after the middle of the fourteenth century. If Chaucer may not properly be taxed with responsibility for the abandonment of the alliterative long-line, his experiments led to synthesis of the syllabic and accentual principles and thus hastened the decay of the older system, which was best suited to recitative uses. With the new lyric mode came the influence of treatises of rhetoric and *Le Roman de la Rose*, the stylebook of allegory. The older tradition, derived partially from trouvère lyric, was forgotten or abandoned. Needless to say, the change was all for the worse, as the restrictions on form brought a corresponding dwindling of the imagination. Inspiration lost, polite lyric was in the time of Chaucer and after seldom meritorious.

At the end of the thirteenth century, the loose long-line was showing symptoms of foot division, whether from direct influence of French syllabic scansion or from the putative effect of the rhyme in forcing the metrical unit into a temporal pattern.[1] Secular lyric was not much affected by eccentric systems of versification, as it developed late and was little cultivated in the alliterative revival.[2] The only important collection written in the older tradition is the

Harleian, and indeed several songs of this manuscript give unmistakable evidence of the development of foot division. As a rule, however, these poems have lines of three or four stresses, with a variable number of unaccented syllables, Saintsbury's assumption of the contrary notwithstanding.[3] Equivalence and substitution[4] may explain the scansion of a given verse—not the characteristic rhythm. Saintsbury leaned too heavily on these principles in striving to establish an early date for the beginnings of modern prosody. The Harleian poets probably composed by ear with a melody running through their heads; if the phrasing were felicitous and the three or four stresses properly distributed, the exigencies of time were satisfied,[5] and nothing mattered further. For example, the following lines illustrate the difficulty of imposing foot scansion on the *Song of Lewes:*

> Sire simond de mountfort hath suore bi ys chyn,
> heuede he nou here the erl of waryn,
> shulde he neuer more come to is yn.

The swinging movement of the first line, which requires but slight confirmation, is virtually repudiated by the second and third lines. This is not to suggest fundamental discord: it must be conceded that the composer knew his business, and, sung or chanted, the *Song of Lewes* doubtless went very well. The basic rhythm of the alliterated long-line is singularly prominent and not infrequently resists attempts at recitation. Thus, the opening couplet of a Harleian *reverdie* compels musical utterance:

> Lenten ys come with loue to toune,
> with blosmen & with briddes roune.

Obviously, art lyric could ill afford to retain a prosodic principle likely at any time to trick reciters into bursts of melody. Elsewhere in the manuscript are lyrics which seem to be constructed by the principle of modern prosody, and it is not unlikely that the collection exemplifies both new and old systems. Foot division was a simple and dependable solution, and southern poets apparently accepted it with alacrity.

As early as the middle of the thirteenth century, passable octosyllables were written by Friar Thomas de Hales, reputedly a Franciscan. The devotional *Love Ron* bespeaks his unconscious knowledge of foot division; more than half of the lines of the fifth stanza are clearly iambic, and the others are probably to be considered acephalous:

> this world fareth hwilynde.
> hwenne on cumeth an other goth.
> that wes bi-fore. nv is bihynde.
> that er was leof nv hit is loth.
> For-thi he doth as the blynde.
> that in this world. his luue doth.
> Ye mowen iseo. the world aswynde.
> that wouh goth forth. abak that soth.[6]

Any doubt about the establishment of foot division vanishes with the appearance of *With longyng y am lad,* written in fairly regular three-foot lines. Saintsbury prefers a much earlier date for the inception of the modern system, but not many such unequivocal demonstrations as this occur before 1300. By the Chaucerian fashion of managing final -*e*'s, the following verses go very well:

> With longyng y am lad,
> on molde y waxe mad,
> a maide marreth me;
> y grede, y grone, vnglad,
> for selden y am sad
> that semly forte se.

Two divergent lines in the following stanza—"les me out of bonde" and "broht icham in wo"—are clearly analogous to Chaucer's acephalous verse, "Twenty bookes, clad in blak or reed."

The limitations imposed upon this study obviate the ne-
cessity of surveying Middle English prosody, even sketchily.[7]
Chaucerian scansion has often been discussed and poses no
special problems in connection with lyric. The knowledge
of foot division granted for the fifteenth century, scholar-
ship has yet to explain the prosodical anarchy of Lydgate
and other courtly makers beside the meticulousness of
Hoccleve and the perfection of Dunbar. It has been sug-
gested that prosodic confusion was owing to the disappear-
ance of final -e from the spoken language; that poets com-
posed by ear without counting syllables; that the surviving
manuscripts are hopelessly corrupt.[8] These hypotheses work
well with certain classes of verse, but not one alone is suffi-
ciently comprehensive to account for any large fraction of
the metrical aberrations of the century.

The significant result of the prosodical and stylistic in-
novations was art lyric, unprovided with music. By Chau-
cer's time, the modern concept of lyric poetry was accepted
by educated men, and courtiers were hardly expected to
fit amorous complaints and extravagant eulogies into musical
settings. In contrast to the new arrangement, words and
melody, if not inseparable, seem to have been closely
associated parts of lyric until the end of the thirteenth cen-
tury. That the short, stanzaic poems of the Harleian and
other early manuscripts were meant for singing is a useful
and legitimate hypothesis, the absence of notation notwith-
standing. If not sung, they were at least chanted, to the
accompaniment of *vieille*, crowd, psaltery, or any of a dozen
other stringed instruments. Although Schipper doubted
that the manner of presentation of the alliterative lyrics
could be determined on internal grounds alone,[9] scattered
references to song and singing in pre-Chaucerian specimens
are not altogether worthless testimonials, since music ac-
tually exists for several religious pieces, the *Cuckoo Song*,
Mirie it is while sumer ilast, and *Foweles in the frith*. Two

lyrics to the Virgin Mary have references to singing: one poet announces at the outset, "On hire is al mi lif ylong/ Of hwam ich wule singe,"[10] and the other in the first line of the second stanza declares, "Of the, suete levedy, my song y wile byginne."[11] Near the conclusion of the *Love Ron,* Thomas advises the maiden for whom the poem is written, "Mid swete stephne thu hit singe," but in this instance *singe* may mean *recite.* The author of *When the nyhtegale singes* states, "y wole mone my song to wham that hit ys on ylong." Incomparable *Alysoun* ends with the injunction, "herkne to my roun," which, in a lyric equipped with a jaunty refrain, argues stoutly for musical recitation. In point of fact, the refrains attached to *Alysoun, Ichot a burde in boure bryht, Lutel wot hit anymon,* and the *Song of Lewes* may be the best evidence that the Harleian lyrics were meant for singing, though melody is latent in the flowing movement of most.

The position of Chaucer in the transition from lyric song to art lyric is complicated by the suspicion, not wholly unfounded, that he composed songs, or at least texts designed for singing, which are now lost. This belief has been encouraged unduly by scholars who were reluctant to accept as the poet's finest lyrical efforts the mediocrity which the shorter poems all too clearly exhibit. The idea implicit in most discussions of the "lost" songs is that they somehow differed from those preserved and were therefore more lyrical and singable. Actually, the extant lyrics are perfectly consistent with French literary standards of the fourteenth century, and Chaucer, it is scarcely necessary to say, was early apprenticed to Guillaume de Machaut. Though Machaut did not himself produce the fracture of words and music,[12] his was the influence which led to the altogether unsingable lyrics of Eustache Deschamps. Chaucer is in England both instrument and victim of the altered tradition; his lyrical poems represent a distinct break with the singing past and constitute the strongest influence on fifteenth-century lyric at the courtly level. The quantity of internal and external evidence and the accumulated scholarly conjecture suggest the need for a close examination of the problem of Chaucer's song writing and his concept of literary "song."

For composing "many a song and many a leccherous lay"[13] Chaucer asks Heaven's forgiveness in the humble retraction appended to the *Parson's Tale;* and in the *Prologue* to the *Legend of Good Women,* he is said by Alceste to be the author of "many an ympne for your [God of Love's] halydayes,/ That highten balades, roundels, virelayes."[14] The eagle who conveys the poet to the House of Fame furnishes further confirmation:

> And never-the-lesse hast set thy wit—
> Although that in thy hed ful lyte is—
> To make bookys, songes, dytees,
> In ryme, or elles in cadence . . .[15]

As John Gower takes leave of Venus in the *Confessio Amantis,* she tells him:

> And gret wel Chaucer whan ye mete,
> As mi disciple and mi poete:
> For in the floures of his youthe
> In sondri wise, as he wel couthe,
> Of Ditees and of songes glade,
> The whiche he for mi sake made:[16]

Since the *House of Fame* was written not later than 1385,[17] Gower is not above suspicion of having taken over Chaucer's own statement for the *Confessio* (1390-93), without himself having any real knowledge of "songes" and "ditees." The same question arises when Lydgate recollects in the *Fall of Princes:*

> This said poete, my maistir in his daies,
> Maad and compiled ful many a fressh dite,
> Compleyntis, baladis, roundelis, virelaies . . .[18]

From these testimonials, scholars have generally agreed that Chaucer did in all probability write lyrics which are now lost. Ten Brink suggested that only a fraction of the poet's lyrics have survived, though he did not suppose that the quality of these pieces was especially high.[19] Lounsbury agreed.[20] Robinson regards no more than ten of the short poems as love lyrics and partly on that account conjectures that as a young courtier Chaucer wrote songs now lost. About the musical setting of the poet's lyrics,[21] Robinson is less confident than Manly,[22] though he is unwilling to close the door on the possibility that Chaucer wrote music: "Chaucer may very well have written some of them for music, if he did not, like a number of his contemporaries, himself compose the melodies. But very few of them would find a place in a song-book."[23] Brusendorff, however, considers the attributions quite conventional and points to parallels in Machaut's *Remède de Fortune* and Froissart's *Le Joli Buisson de Jonece*.[24] Two questions, at least, are suggested by this array of contemporary testimony and scholarly conjecture. What did the term *song* mean to the fourteenth-century poet? And how much of Chaucer's verse is to be regarded as song by fourteenth-century standards? Even tentative answers to these questions may clarify the problem of the "lost" songs.

The question of music aside for the moment, the inclusion in the list of Chaucer's lyrics of all those complete "songs" imbedded in longer works increases the poet's lyrics by more than fifty per cent. At least twelve lyrics or lyrical pieces— over half the number existing separately—are scattered through *Troilus and Criseyde,* the *Book of the Duchess,* the *Parliament of Foules,* and the *Legend of Good Women,* and these poems, usually in the French style, are generally shorter and more lyrical than the others. There is no valid reason for denying the intercalated lyrics a place beside the separate short pieces. Guillaume de Machaut, with whose verse Chaucer was quite familiar, employed in *Le Remède de Fortune* a total of seven lyrics: two ballades, a *lay, complainte, chanson royal, chanson baladée* (virelay), and rondelet.[25] One of the earliest French poets to use such ornamentation was the author of *Guillaume de Dole*,[26] now known to have been Jehan Renart; others followed the practice,[27] including Froissart.[28] The lyrics which were interspersed through *Le Remède* were certainly regarded by Machaut as separable from the body of the long poem, as he composed music for them.[29] If as much be allowed for Chaucer, to the twenty short poems[30] known or thought to be his should be added the following:

The roundel at the end of the *Parliament of Foules:* "Now welcome, somer, with thy sonne softe."[31]

The ballade sung by the followers of Alceste in the *Prologue* to the *Legend of Good Women:* "Hyd, Absolon, thy gilte tresses clere."[32]

Two songs attributed to the Black Knight in the *Book of the Duchess:* "I have of sorwe so gret won" and "Lord, hyt maketh myn herte lyght."[33]

At least nine segments of *Troilus and Criseyde* have some claim to lyric quality: Antigone's "Troian song"—"O Love, to whom I have and shal";[34] "Canticus Troilii"—"If no love is, O God, what fele I so?";[35] another song of Troilus on love—"Love, that of erthe and se hath governaunce";[36] and the doleful complaint of the last book, also called "Canticus Troilii"—"O sterre, of which I lost have al the light,"[37] and the verse epistles exchanged by the lovers.[38]

The *aube*-like sections[39] of the third book are less certainly to be regarded as songs. Troilus and Criseyde are not represented as singing them, it is true, but the situation calls for the traditional song.[40] If not like the more popular *aubes*, such as *Gaite de la tor*[41] or the English ballad *Grey Cock*,[42] the *Troilus* songs are nevertheless expressions of the same disgust that lovers the world over might feel with the coming of dawn. Besides, the pieces exhibit a fairly high and sustained lyric quality.

Regardless of their originality, some of these lyrics are excellent, and most of them achieve a level quite above the separate short poems, with the exceptions of *Merciles Beaute* and *To Rosemounde*. The number of lyrics of fixed form is increased to the extent of one ballade and one roundel, and most of these intercalated poems could be regarded loosely as hymns for the God of Love's "halydayes,"[43] revealing as they do the poet's devotion to the service of Love. All of the thirty-odd poems are lyrics by virtue of form or content, or both, and should be so considered. That most of them are less imaginative and spirited than the best lyrics of the thirteenth and sixteenth centuries is the fault of the times. It is probably true that the measure of lyric excellence was conformity to fixed structural patterns and the decorum of court society.[44] Chaucer and his fifteenth-century followers usually seem more concerned with convention than with feeling.

For the fourteenth century, Chaucer's attempts at lyric expression are numerous. The virelais excepted, all of the clearly defined types mentioned as being cultivated by the poet are illustrated by several specimens. These lyrics, moreover, cover ranges of interests and degrees of excellence so wide as to represent the poet quite adequately. That some lyrics have not survived is conceivable; that they would differ in any important respects from those which have been saved is altogether improbable. There is no reason to believe that Chaucer ever departed radically from the lyric conventions learned in the school of Machaut. If these lyrical poems then can be shown to fall within the limits of the conception of song held generally in the late fourteenth century, the question of lost pieces will of necessity decline in significance.

Whether Chaucer composed music for any of his extant

lyrics or for lost songs cannot be determined with absolute certainty. Two points, at least, are clear: no music has survived with his poetry, and none of his contemporaries describes him as a composer. He manifests, moreover, little real interest in professional musicians and speaks of minstrelsy in very general terms.[45] His references to instruments and instrumental music are probably conventional[46] and do not prove that he had a technical knowledge of the art. Why, then, have both Manly and Robinson toyed with the idea that Chaucer may have joined the ability to compose music to the gift of poetry? The eagle of the *House of Fame* credited him with songs, and Gower echoed the attribution. Furthermore, Chaucer was strongly influenced by Machaut, who in a sense revived the trouvère art in the fourteenth century. The evidence forces a consideration of the question.

French lyric of the twelfth and thirteenth centuries was inevitably designed for singing,[47] and much of the music has been preserved. The trouvères were both poets and musicians. The decline of this class, however, opened the way to a fracture of the art: melody went one way and lyric another. Miss Cohen refers to the opinion of Pierre Champion *(Vie de Charles d'Orléans)* that in the early fourteenth century—the period of Machaut—rondeaux, ballades, and chansons were sung, but by the beginning of the fifteenth century only the last were provided with music.[48] *Chanson* in the fifteenth century acquired a specialized use in the field of music. Ballades and rondeaux became strictly literary lyric, notwithstanding an occasional specimen set to music.[49] Chaucer stands about midway in this transition period, and on that account his use of the term *song* is often puzzling. Certainly, in some instances there is no way of determining whether he means song with or without music.

Clear-cut cases there are. Chaucer frequently speaks of the singing of the Canterbury pilgrims or characters in the tales and occasionally quotes snatches of the songs they sang. In such circumstances, there can be no doubt of the poet's meaning. The Pardoner sang as he rode, "Com hider, love, to me,"[50] and the Friar "Of yeddynges he baar outrely the pris."[51] Courteous Nicholas of the *Miller's Tale* knew the *Angelus ad virginem* and also the "kynges noote."[52] For the benefit of the carpenter's wife, whose song was "loude and yerne,"[53] the clerk Absolon sang a love song of which Chaucer has quoted the first two lines: "Now, deere lady, if thy wille be,/ I praye yow that ye wole rewe on me."[54] A half century ago, Skeat discovered six additional lines to a song[55] which is mentioned in the *Nun's Priest's Tale*—"My lief is faren in londe!"[56] These are in all probability songs so widely known in Chaucer's day as to require only a reference. There is no question about their musical quality. To these should be added the courtly roundel, "Now welcome, somer, with thy sonne softe,"[57] and less certainly the fragment of another roundel which Arcite sang, "May, with alle thy floures and thy grene."[58]

Elsewhere, Chaucer's intention is much less clear. The paraphrase of a prayer to the Blessed Virgin from Deguilleville's *Pèlerinage de la Vie Humaine* is headed by the rubric, "Incipit carmen secundum ordinem litterarum alphabeti." In the envoy to the *Complaint of Chaucer to His Purse*, the poet announces, "this song to yow I sende." It is "This woful song and this compleynte I make" in the *Complaynt d'Amours*. Chaucer proposes in the rather long *Complaint of Mars* to "synge / The sentence of the compleynt." It is, however, conceivable that "Hyd, Absalon, thy gilte tresses clere," which is described as a song, was actually sung, as the rhythm is not incompatible with a musical setting. Antigone, according to Chaucer, sang the "Troian song"— "O Love, to whom I have and shal," and Troilus himself bursts into melody on three occasions. Multiplying problematical uses of *song* would serve no good purpose; the

examples are sufficient to show that the term in the four-
teenth century was applied to markedly different kinds of
poetry.[59]

Chaucer, then, rather consistently applies the term *song*
to poems that strike eye and ear as utterly unsuitable for
singing. The high incidence of the examples suggests on
the one hand a convention and on the other a concept of
music so extensive as to embrace lyric not designed for
singing. When Chaucer declares in the envoy to *Complaint
of Chaucer to His Purse,* "this song to yow I sende," there
is no question but that he has used a modification of the
popular "Go little bill" form of address, and no source need
be sought.[60] The point is that Chaucer probably does not
mean song in the same sense as the unknown poet-musician
who in an early lyrical romance thus addresses his handi-
work:

> Chanconete, tu iras
> en mon pais
> et si me diras a cele
> qui m'a trais
> que j'amoie loiaument . . .[61]

Trans. Little song, you will go into my country, and so you
will say to that one who has betrayed me that I love
loyally . . .

Thibaut de Champagne in the early thirteenth century em-
ployed this device a number of times. In the following ex-
ample, there seems to be no doubt that the poet means song
in the usual sense. One might also guess that the musical
notation accompanied the chanson sent to the *dame:*

> Dame, vers vous n'ai autre messagier
> Par cui vous os mon corage envoier
> Fors ma chançon, se la volez chanter.[62]

Trans. Lady, for you I have no other messenger by which
I dare to send my heart to you, except my song, if
you wish to sing it.

For the best trouvère lyric no internal proof of musical set-
ting is at all necessary, as the scores have been saved in
large numbers.

By these precedents, one might conjecture that the chan-
sons scattered through MS. Harley 2253 were likewise in-
tended for singing, though no music has survived. The
Anglo-Norman poet who wrote,

> Ferroy chaunsoun que bien doit estre oye,
> De ma amie chaunterai qe m'ad deguerpie.[63]

Trans. I shall make a song which deserves to be heard; of
my lady I shall sing who has abandoned me.

undoubtedly sang this love song. He finished it with a
"bill"—"Par cest chaunsoun portez salutz à ma tresdouce
amye." It is not to be supposed, however, that Chaucer
was indebted for this and other conventions directly to
French poetry of the twelfth and thirteenth centuries or to
the transplanted trouvère tradition exemplified by the songs
of MS. Harley 2253.[64] His French teachers, particularly
Machaut and Deschamps, are no doubt responsible for most
of the ideas that go into his conception of song and literary
lyric.

In one respect, at least, Machaut continued the older
tradition: he wrote music for many of his lyrics; but in
other matters his work belongs to the new poetry, which
began developing about the time of the succession of the
Valois in 1328.[65] Lyric moved away from the metrical
variety allowable in the preceding period and tended to
become fixed structurally, as in the ballade and rondeau.
And as the century advanced, less need was felt by the new
poets—really men of letters—to provide music for their
verse. But there would be no question on any account about
the meaning of *chant*, when *Espérance* of *Le Remède de
Fortune* begins "Joliement son chant nouvel,"[66] which hap-
pens to be a *chanson royal*. Nor is there any doubt that the

chant, "Dame, de qui toute ma joie vient,"[67] was likewise sung. Notation exists for both.

The state of lyric poetry in the last half of the fourteenth century is best seen in the verse of Eustache Deschamps, Machaut's most prolific follower. The ballade and other genres of fixed form are with him certainly not designed for singing. They have become literary lyrics in the modern sense. Yet Deschamps was disposed to consider them music and on two occasions followed the old convention by referring to ballades as chansons, which they clearly are not by any recognized standards. Undoubtedly, the court circles for which Deschamps wrote understood quite well that by *chanson* he did not mean *song* in a musical sense:

> Grace et Octroy, Maniere et Contenance,
> Vueillés pour moy a ma dame parler,
> Ou il me fault mes dolens jours finer,
> Se ne reçoit mon offre et ma chançon.[68]

Trans. Grace and Agreement, Manner and Countenance, may it please you to speak to my lady for me; or it is necessary for me to end my unhappy days, if she receives not my offer and my song.

And again in the envoy to Ballade No. 546:

> Dame, au jour d'uy vous doing cuer et pensée,
> Ceste chançon pour vo bien figurée,
> Qu'aux grans vertus de ces dames [Judith, Hester,
>   et al.] descrips:[69]

Trans. Lady, today I give you heart and thought, this song for you well composed, which describes the great virtues of these ladies:

This versifier is nevertheless convinced that his 1,100-odd ballades and other short poems are music, unlyrical and unsingable though they be; and in *L'Art de dictier* (1392) he presents his reasons. He conceives of two kinds of music—

artificiele and *naturele,* which could be united or left sepa-
rate.[70] Though granting that *musique naturele,* the voice
reciting poetry, was effective when joined with *musique
artificiele,* the music of notes, he nevertheless maintains that
the former is a higher kind of art.[71] What is especially im-
portant, Deschamps believed that the practitioners of
musique naturele, the poets, did not commonly know the
music of notes. In the *puis,* according to him, it had long
been customary for contestants to recite rather than to sing
their poetry.[72] His insistence upon "les douces paroles"
suggests that very orotund recitative was fashionable.

For a number of reasons now apparent, one might ven-
ture to say that Chaucer subscribed to the view that oral
delivery was fundamentally musical. He was not neces-
sarily influenced by Deschamps in this belief, which may
have been a commonplace, though much of the verse of the
French poet seems to have been known to him. Chaucer
was likewise known to Deschamps, who has left a slight
memorial to his English friend. A comparison of the ballade
to Chaucer with two on Machaut discloses that Deschamps
recognizes both poets as noble rhetoricians, but only Ma-
chaut certainly as a musician. Writing in Ballade No. 127,
he says:

> Treschiers sires, vueillez remercier
> L'art de musique et le gay sentement
> Que Orpheus fist en vous commencier,
> Dont vous estes honouriez haultement:[73]

Trans. Most honorable sir, may you wish to give thanks for
the art of music and the pleasant thought which
Orpheus caused in you to begin, for which you are
honored highly.

But of Chaucer, "saiges en rethorique," Deschamps merely
remarks:

> Poete hault, loenge destruye,
> En ton jardin ne seroye qu'ortie:

> Considere ce que j'ay dit premier,
> Ton noble plant, ta douce mélodie:[74]

Trans. Noble poet, I am unworthy of praise; in your garden
I should be only a nettle. Consider what I said first,
your noble plaint, your sweet melody.

The "douce mélodie" for the French poet is undoubtedly
musique naturele. Certainly, no evidence actually coun-
tervails this supposition. Dunbar in the *Goldyn Targe*
commended Chaucer for the "fresch anamalit termes celi-
call" of his diction,[75] and Lydgate praised his "colours of
suetnesse";[76] but of music the fifteenth-century Chaucerians
have no more to say than Deschamps.

If Chaucer considered oral recitation a division of music,
here and there should occur some internal indication in
addition to the use of the term *song* in connection with lit-
erary lyric. The poet appears to make the desired differen-
tiation in a poem clearly not designed for singing. After
commenting on the dialectal diversity of the English lan-
guage in the epilogue to *Troilus and Criseyde,* he expresses
a wish about his book: "And red wherso thow be, or elles
songe,/ That thow be understonde, God I biseche!"[77] The
distinction Chaucer wishes to make here, it seems, is be-
tween silent reading and recitation.[78] That he considered
the *Troilus* a song, long as it is, bespeaks a concept that has
been too little noticed. This view of literature, shared by
Deschamps, explains Chaucer's readiness to call his lyrical
pieces songs. The attitude seems not to be a development
of the later years, for in the *Book of the Duchess* Chaucer
clearly conceives of song without music. Of the first com-
plaint of the sorrowing Black Knight, the poet says,

> He sayd a lay, a maner song,
> Withoute noote, withoute song;
> And was thys, for ful wel I kan
> Reherse hyt; ryght thus hyt began:[79]

The first element of the rich rhyme *song:song* signifies *poem*, the second, *music*. The complaint of eleven lines follows.

Chaucer appears to stand in English poetry at the end of a period of transition, which was initiated and carried through largely by French poets of the fourteenth century. In the process, song became lyric; and the practitioners were not minstrels or *clerici vagantes*, but respectable and erudite men of letters. The more than thirty lyrical poems which have been preserved are all consistent with the new conventions established in France, and their number is sufficient to justify the attributions of Gower and Lydgate, whatever they are worth. If Chaucer's view of lyric corresponds to that of Deschamps, as seems likely, no lost "songs" with music need be sought. Lost lyrics there may be, but other grounds are required than those upon which their existence has generally been postulated.

In point of form, the new lyric departs markedly from pre-Chaucerian song. Whereas the older lyric was composed in a tradition allowing great liberty in the management of stanzaic patterns, that of the fifteenth century is scarcely less restricted than the French out of which it grew. Both in Le Midi and later in northern France, poets sought infinite variety of rhyme scheme; in fact, nearly a thousand stanza arrangements have been counted in Provençal.[80] English lyric before Chaucer—an after-blooming of trouvère song—exhibits the diversity characteristic of its stock.

However much researchers have desired to find a direct connection between early English and troubadour verse, the exact correspondence of rhyme patterns can in no way further their case for borrowing. Poets of both lands wished to achieve unique stanzas and inevitably hit upon common schemes. Thirteenth- and fourteenth-century English lyrics, secular and religious, afford twice as many unduplicated as duplicated arrangements,[81] and only three of the latter are especially common—aaaa, aabccb, and abababab, of which the last leads all others. The degree of concord is considerably reduced if verse length and alliteration are taken into account. Though agreement in form is not the rule, three Harleian lyrics—*Lenten ys come with loue to toune, Mosti ryden bi ribbesdale,* and *In may hit murgeth when hit dawes*—are an interesting exception. Line length and rhyme scheme—aabccbddbeeb—agree, and all three are alliterated. The lack of dialectal and verbal resemblance is, however, a check on the deduction almost compelled by the singular physical correspondence, though common authorship is not the only possible explanation of the phenomenon. From the same manuscript *De Clerico et Puella* invites comparison with *When the nyhtegale singes,* as both are written in monorhymed quatrains. A superficial correspondence between *Mirie it is while sumer ilast* and the Lincoln's Inn *pastourelle, Als i me rod this ender dai,* is probably accidental, and nothing need be made of it.

The new lyric mode gave prominence to two patterns affected by Chaucer; courtly verse of the fifteenth century is all too frequently in rhyme royal and *Monk's Tale* octaves. So negligent were the poets, however, that few specimens are consistently octosyllabic or decasyllabic. Semipopular verse, other than the carol, which has fairly distinctive form, is likely to show greater variety. But in this as in other matters, convention accomplished its deadly work, and, the exceptions notwithstanding, the century was as slavishly devoted to Chaucerian arrangements as to artificial diction.

The ballade as such was cultivated far less in England than in France during the transition, but had nevertheless a pervasive influence on courtly lyric. Though Miss Cohen expresses wonderment that Middle English should afford no more than 220 specimens (her count),[82] including the ballades associated with Orléans, Quixley's translations,[83] and some doubtful examples, the reason, as Chaucer remarks, is to be found in the scarcity of rhymes. At all events, the ballade is less restrictive than roundel[84] or virelai, both popular in France but of little consequence in England. The rules promulgated by Deschamps permit endless variation of the ballade pattern, but invariably in the direction of further complication.[85] Some of his examples are utterly impossible in English, as the experimental *Balade coulourd and Reuersid* of MS. Arundel 26[86] shows all too well. Saving the sonnet, more often modified than not, no strictly fixed genre has ever caught on with English writers. This native repugnance to discipline expresses itself in the neglect of the roundel and the severe alteration of the ballade. Thus, Miss Cohen will admit as ballade any poem in three stanzas with refrain, whether it has common rhymes or not.

Neither Chaucer in English nor Gower in French was in any way responsible for the radical modification of the ballade or the random application of the term to lyric of all sorts, for both adhered rather strictly to the rules. But Lydgate, quite as influential in his own day as his worthier predecessors, injudiciously tagged as *ballade* almost every variety of courtly lyric in stanzas, whether ballade by the French standard or not.[87] In the lack of an unequivocal term for lyric (that is, song without music), there was a real need underlying the apparent carelessness. The century probably followed Lydgate in this matter, for he seems to have been among the first to use *ballade* in the broad sense, and he did it often, as his minor poems attest. Lydgate, like other English poets, found the fixed form much too binding. A case in point is his expansion of a French ballade into the six stanzas and envoy of *So As the Crabbe Goth Forward*. Not all writers of the period were as prolix as he, but all found too straitened the form in which an Orléans could maneuver in well-turned, succinct accents. Otherwise, the preciosity, artificiality, and diffuseness of the French are translated only too well.

Of course, not all poets of the period followed Chaucerian arrangements. The miscellaneous lyrics of MS. Cambridge Univ. Lib. Ff. I. 6, however conventional in other respects, are often structurally eccentric. Too, the semipopular songs of MS. Sloane 2593 use simple structures, as do many religious lyrics. Toward the end of the century, greater variety is evident, and Dunbar was as much concerned with creating novel metrical schemes as any troubadour.

The ascendancy of form over matter was encouraged by the textbooks of rhetoric which seem to have been widely employed in the schools from the thirteenth to the fifteenth century. Doubtless, the study of literary organization, amplification, and ornamentation was a legitimate discipline and within limits did effect stylistic improvements. The perfection of form in the Age of Reason may have been an ultimate benefit from the study of this fraction of the trivium. In Chaucer's time and after, however, the "colours" of rhetoric, consciously applied, merely freighted the poetic muse with a burden additional to allegory, *amour courtois*, and abstractness. The salutary effect of sound rhetoric was offset by abuse or obscured by wretched habits of one kind or another.

Several manuscripts attest the popularity of the *Ars Versificatoria* of Matthieu de Vendôme; the *Poetria Nova, Documentum de Modo et Arte Dictandi et Versificandi,* and *Summa de Coloribus Rhetoricis* of Geoffroi de Vinsauf.[88] These and other twelfth- and thirteenth-century manuals were derived ultimately from Cicero's *De Inventione,* the ever-popular *De Rhetorica, ad Herennium,* and Horace's *Ars Poetica*—in Manly's opinion the main sources of medieval rhetoric.[89] By using the formulas set out in the textbooks, poets could refurbish an old story, superimpose a high gloss of "colours" upon a plain surface, and expand a thin sentiment or narrative core into a substantial poem. The formulas of amplification were to the lyric poet of great interest, for with these artifices he was able to continue indefinitely on a single theme, without introducing narrative matter. Manly declares the conventional complaint to be a product of the schools of rhetoric,[90] and there is little doubt that most of the courtiers following Chaucer sought to be "gay of eloquence"[91] after the best manner of models of rhetoric.

Rhetoricians concerned themselves with the whole mechanical problem of composition. Two ways of beginning were projected, the natural and the artificial, of which Geoffroi de Vinsauf preferred the latter, that is, the beginning with *sententia* or *exemplum*. Geoffroi maintained that the conclusion should balance the beginning with a general idea or an example.[92] Various means of amplification were accepted. A common method was the accumulation of ideas around a central theme by means of *interpretatio* and *expolitio*, periphrasis, and comparison.[93] The figures of words and of thoughts *(figurae verborum, figurae sententiarum)* were regarded as "facile" ornamentation; these are the "colours" of rhetoric. "Difficile" ornamentation consisted in the use of the ten tropes, among which onomatopœia, metonymy, hyperbole, synecdoche, and metaphor, at least, are the property of good poetry everywhere.[94]

The wholesale dependence upon formalized structure was not without its critics. Manly's examination of Chaucer's poetry reveals the satirical intent of the poet in embellishing the account of Chauntecleer's capture with highly inflated apostrophe.[95] The allusion to "Gaufred"[96] clearly identifies Geoffroi de Vinsauf with the passage; and Robinson,[97] describing as "lamentation" this particular variety of address, points out the passage in the *Poetria Nova* which Chaucer surely had in mind.[98] Manly believed that Chaucer, though willing to parody rhetorical excess, was nevertheless convinced of the efficacy of apostrophe, *sententia*, and *exemplum*.[99]

The Chaucerian *Craft of Lovers*, a fifteenth-century rhyme-royal dialogue, bears directly on the abuse of rhetoric, as the unidentified author clearly intended to parody the inflated style of courtly complaints. Despite the editorial obfuscations of the *Works of the English Poets*,[100] it is apparent that the poem begins in the so-called artificial manner, that is, with a *sententia*, in this case a general statement about the character of love complaints. The conclusion is a conventional address, probably to Venus, "O potent princesse conserue true louers all,/ And grant them thy region and blisse celestiall";[101] this is a prescribed way of ending a poem. The self-depreciation of the second stanza calls to mind the Franklin's disclaimer. According to marginal notes in MS. Brit. Mus. Addit. 34360, f. 73b, tne man is Cupido and the woman Diana. In alternate stanzas, he complains in the usual manner, and the lady, acting the part of the reluctant fair, comments on the style of the address. Thus, the third and fifth stanzas are extended apostrophes[102] employing numerous "colours."[103]

In stanza four the woman praises his "painted eloquence,/ So gay, so fresh and eke so talcatife," and expresses the fear that she will be "shent" by the persuasiveness of his "conceit," "thought," and "entent." The woman warns her opposite in the eighth stanza, "At your beginning thinke on the terminacion," an injunction reflecting prescriptions of the rhetorics. Much else bearing the stamp of rhetorical doctrine might be here indicated, for the *Craft of Lovers* is crowded with artifices. It is sufficient to observe that the author has concentrated in the parody what occurs regularly in the vapid courtly stuff of the period. Rhetoric enabled the poet to expand a thin sentiment into a good many stanzas, but not to sustain a true lyric note.

Hand in hand with "rhetorication" goes "flourishing," or the affectation of a Latinical vocabulary, which, by Mendenhall's calculations, is most apparent between 1350 and

1530,[104] though the poets of the fifteenth century are pos-
sibly the worst offenders.   The so-called aureate terms were
born of the poets' delight in certain melodious terminations
and rhythmical polysyllables of Latin origin, and, more
significantly, of the exigencies of rhyme.[105]   One recalls the
high incidence of such rhyme suffixes as *-ure, -ite, -oun,
-aunce, -esse, -ment,* and *-ence.*   Many of the curiosities
happily did not survive, although the learned writers of
the period enriched, or "aureated," the language by hun-
dreds of words.[106]   In Dunbar this sort of thing is brought
to perfection.   "Painted eloquence" was all the fashion, and
"sentence," provided that it was reasonably moral or con-
ventional, could well take care of itself.   It is now difficult
to believe that style could so blind a class of poets to other
considerations; yet there is no alternative explanation of the
ornamental vaporings of the period.

CHAPTER FIVE

THE CHAUCERIAN LYRIC
MODE

THREE TIMES IN A SPACE OF FOUR HUNDRED YEARS PRO-
vençal lyric art indirectly colored English literature: twice
medieval French poetry was the transmitting agency, and
once Petrarchan sonnets and *canzoni*, which resuscitated
the moribund lyric tradition in the Renaissance. The sec-
ond impulse, severely vitiated in passing through the con-
servative milieu of fourteenth-century France, reached
England with the ethical inspiration already translated into
conventionalized pretense and the rich, metaphorical state-
ments of troubadour *cansos* reduced to plethoric generali-
ties. The scion upon which the Harleian lyrics had prev-
iously blossomed was detached before the songs of Gace
Brulé, Conon de Béthune, Blondel de Nesle, and the
Châtelain de Coucy were faded on the stock of French
literature[1] and obviously before *Le Roman de la Rose* had
infected the craft of poetry with the virus of allegory. The
troubadour lyric which Chaucer introduced was twice re-
moved from the source and once removed from the inspired
trouvère imitations. Lyric had degenerated progressively
in the keeping of unimaginative French poets after the mid-
dle of the thirteenth century, and the models available in
England were irreparably damaged by formalism and ab-
stractness, vices inherent in Middle English lyric from Chau-
cer to Dunbar. Machaut was doubtless familiar with the
spirit of the older lyric, but his followers apparently re-
garded lyric forms as legitimate vehicles for even the driest
discussions. The hundreds of ballades written by Des-

champs, for example, range in subject from religious dogma to the iniquity of womankind. As others of his time, he used lyric patterns to demonstrate dull propositions by logical procedures and did not often regard the communication of particular experience as his main obligation.

The lyric impulse in Chaucer and most of his disciples, acknowledged or otherwise, is admittedly weak, but the excess of defects in their shorter poems is partially owing to the decline of the trouvères and to the fragmentation of the whole art in the practice of fourteenth-century French poets, who abandoned musical accompaniment and extirpated metrical and emotional license. Chaucer was probably the first to affect the new manner in England, though Gower's French ballades may be as early as those of his contemporary.[2] It is hardly necessary to add that for all the metrical regularity of the *Cinkante Balades* no great merit attaches to the sequence. In any event, it was the master's example which counted. His lyrical pieces—ballades, roundels, and complaints—urged upon the courtly practitioners of the craft a lyric mode compounded of the synthetic emotion of the later *chansons d'amour*, the habit of allegory spread abroad by Guillaume de Lorris, and chivalric decorum tinctured with straitened moral and religious propriety. Within this tradition, first given prominence by Machaut and confirmed by Deschamps, the lyric spirit could not thrive; in his short poems Chaucer's genius shines feebly. Less blame attaches to him for failing with a style which was fundamentally inefficacious than for attempting it at all.

European society altered appreciably in the last two hundred years of the Middle Ages. Feudalism died, and with it the amiable half-truth of chivalry. Courtly and Ovidian love coalesced in a hypocritical union. The bourgeoisie arose as an articulate segment, sardonic and realistic. The tone of the literature became increasingly moral and therefore poorly reflected a society in which the clergy vied with rising commoners in acts of vulgarity and expressions of rank materialism. Whatever the causes—the decay of the intellectual fiber of the Church, the Hundred Years' War, the suppression of Lollardry and other forms of religious and social protest—the long transition to the Renaissance is in England a sorry spectacle.

Lyric passed from the possession of minstrels to professional men of letters, who catered not to a fairly homogeneous populace,[3] but to what must have been a very small circle of the select, educated and sophisticated, people disposed by training to esteem the abstract, the subtle, the moral. The taste of court society was not then sufficiently sharp to relish the obscure relations of *trobar clus,* but the literary coterie had nevertheless made a beginning by the time Chaucer set to work on the *Canterbury Tales.* If the form of courtly love yet lingered, the substance had long since vanished; Chaucer and his followers could not summon the rapture and enthusiasm of the Bernart de Ventadours for the condition of permanently unrewarded adoration. Moreover, the surface morality of the times, a simulated puritanism, drained passion out of literary love, with the result that a respectable monk like Lydgate could compose amorous complaints without fear of reprimand. The lady of this anemic love poetry remains so ill defined as to breed doubt of her existence outside of the poet's mind. Even when real, she is likely to become a mere symbol of love abstracted to an atmosphere so rarefied that the treatment is less emotional than metaphysical. The disciplined passions and religious leanings of the majority of transition poets are doubtless responsible for the exclusion of the sensual. After all, the Church for centuries had labored mightily to banish the secularity which animated the lush climate where *clerici vagantes* sang of unholy love and deemed "dulcissimum est ludere cum virgine formosa," and *chevaliers* rode "en la praele" seeking the shepherdess with "color vermeil-lete" and "euz verz."

In laboring to express the commonplace truths of life, death, immortality, and love, poets of the transition in England as in France brought to the task rhetorical artifices, inflated diction, and allegory, such heavy equipment as all great writers have used with the utmost discretion. As a rule, the Machauts and the Lydgates abhorred the particular and delighted in generalities, neglected concrete representation in their preoccupation with abstract ideas. If the poetry is turgid and discursive, the reason is that the times afforded few minds capable of fashioning sublimity with the difficult tools at hand. It is probably correct to say that the learned poets often mistook the symbol for the fact, and it is undoubtedly true that more time was expended in the management of the pasteboard personages of allegory, whether from the Classics or not, than on the central truth behind the fiction. Dangier, Espoir, Pitee, and the entire roster of capering personifications assumed a significance barely comprehensible at a later day, such was the mental discipline that prepared the medieval mind to leap from abstraction to abstraction without benefit of concrete referents. Chaucer easily visualized "Beute withouten any atyr" and "Youthe, ful of game and jolyte,"[4] but only the "fresshe fetures" and "comlynesse" of the subject of *Womanly Noblesse*. In a lyric inserted in *Le Remède de Fortune*, Machaut became so engrossed with the manipulation of the allegory designed to explain the physiology of love that he quite neglected the passion itself:

> Car vraie Amour en cuer d'amant figure
> Trés dous Espoir et gracieus Penser:
> Espoirs attrait Joie et bonne Aventure;
> Dous Pensers fait Plaisence en cuer entrer;
>   Si ne doit plus demander
> Cils qui a bonne Esperence,

Dous Penser, Joie et Plaisence,
Car qui plus requiert, je di
Qu'Amours l'a guerpi.[5]   ll. 1994-2002

Trans. For true Love in the heart of the lover fashions very
sweet Hope and gracious Thought; Hope attracts
Joy and good Adventure; sweet Thought causes De-
light in the heart to enter. So he should demand no
more this one who has good Hope, sweet Thought,
Joy, and Delight. For who requires more, I say that
Love has abandoned him.

Verse of this sort is based on a defective principle of ob-
jectification, for the prime motive is always ulterior and the
surface drama inconsequential. Tension cannot be main-
tained in a frame compounded of nine-tenths inorganic
matter.

Poetic thought was not always expanded by allegory and
discussion. The *chanson populaire* antedating trouvère lyric
shows a large narrative and descriptive content, as do many
lyrics of MS. Harley 2253. Emotional tension, if present, is
necessarily the product of situation or laconic commentary,
not of prolonged discussion or subjective analysis. The
difficulty with poetry which develops by this means is that
the special feeling of the author is of necessity a subordinate
factor. As a consequence of this limitation, the issues of
the Harleian songs are relatively simple. With the increase
of literary self-consciousness and the narrowing of the audi-
ence, the problem became one of spinning lyric on a thread
of pure sentiment. Both the troubadours and trouvères un-
derstood the technique of maintaining subjectivity by the
use of rhetorical devices, and Middle English poets acquired
the knack in due course. In the fourteenth century, France
communicated to England a vocabulary of abstract and
affective language, thus supplying a need existing from the
time of the Conquest, when educated men, turning to Latin
and French, permitted the learned and technical terms of

Old English to fall into disuse. With this deficiency in the terms of complex feeling repaired, the English language was once more a serviceable instrument for a poet who regarded the unique reaction to experience (ordinarily his own) as independently significant. The reaction is basically the naked exclamation of embryo lyric, but the emphasis rests on the effect of the situation on the poet. He explicitly states his emotion and around this central point accumulates associated ideas until the lyric has reached an appointed limit. The audience is called upon to follow the analysis and to appreciate the elaborate account of feeling in action which the expanded vocabulary makes possible, but not necessarily to participate in the experience.

Popular song requires the audience to react to a situation clearly outlined, limiting the reaction only in a general way; abstract lyric, like Chaucer's *Womanly Noblesse*, does little more than describe the reaction, leaving the audience to correlate the effect with a logical cause, which the poem merely suggests. Lyric with a large dramatic core compels vigorous generalizing; but the poetry of personal, explicit emotion requires strenuous intellectual activity directed toward finding segments of experience to fit abstract concepts. That the human mind performs this last task with reluctance the medieval Church soon learned and wisely equipped sermons with *exempla* to tie down general statements of principle. But the value of concrete referents in lyric poetry was never fully understood by English poets of the Middle Ages. Pre-Chaucerian song is fairly concrete, as lately seen, but the poet's emotion is not often articulated satisfactorily with physical content. Allegory as it is used by transition versifiers is only quasi-objective and wholly lacks the power of physical entities to provoke emotional response. The fundamental problems of holding situation in suspense (that is, preventing narrative development) and amplifying personal emotion aroused by the static situation have been solved to some extent in modern times by metaphor, but this convenient artifice is with Chaucer and his age merely a means of ornamentation.

The shorter pieces, usually in rhyme royal or *Monk's Tale* octaves, which have been attributed with more or less confidence to Chaucer divide loosely into poems of love and of moral philosophy. The serious Boethian ballades read rather well, even if the tone is usually homiletical. Nevertheless, such exercises as *Gentilesse, Fortune,* and *Truth,* though phrased with dignity and economy, are in large part pious essays trimmed to fit the ballade framework and are lyrical only in a limited sense. They illustrate the inclination of medieval poets to allow abstractions to drift about without appreciable mooring. Where Wordsworth will struggle to project "a motion and a spirit" through material forms, Chaucer is usually content with statement. Yet his choice and management of Boethian themes was conventional, for lyric frames were forced to accommodate a wide variety of prosaic subjects.[6] An age which wrote prose with a cramped hand used meter of necessity for commonplace purposes.

Large, dramatic canvasses best suited Chaucer's special talents. *Troilus and Criseyde* is a masterpiece precisely because it afforded the poet adequate space for close examinations of human conduct, the kind of literary work at which he excelled. On the other hand, his lyrical exclamation seldom rings out true and clear, whether from native reticence or formal restraints. Chaucer's love lyric, a genre by nature autobiographical, reveals virtually nothing of the life of the man. Real experience doubtless lies behind the facades of the complaints, but it is not soon discovered from the conventional utterances of the *Complaint to Pity, Complaint to His Lady,* and *Complaynt d'Amours.* There is no evidence, moreover, that Chaucer's contemporaries succeeded in penetrating the disguise.

Womanly Noblesse, an inferior performance by modern standards, illustrates not only the defective technique of *vers de société*, but also Chaucer's reluctance to engage his own sympathies. He dilates the exhausted theme of un-rewarded devotion: Your beauty and your virtue have cap-tivated me; since I shall be your servant all my life, I deserve some solace for the pangs I endure. The first stanza states that the lady's beauty and virtue have caught the poet's heart "in remembraunce" and that the image cannot be extinguished. Stanza two calls attention to the lover's distress, issuing at the same time an oblique appeal for relief. In the third stanza, the poet justifies his petition on logical grounds:

> Considryng eke how I hange in balaunce,
> In your service, such, lo! is my chaunce,
> Abidyng grace, whan that your gentilnesse,
> Of my grete wo listeth don alleggeaunce,
> And wyth your pite me som wise avaunce,
> In ful rebatyng of myn hevynesse,
> And thynketh by resoun that wommanly noblesse
> Shulde nat desire for to do the outrance
> Ther as she fyndeth non unbuxumnesse.

The advance in technique conceded, Chaucer nevertheless fails of lyric excellence because the emotion he feels or simulates remains in a fluid state. *Womanly Noblesse* is deficient in figures which should measure the depth of the poet's distress and the intensity of his desire for favor. The stale metaphor, "Considryng eke how I hange in balaunce," is not only weak but also elliptical; the presumably awful consequence of her coolness is unspecified. The lady's "governaunce," "noblesse," and "gentilnesse" and his "dur-esse" and "hevynesse" are all quite general and contribute little to the reader's understanding, although these and kin-dred abstractions to the medieval intelligence would be more or less animated. The inevitable conclusion is that the poet's inability to define his love proves there is no love—perhaps not even a lady; and this suspicion attaches to most love lyric from Chaucer to Wyatt. The diffuseness, vague imagery, and stylistic preciosity suggest not only that poets were incompetent to communicate such experience as lyric best handles, but that decorum discouraged particularity in poetic representations of love situations. Even in the autobiographical ballade sequence of Charles d'Orléans, for instance, an intimate passage with Lady Beauty is rare.

Chaucer at his serious best in love lyric is then not very stimulating; yet given the shadow of a jest, he writes with a deft hand. *To Rosemounde* probably contains an element of seriousness, but Chaucer treats the conventional love relationship jokingly. True, Rosemounde is vaguely drawn—any lovely lady who shines as the "cristal glorious." In this instance, however, the woman is unimportant, for the central interest is the poet's humorous revelation of a half-serious, middle-age passion. The poet is fascinated by Rosemounde, possibly a vivacious coquette of the court, because, as he confesses, she is

> . . . so mery and so jocounde
> That at a revel whan that I see you daunce,
> It is an oynement unto my wounde.

But no real attachment is implied. The extravagant imagery of the last stanza confirms the jesting tone established at the outset:

> Nas never pyk walwed in galauntyne
> As I in love am walwed and ywounde,
> For which ful ofte I of myself devyne
> That I am trewe Tristam the secounde.
> My love may not refreyd be nor affounde;
> I brenne ay in an amorous plesaunce.
> Do what you lyst, I wyl your thral be founde,
> Thogh ye to me ne do no daliaunce.

The portrait of Chaucer as a second Tristram (a common-place, incidentally) is amusing, but the resemblance of his state to a pike wallowing in sauce is nothing short of ludicrous. "Daliaunce" has here a playfully sinister connotation and therefore accords with the half-joking tone of the poem. It is possible that Chaucer, as a middle-aged lover, is describing his own waning amativeness as a good deal more fevered than was actually the case; by this view, the sad humor of irony is a significant thread of the poem. The lyric, in any event, is hardly the work of a young squire who "sleep namoore than dooth a nyghtyngale," but of a mature fancy, like Chaucer's in the *Troilus* period, when the poem by Robinson's estimate was probably written.[7]

Chaucerian wit sparkles again in the triple roundel *Merciles Beaute*. In the first section, the poet remarks the power of the lady's eyes to kill him. The second part is a carefully wrought design, in which Pitee and Daunger play hide-and-seek in the lady's cardiac region. Thus, two thirds of the poem follow a conventional pattern. In the concluding roundel, for contrast, Chaucer reacts mildly against both the artificial diction and the synthetic emotion of such complaints:

> Sin I fro Love escaped am so fat,
> I never thenk to ben in his prison lene;
> Sin I am free, I counte him not a bene.
> He may answere, and seye this and that;
> I do no fors, I speke right as I mene.

This muscular heresy comes as a pleasant antidote, hinting as it does that Chaucer placed no high value on the lyric in favor with the effete aristocracy. Although the spirit of rebellion was unfortunately not encouraged by either the master or his fifteenth-century disciples, renunciations of love were composed extensively during the Renaissance.

The two best-known English Chaucerians were men of strong religious inclinations: John Lydgate spent most of

his life at the abbey of Bury St. Edmunds, and Thomas
Hoccleve early intended to become a priest, an ambition
which, however, was never realized. They are linked by
their literary relationship to Chaucer and unfortunately by
a common mediocrity, the like of which in other centuries
would surely be denied a complete edition. With Lydgate
and Hoccleve and the amateur versifiers among the nobility,
the worst tendencies of precedent lyric were confirmed and
the saving graces of traditional song entirely ignored in the
tedious metrical exercises which passed as poetry in the
fifteenth century. Miss Hammond blames the sterility on
the times. War and tyranny sapped the intellectual strength
of England. The unending struggle with France blocked
the exchange of ideas; and the Church, supported by the
crown, crushed Lollardry and channeled thought along
orthodox lines.[8] Hoccleve and Lydgate are entirely repre-
sentative of the period, conforming as servilely to accepted
literary style as to religious dogma.[9] Whatever merit his-
tory finds in their works is Chaucer's reflected excellence.
Though both wrote lyrical poems, the rich possibilities of
the form seem never to have occurred to either.

In *La Male Regle,* Hoccleve regrets the excesses of a mis-
spent youth;[10] according to contemporary records, however,
he was an unexceptional clerk in the office of the Privy
Seal, where he seems to have commenced working about
1387.[11] Hoccleve's importance now rests on the interesting
testimonials he has left of Chaucer, whom he seems to have
known reasonably well. The dates agree. If born in 1368,
or thereabouts, he would have reached maturity a good ten
years before Geoffrey's death. The relationship is strength-
ened by the humble confession in the *Regement of Princes*
that his master was unable to communicate his art to him
"And fadir, Chaucer, fayn wolde han me taght;/ But I was
dul, and lerned lite or naght."[12] One reason for the clerk's
failure is not far to seek; like most poets of the period, he

praised Chaucer for "ornat endytyng" and "swetnesse of rethorik," qualities far less admired by posterity than the muscularity of the Canterbury period. Such a literary judgment as this discloses how completely formal problems occupied the attention of poets in this century, and it suggests that the questions with which poetry ordinarily deals were answered to the satisfaction of most educated men by the constituted authority of state, Church, and society. Hoccleve, needless to say, lacked the stomach for dissent.

What little talent Hoccleve possessed was expended on religious poetry, of which the hymns to the Virgin have been reckoned his best; the lyrical pieces of a secular character are occasional and uninspired by any commendable motives. He addressed servile petitions in rhyme royal and *Monk's Tale* octaves to his patrons, including Henry V, the Duke of York, and the Duke of Bedford.[13] Heresy is the subject of two ballades addressed to Henry and the Knights of the Garter; these belong, therefore, with the longer poem *To Sir John Oldcastle*, in which the poet censures the ill-starred dissenter.[14]

Three of Hoccleve's poems are requests for money sent to Henry V; Sir Henry Somer, chancellor (afterwards baron) of the Exchequer; and John Carpenter, described by Furnivall as the famous town clerk of London.[15] The *Complaint of Chaucer to His Purse* doubtless prompted Hoccleve's poems, Lydgate's *Letter to Gloucester*, and Dunbar's *To the King* and *To the Lordis of the Kingis Chalker*, but the begging song was an ancient type.[16] Two roundels, Hoccleve's *Appeal to Lady Money* and *Lady Money's Scornful Answer*, are in a jocular vein.[17] Humor occasionally creeps into the stilted verse. The first stanza of a begging poem to Henry, though characteristically humble, ends on a ruefully funny note:

> Victorious Kyng, our lord ful gracious,
> We, humble lige men to your hynesse,

Meekly byseechen yow (o kyng pitous!)
Tendre pitee haue on our sharp distresse;
For, but the flood of your rial largesse
Flowe vp on vs / gold hath vs in swich hate,
That of his loue and cheertee the scantnesse
Wole arte vs three to trotte vn-to Newgate.[18]

Though satire is even rarer than humor in Hoccleve's verse,
the roundel *Humorous Praise of His Lady* is a mildly di-
verting parodical inversion of the ideal of feminine beauty
in the Middle Ages. The last four lines are the repeated
element:

Hir mowth is nothyng scant / with lippes gray;
Hir chin vnnethe / may be seen at al;
Hir comly body / shape as a foot-bal;
And shee syngith / ful lyk a papeJay.
Of my lady, wel me reioise I may:
hir golden forheed is ful narw & smal;
hir browes been lyk to dym reed coral;
And as the Ieet / hir yen glistren ay.[19]

Prosodically, Hoccleve's verse is passable, though word ac-
cent and metrical stress are not always in accord; he at
least counts syllables, an observation which cannot properly
be made of Lydgate.

The life of the second Chaucerian is known imperfectly,
notwithstanding his excellent contemporary reputation and
the amazing quantity of verse now regarded as his. John
Lydgate was probably born in 1370, a year or two after
Hoccleve. He seems for limited periods to have attended
Oxford and schools in France and Italy; most of his long
life, estimated at eighty years, was spent in and around the
abbey of Bury St. Edmunds.[20] Critics have not been kind
to this monk who numbered among his illustrious patrons
the bibliophile Humphrey of Gloucester, and few defenders
have attempted to relieve him of the invidious judgment
uttered long ago by acidulous Joseph Ritson.[21] By virtue

of having written a minimum of 140,000 lines of verse, which contain scattered testimonials of Chaucer, Lydgate has commanded attention far in excess of the intrinsic merit of anything he composed. That he was ranked in his own time with Chaucer and Gower bespeaks an eccentric view of poetry. The long poems—notably the *Fall of Princes* and the *Troy Book*—are loose translations or prolix paraphrases; much of the rest is devotional poetry and *vers de société*. To the familiar defects of courtly poetry of the times, he added prosodic anarchy; and the generous emendations of apologetic editors have not much availed to straighten up his sprawling verse.

Both Hoccleve and Lydgate admired the artificial diction of Chaucer's dream-allegories and tried with little success to imitate it. The effort carried Lydgate to the extreme stylistic affectation properly called aureatism. Polysyllabic Latin and Romance forms, which were valued for sound, sense, or rhyme, had been entering the language since several decades before Chaucer, but Lydgate carried the practice to excess. He is credited by the *New English Dictionary* with introducing about eight hundred words.[22] This in itself is not fatal to the monk's verse, no more than to Chaucer's *Troilus;* it does, however, disclose in Lydgate an effort to conceal the poverty of ideas with rich ornamentation. Yet, Lydgate realized, if his century did not, that he fell far short of his master; in the *Floure of Curtesye* he sized up the transition with remarkable acumen:

> We may assay for to countrefete
>   His [Chaucer's] gaye style, but it wyl not be;
> The welle is drie, with the lycoure swete,
>   Bothe of Clye and of Caliope.[23]

In contrast to this honest appraisal stands the nauseating paean of Benedict Burgh to Lydgate: "ye be the flowre and tresure of poise, / the garland of Ive, and laure of victorye."[24]

With an unimaginable lack of discernment, Burgh ranks the monk above Aristotle, Cicero, Virgil, Homer, and Horace. His ballade were not worth the mentioning did it not so well represent the uncritical opinion of the times.

J. O. Halliwell-Phillipps published a batch of Lydgate's shorter poems in the last century,[25] and the Early English Text Society has recently brought out the last of the minor verse, a volume which contains all that may by courtesy be called secular lyric. Nothing in the collection compensates Lydgate for the loss of *London Lickpenny* and the *Lover's Mass*,[26] which alert scholarship has emphatically denied him. Much of the verse is occasional, and all of it shows the effect of hasty workmanship. The same vague images, unattached abstractions, and precious language which mar Chaucer's lyrics are magnified in Lydgate. The opening stanza of a ballade written for an unidentified squire, who apparently intended to send it to his lady, illustrates Dan John's prodigious gift for twaddle:

> Fresshe lusty beaute, ioyned with gentylesse,
>   Demure appert, glad chere with gouuernaunce,
> Yche thing demenid by avysinesse,
>   Prudent of speeche, wisdam of dalyaunce,
>   Gentylesse, with wommanly plesaunce,
> Hevenly eyeghen, aungellyk of vysage:
> Al this hathe nature sette in youre ymage.

The monk is not always so incoherent; *A Gentlewoman's Lament*, for all the familiar furniture, achieves some feeling. Warton long ago culled a few ecstatic passages from the *Life of Our Lady*.[27] The much-abused *Complaint of the Black Knight* has some good lines. There are a number of amusing antifeminist poems, which hardly reflect Lydgate's real views. The *Servant of Cupyde Forsaken*, though purporting to reveal the monk's experiences in the Court of Love, is certainly an untrustworthy document. *A Praise of Peace* is didactic and sententious.

Perhaps the *Ballade on an Ale-Seller* is Lydgate's most honest lyrical piece. The conviction is hard to avoid that for once the monk has presented a real situation. From the rubric, it appears that the barmaid waited on the trade in Canterbury. What relations the poet had with her cannot be known, although the vigor of his complaint suggests a discomfiting experience. "Stondyng in a traunce," the monk reflects bitterly on her "feyned plesaunce / Venus to serue." At one point he looks directly at the object of his wrath and writes what he sees and feels of the woman's deceitful practice. The product of this uncourtly reaction is a sharp description which has even now the power to re-create the portrait of a brazen flirt:

> Your callyng look, the sholdres ofte thwertyng,
> Your brestis bare, I dar riht weel assur,
> Your lauhtir, and your sadde kissyng,
> And I shold sey, be moste for to recure
> Money out of purs, and call men to your lur;
> Thes snaris leyd, withe guyle and trecherie
> Makethe men to fonne, in you ther tryst taffie.

The frankness is exceptional to say the least. Lydgate undoubtedly wrote the poem to express a real or imagined personal grievance and for the moment cared little for propriety. At the same time, his own good taste saved the poem from the vulgarity which in the fifteenth century mars a number of pieces in the popular idiom. This disclosure reveals the old celibate as a bit more human than should ever be surmised from his religious and didactic musings.

If sporadic remembrances of Chaucer save the verse of Hoccleve and Lydgate from utter neglect, no such interest attaches to the rest of the courtly poetry of the fifteenth century. Nevertheless, the abominable ballades and ballade-like pieces of the Duke of Suffolk and the unidentified courtly poetasters stem just as certainly from the dream-

allegories and the lyrical poems of Chaucer as do the
equally inept performances of the acknowledged disciples.
Though the century may have imitated in Chaucer what
was actually imitable, the choice could only be unfortunate,
seeing that the themes of fortune, death, polite love, and
the Blessed Virgin were long since bled of vitality in bal-
lades of the school of Machaut. The fixed forms remained
in vogue in France and doubtless continued to influence
English poetry. The verse of the two nations differs in
degree, not kind, the French having a superior finish and
somewhat more elegance and variety. No further develop-
ment of the vague, expository style was possible, despite the
fact that courtly lyric took a century to suffocate in its own
conventionality. Few poets realized that form had extin-
guished the spirit of the lyric. If the genius of Charles
d'Orléans temporarily revivified the fixed forms, little was
gained. English poets held to the outmoded style and
therefore left little worthy of anthologizing. The transition
in its main stream simply could not see the possibilities of
lyric expression, nor was there then in England a Villon to
enlarge and enrich the field.

In actuality, then, France had little to contribute to the
lyric art of Britain: the courtly verse of the two countries
acknowledges the same ideals during the fifteenth century—
stylistic facility and decorous statement. Chaucer was
himself a victim of the transitional French mode, which
prevailed in England at least until the Tudors. In France,
form triumphed rather completely over matter from the
accession of the Valois to Villon, and Villon was rather a
mutation without issue than the first of a new race of poets.
Charles d'Orléans, who survived Villon, took as his point
of departure the style of Guillaume de Machaut and blithely
cultivated a decadent medievalism among his circle at Blois,
though not without occasional achievement.

Ironically enough, the most expert manipulator of syllable

and sentiment during the period was not an Englishman but Orléans himself, the fastidious captive of Agincourt,[28] who spent twenty-five years of fairly easy confinement in England. Whatever the distinction is worth, the ballades and roundels associated with his name are unquestionably the best *vers de société* between Chaucer and Dunbar, despite the inevitable loss in translation, or "re-handling," as the recent editor of the English poems would have it.[29] Steele urges the conjecture that many of Charles' poems were composed originally in English, especially those dedicated to Lady Beauty. There is no strong evidence against the view, since the poet is known to have mastered English. Though there are no good criteria for judging priority where two versions of the same lyric exist, as in the case of half the contents of MS. Harley 682, the corresponding French poems, generally more polished, have the appearance of revisions.[30]

The ballades and roundels, arranged in a loose sequence of 6531 lines, are a vague record of two love adventures in England. Ever mindful of the statutes of that antiquated cult to which he adhered as faithfully as Machaut, Charles took precautions quite adequate to forestall researchers of a later day who would pry into his affairs. Therefore, the identification of Lady Beauty with Maud, countess of Arundel, and of the second love with Anne Moleyns, widow of Lord Moleyns and cousin of Alice Chaucer, duchess of Suffolk,[31] is highly conjectural. Notwithstanding several intimacies mentioned in the poetry, the precise relationships remain unclear, though Charles seems to have fared less advantageously with the second lady. The elegiac ballades on the death of Lady Beauty connote a strong affection and are reason enough for thinking the one attachment at least perfectly real.[32]

The staple arrangement of the ballades consists of three octaves, rhyming ababbcbc, with envoy, bcbc, though there are numerous variations in stanza length. The normal roundel has fourteen decasyllabic lines.

Charles' vocabulary has been described as Chaucerian by Steele,[33] though the verse is studded with numerous fanciful inventions which Geoffrey would not have relished. Unlike Lydgate's aureate terms, these have made no impression on the language. Stylistically, the verse suffers the defects of the age: artificialty, diffuseness; and is seldom exceptional. An excessive number of chevilles—notably *lo, mafay, fy, parde*—are required to fill out short lines, a matter to which the French poet, disciplined in the syllabic principle, was extremely attentive. Many of the English poems (though none with French counterpart)[34] violate the rule of *unissonans,* since, as Chaucer observed in the *Complaint of Venus,* rhymes are scarce in English. This liberty notwithstanding, Charles cannot avoid a plethora of terminations in *-aunce, -ight, -ly, -es, -yng, -ure,* and *-esse,* which indeed dog the meters of every courtly poet in the period. The syntax is sometimes un-English, as in "Vnto y may hir fauoure more purchase" or "I nolde it happe shuld for a thousand pound."[35] But for all the instances of unorthodox phrasing, there is less cause to quarrel with the poet's diction than with his commonplace management of stereotyped themes. In this matter he proves himself hopelessly unoriginal.

The trite artifices of the period are with few omissions unexceptionally represented in the ballades and roundels. The metaphorical ship carries the poet's trivial sentiment in Ballade 28 and Roundel 49,[36] while the lovers' compact is likened to a treaty in Ballade 30. Further examples of the conceited style appear in Roundel 41, where the poet offers his "hert as in morgage" for his lady's kisses. Ballade 61, reminiscent of the *Book of the Duchess,* represents the poet's losing Lady Beauty in a chess game with "cursid false daungere." Ballades 65 and 66 reflect the "Flower and Leaf" contention,[37] Ballade 78 a parliament of love,[38] and Ballade 72 a parliament of birds, with some verbal echoes of Chaucer. Needless to say, "bill" envoys are numerous.

The language of several ballades in the Lady Beauty sequence suggests a degree of intimacy inconsistent with *amour courtois*, though such a regret in Ballade 11 as "That y ne may now stroke yowre sidis pleyne," written in the lady's absence, may be innocent. In any event, Charles' passion led him to write ridiculous lines of confession in Ballade 12:

> In which thought oft y thynke and neuer the ner
> That y in armes haue yow my lady,
> For which y clippe my pylow lo and cry:
> "O mercy loue and make me so happy
> That y may see this thought or that y dy!"

The ludicrous exclamation prompted by a severe attack of "lovis malady" in Ballade 26, "I brenne! y brenne! o frendis come rennyng / And helpe alas this fyre were fro me rent," is not less extravagant than the unfortunate exclamation "I die! I faint! I fail!" of the *Indian Serenade*. Whether these effusions are altogether meaningful remains uncertain.

This is not to say that Charles d'Orléans was a mean poet, for within the limits which he accepted his verse is elsewhere scarcely excelled. The fault was his unwillingness to break out of the medieval tradition of love poetry; even for the mid-fifteenth century he was something of an anachronism. In fact, the absence of particularity and well-defined images, the reliance upon conventional generalities, the stuffy decorum, the denial of the flesh in amatory relationships[39] are the failings of transition verse, not Charles' alone. He sometimes proves superior to the age and sings in a clear, unrestrained voice. That despairing ballade, *En regardant vers le pais de France,* filled with nostalgic remembrance of other years, speaks in its passionate envoy to all times: "Paix est tresor qu'on ne peut trop löer: / je hé guerre, point ne la doy priser . . ." Just as Orléans forgot in the ballade to act the part of a militant *chevalier*, so in Roundel 57 he dispensed for the moment with the elegant diction becoming a courtier-poet:

> My gostly fadir, y me confesse
> First to god and then to yow,
> That at a wyndow—wot ye how?—
> I stale a cosse of gret swetnes,
> Which don was out avisynes,
> But hit is doon not vndoon now . . .

The simple language reinforces the tone of dignity and innocence established by the fiction of the confessional. Bowed before the priest, the poet reveals the kiss as if it were a sin of the first magnitude. But contrition is really no part of his attitude. The next statement is a superb piece of wit:

> But y restore it shalle dowtles
> Ageyn if so be that y mow.
> And that, god, y make a vow,
> And ellis y axe foryefnes.

Despite an occasional good poem, Charles failed to renew the life of medieval lyric, so strong were the influences bearing on him during the twenty-five years of captivity in England and afterward at Blois.[40] Neither he nor any courtly poet of the preceding hundred years had Villon's intense awareness of the beauty and tragedy of real life.

William de la Pole, duke of Suffolk, to whose custody Orléans was entrusted in 1432, has been tentatively identified by MacCracken as the author of twenty undistinguished specimens of *vers de société* in Bodleian MS. Fairfax 16.[41] It was in the company of Suffolk and his wife, Alice Chaucer, probably Geoffrey's granddaughter, that Charles is supposed to have written his English poems. Suffolk's English verse, as well as six roundels and a ballade in French attributed to him in MS. Trinity College Cambridge R.3.20, are no better than the average for the century, which is an extremely low mark. *Not far fro marche, in the ende of feueryere* has the merit of sincerity and possibly some historical interest, as it may reflect the poet's dismay over the general misunderstanding of his foreign policy. Though time has vindicated the peace-loving noble, in the 1440's the public regarded him as traitorous for making great concessions to France in the interest of peace and for effecting the release by ransom of the Duke of Orléans.[42] Suffolk was also blamed for the death of Humphrey, duke of Gloucester,[43] who died shortly after being arrested while en route to a session of Parliament at Bury St. Edmunds in 1447. Put under five years' banishment in 1450, the duke sailed for Calais; he was intercepted by a ship named, ironically, *Nicholas of the Tower* and was promptly beheaded by his political enemies. The public seems to have regarded this catastrophe as not undeserved, or so the poetry of the period evidences. Shortly afterward, there appeared a mock elegy larded with phrases from the Service of the Dead; thus, "For Jac Napes soule, *Placebo* and *Dirige*."[44] The humor of this ragged piece is at best grim. Wright printed a poor speciment of political allegory from Cotton Rolls ii, apparently written soon after Suffolk's arrest in 1449.[45] However interesting the Suffolk-Orléans relationship may be for political and historical uses, lyric gained little of consequence from it.

The century brought forth numerous addresses to princes of the blood, laudatory verses designed for use in pageants provided along the routes of royal progresses. Even if only a fraction of this matter has survived, the language could hardly be the richer for having it all. The Coventry Corporation Leet Book preserves ceremonial verses from three pageants of the second half of the fifteenth century. Queen

Margaret was welcomed in 1456 by a poem in sixteen rhyme-royal stanzas and three quatrains.[46]   In 1474, Prince Edward was similarly received,[47] and in 1498, Prince Arthur.[48] Elaborate pageantry marked the entrance of Henry VII into York in 1486, and three metrical addresses are preserved from the occasion in York City House Book No. VI.[49] The first piece was recited by a person representing "Ebrauk," the legendary founder of the city, anciently called Eboracum.   The introductory formula is familiar:

> Most reverend, rightwose regent of this rigalitie,
> Whos primative patrone I peyre to your presence,
> Ebraunk of Britane, I sitt nat this citie
> For a place to my pleasour of moost prehemynence . . .

This is the inflated manner of Hoccleve's numerous petitions to royalty[50] and of Lydgate's ceremonial poetry, much of which was surely purchased from the monk.   Lydgate excels at this sort of thing, as the opening of a piece written for the coronation of Henry VI shows:

> Moost noble prynce of Cristin prynces alle,
> Flouring in youthe and vertuous innocence,
> Whome God aboue list of his grace calle
> This day testaate of knyghtly excellence . . .[51]

This is laureate drivel, but unquestionably what such occasions demanded.

Another artifice of the fifteenth century was the love epistle, nothing more than the conventional complaint, with salutation or complimentary close or both tacked on.   It is an outgrowth of the "Go little bill" formula affected by troubadour and trouvère and claims certain affinities with the "Prince" envoys, through which the presidents of the *puys* were addressed by contestants submitting their ballades for judging.[52]   The number of epistolary poems written in the late fourteenth and fifteenth centuries must have been great, though Robbins reports only thirty-nine specimens, of which fourteen are as yet unpublished.[53] Orléans wrote six of these poems, and Suffolk two others; two unexceptional examples are among the Paston Letters. To the list compiled by Robbins should be added six others.

Three lyrics of MS. Rawlinson C.813, exclusive of five listed by Robbins, are surely to be regarded as love epistles. The composer of *O loue most dere, o loue most nere my harte*[54] so defines his lyric in l. 54: "and thys my letter full priuely yow grete." *Entierly belouyd & most yn my mynde*[55] opens with a salutation. In l. 7, the author speaks of "this lyttle byll" and at l. 25 announces, "No more to yow I wryte for lacke of scyence." The complaint, *Hevy thoughtes & longe depe sykyng*,[56] ends with a "bill," "Goo, lytle byll, & recommende thow me" (l. 17), as does *I loue on louyd, I wotte nott what loue may be*,[57] which Robbins includes.

That Pasaunt Goodnes, the Rote of all vertve (MS. Lambeth 306),[58] though in close proximity to two other letters in the manuscript, is omitted by Robbins. It has the simple "Go litill bill" envoy, but is clearly meant to be an epistle. ME *bille,* however, has not always the meaning of letter. According to the *NED, bille,* from L. *bulla,* could signify "a written document . . . statement in writing . . . ; a letter, note, memorandum."[59] Some lyrics with "bill" envoys are hardly to be reckoned letters, since they are written about and not to the subject. Thus, Lydgate's *My Lady Dere,* though provided with a "bill," is not actually designed as a letter, nor for that matter is his *A Lover's New Year's Gift,*[60] which has a variant of the formula.

From the fourteenth century should be included two letters intercalated in *Troilus and Criseyde.*[61] The first—from Troilus to Criseyde, beginning "Right fresshe flour, whos I ben have and shal"—may have suggested the salutations of *Frische flour of womanly nature* and *O resplendent floure! prynte this yn your mynde,* both indexed by Robbins. Indeed, the Chaucerian epistles are written in the same artificial style as many fifteenth-century letters and were probably known to most of those poets who attempted the form after 1400.

The love epistle, with its "Go little bill" formula, appears to be a mere refinement of a very old convention, the "Go little book" envoy, which, according to Tatlock, is to be referred ultimately to Ovid.[62] Trouvères and troubadours[63] employed a variant of the conceit extensively in chanson and *canso*. Thibaut de Champagne was particularly fond of the device,[64] and Blondel de Nesle occasionally used it, as in the lyric *Se savoient mon tourment:*

> Chançons, va isnelement
> A la bele au cler viaire . . .[65]

Trans. Song, go quickly to the lovely one with the clear visage . . .

One of the French poems in MS. Harley 2253 was apparently regarded as a message by the author:

> Par cest chaunsoun portez salutz à ma tresdouce amye;
> Quar ne vueil autre message, quei que je me afye.[66]

Trans. By means of this song bear greetings to my very dear friend; for I desire no other message, although I give myself up.

The lyric as message shows full development in three French ballades of John Gower,[67] which are internally described as letters and written directly to the *doulce dame*. The envoys serve as complimentary closes, as in No. 2:

> O noble dame, a vous ce lettre irra,
> Et quant dieu plest, jeo vous verrai apres:
> Par cest escrit il vous remembrera,
> Quant dolour vait, les joies vienont pres.[68]

Trans. O, noble lady, to you this letter will go, and if God grant, I shall see you afterwards. By this writing you will be reminded, when sadness goes, pleasures soon come.

In a similar manner, English poets of the fifteenth century employed the "Go little bill" convention in the closing stanzas of their ballade-like epistles. Meanwhile, the "Go little book" envoy, first used by Boccaccio as a conclusion for long, non-lyrical poems,[69] developed independently of the epistle. It was popularized by Chaucer in *Troilus and Criseyde*[70] and thoroughly conventionalized by his followers in the next century.

A variant form of the amatory epistle was the versified Valentine, which seems to have originated in France, possibly with Otes de Graunson.[71] Chaucer, who knew the poetry of the ill-fated French poet, celebrated St. Valentine's Day in the *Complaint of Mars,* the *Complaynt d'Amours,* and the *Parliament of Foules.*[72] Lydgate composed *A Valentine to Her That Excelleth All,* appropriately dedicated to the Blessed Virgin. Although few examples of this occasional type have survived from the medieval period, the custom of sending anonymous love verses on St. Valentine's Day was probably widespread. This practice was based on the ancient tradition that all creatures chose mates at this time; originally there was no connection between the mating period and the festival of St. Valentine.[73] But besides Chaucer's *Parliament,* which is not lyrical, the curious convention has left nothing in English of enduring interest.

Some antiquarian significance attaches to the metrical curiosities of the period, and literary history finds them further proof of perverted taste. An antifeminist punctuation poem of three rhyme-royal stanzas (attributed to Richard Hatfield) is a damning commentary on fifteenth-century literary ideals:

> All women have vertues noble & excelent
> Who can perceyve that / they do offend

dayly / they prove god wt good intent
Seldome / they dysplease there husbond /
    to theyr lyves end
Always / to plese them they do intend /
never / man may fynd in them shrewdnes
comonly / suche condycyons they haue more
        or lesse . . .[74]

To this same tendency may be attributed an anagram on
"Love"[75] and a ballade with an acrostic on "Alison."[76] Des-
champs and Christine de Pisan are not without guilt in
encouraging this deplorable tendency. One recalls Des-
champs' two ballades which could be read in eight different
ways.[77] Christine's "balade retrograde qui se dit a droit et
a rebours"[78] recalls a specimen attributed to Suffolk, "Balade
coulourd and Reuersid,"[79] which in the balanced structure
required to produce such effects travesties lyric poetry.

The sincerity and richness of texture which distinguished
the *chansons d'amour* of the late twelfth century were by the
fifteenth century completely vanished. What is praiseworthy
even in contemporary French lyric of the fixed forms—de-
votion to phrasal felicity and metrical regularity—counted
for little with the inept writers, happily unknown for the
most part, who swelled the book of turgid verse at the close
of the Middle Ages. The ballade is probably the parent of
these pieces, though the spawn resembles the progenitor
in few physical respects; in any event, the period referred
to its lyrics as ballades for lack of a more precise term. Most
of the complaints fail in one or more requirements to con-
form to ballade rules—number of stanzas, refrain, envoy, or
stanzaic *unissonans*. The stanzas vary from the standard
three to a dozen or more, and of an envoy there is usually
no sign. Though rhyme royal and *Monk's Tale* octaves
are favorite arrangements, stress and accent seldom agree,
and a consistently decasyllabic or octosyllabic stanza is
rare.[80]

The placid well of synthetic emotion is seldom ruffled by a novel idea, an improper thought, or a startling figure. The portrait of the humble lover in the anonymous complaints of the period is a redundant image, diluted of the striking characteristics of the archetype and adumbrated by a misty overlay of conventional attitudinizing. Always, the faithful courtier entreats the "frische flour of womanly nature," "fullfyled with all benyngnete, / And an Exsample of all worthynes,"[81] to relieve his "gref" and "aduersite." If the circumstances are for the lover more propitious, he swears eternal service,

> And I to hir for to be trew,
> And never chaung her for noon new,
>   unto myne end;
> And that I may in her servise
>   for evyr amend.[82]

So wrote a poet who styled himself A. Godwhen, otherwise unidentified, in an unusual lyric of MS. Cambridge Univ. Lib. Ff. 1.6,[83] where two less attractive pieces are signed by the same hand.[84] The song has six five-line stanzas. The first, second, and fourth lines are octosyllabic, and the others two feet in length. The syllabic exactness is gratifying, though the sentiment is commonplace. From the same manuscript comes another complaint, ostensibly by a woman, but the manner is in no way unusual; like others of this collection, the lyric *My woofull hert thus clad in payn*[85] shows metrical variety, having twenty-one lines, with every third line a foot shorter than the octosyllabic staple. Brown holds[86] that three rhymes are employed, though the poet apparently intended to write seven triplets on the same rhymes, aab. The feminine point of view appears in several other poems of the century,[87] and it may well be that women had come to take an active part in literature. If Margery Brews could write a metrical epistle to John Paston,[88] other women could doubtless manage the none too difficult technique of courtly verse.

The transition manuscript Rawlinson C.813 retains much of the old style and yet points the way to the simpler language and structure of sixteenth-century poetry. Trite formulas of the traditional compositions are nevertheless amazingly viable. Three poems clearly echo the ancient "riding out" introduction of *chansons d'aventure*,[89] and three others possess catalogues of feminine charms.[90] The poet who wrote *Iesue, that ys most of myght* was unquestionably steeped in medieval romance and lyric, for his description of a lady tallies with the prescribed form:

> Hur lyppes ar lyke vnto cherye,
> with tethe as whyte as whalles bone,
> hur browes bente as any can be,
> with eyes clere as crystall stoune.
> Hur fyngers be bothe large & longe,
> with pappes rounde as any ball;
> no-thyng me thynke on hur ys wronge,
> hur medyll ys bothe gaunte & small.

Another singer burlesques the formula, perhaps unintentionally:

> Your fair here hengyng downe to your knee
> with your rollyng eyes whyche ar as glasse grey,
> & your strawbery lyppes as swete as honye,
> with roose rede yn your chekes, ye haue no pere.[91]

Everywhere stylistic flourishes reveal the major interests of transition poets. The ancient concept of the dart of love, employed again and again by Continental poets, is given highly conceited expression in an extravagant complaint of the Bannatyne Manuscript. *Off lufe and trewt wt lang continuans*, appreciably influenced by formal rhetoric, employs the *Troilus* stanza with an exactness unusual for the times, though the language is a palpable travesty of the master's "gay" style. Ornamentation reaches a ridiculous

extreme in the last of seven stanzas, in which the figure of
the dart is fully embellished:

> The figurat dairt Invennomit wt bliss,
> forgit wt lufe, and fedderit wt delyt
> Wtowttin wame hes wondit me, I wiss;
> The harme of quhilk will nevir moir be quyt,
> quhois grundin point vnto my hairt did wryt
> In to my mynd evir In remenbrans
> off lufe and trewt wt lang continwans.[92]

The drift toward simplicity at century's end carried over
occasionally into the treatment of love. The Rawlinson
lyric *As I my-selfe lay thys enderz nyght* departs in a few
noteworthy respects from the conventional manner. The
dream setting and *chanson d'aventure* prelude are of course
nothing new, nor for that matter is the epistolary character
of the piece, which the last stanza indicates. It is moreover
metrically as defective as the usual complaint of this kind.
Nevertheless, the intimacy of tone strikes a pleasant note
in the decorous chambers of transition society, and here for
once may be a testimonial of real love. If the poet does
not free himself entirely from the artificialities of the age,
he is at least convincing. Even the dream is functional,
fulfilling the wishful thinking of the melancholic lover. This
is romantic love, sentimental and not a little lugubrious,
but genuine for all that. Though the tenth and eleventh
quatrains are not particularly memorable, they demand some
consideration for mirroring a plausible passion:

> I haue pryntyd yow yn my harte soo depe,
> wold to God I were able your seruant to be;
> euery nyght yn your armes that I myght slepe!
> Rewarde me with your loue, I aske non other fee.
> Onys ye promysyde me for to be trew,
> & we were neuer soo farre betweyne;
> & now ye haue refusyd me for a new.
> Alas! my harte dothe blede with you.[93]

Had this tendency been confirmed a century earlier, English verse in the fifteenth century might have run a different course. The remains allow no alternative to the conclusion that educated Middle English poets stubbornly refused to discard worn-out formulas, so that the period is not noted for high lyric achievement. It is probably correct to say, therefore, that the merit of the verse increases in direct ratio to the distance of its removal from the influence of that *vers de société* which Chaucer and Gower first imported from France.

CHAPTER SIX

THE DEBRIS OF THE
TRANSITION

THE HISTORY OF FIFTEENTH-CENTURY LIFE AND MAN-
ners as reflected by the poetry of the period is both incom-
plete and distorted, a vague account compounded of ideals
and half-truths, misrepresentation and willful disguise of un-
pleasant circumstances. Poets were astonishingly indiffer-
ent to the slaughter of the War of the Roses, the mounting
social tensions, and the basic considerations of human
existence. Hoccleve and Lydgate were dependent upon
patrons who refused to believe the Middle Ages were very
nearly over, and the nobles themselves maintained a syn-
thetic chivalry in the versified complaints and compliments
which they wrote for circulation among their friends. Wil-
liam de la Pole and Charles d'Orléans, wise and experienced
men both, possessed the raw materials and the sensibilities
for enduring poetic expression; but the contributions as-
sociated with their names, as lately seen, are totally unrepre-
sentative of the times, really of a sort gone to seed a century
and a half before. If it may be alleged that the book of
transition verse is incomplete, the statement holds in prin-
ciple only for minstrel song; no one can complain of a dearth
of art lyric or of songs of religious devotion. The cautious
and uninspired versifiers of the period blasted the modest
promise which poetry had held out at the death of Chaucer.
What remains to be considered is probably better than the
courtly lyric, but the debris rarely yields a treasure even of
minor importance.

If an appreciable segment of that verse which avoids the

courtly blight is fairly popular in spirit, none of it is demonstrably folk song, and the larger fraction is not above suspicion of learned handling. The carol, which is the most numerous genre, owns an attachment to the Church so intimate that one hesitates to assign a minstrel origin even to the most indecent example, though clericals are surely not to be taxed with every song which has come down in carol form. Official pronouncements tell of a popular minstrelsy whose work has all but vanished; the chroniclers of the times occasionally speak of wandering singers, but remain as silent as their predecessors about the repertoires of the entertainers. It may be that what Chambers calls the *scop* tradition[1] had been absorbed in large part by the new class of educated poets, leaving the hapless remnants to seek the company of the lower class of minstrels of the disreputable *mimus* tradition, who had never boasted of conspicuous literary talent. Those who in Elizabeth's reign were ordered punished as "rogues, vagabonds, and sturdy beggars"[2] retained few features of the fabulous Ancient Minstrel. That the wayfarers survived at all is remarkable, for their traditional enemies of Church and State had been joined before the fifteenth century by even more redoubtable foes, men of letters and professional musicians, both specialized products of the fractured art of lyric song.

The survivors of the once thriving army of entertainers surely retained in the decline some vestiges of the inspired lyric which enlivened hall and bower in the days of Coeur-de-Lion and Edward Longshanks. In France, twelfth- and early thirteenth-century lyric endured in oral tradition at least two centuries after the primary impulse was spent, as the important collection of Gaston Paris, *Chansons du XVe siècle,* fortunately demonstrates. Though Britain has now no comparable trove of *chanson populaire,* medieval authors attest to an abundance of unrecorded song, possibly better on the average than those few which have survived.

The lost songs mentioned in the Scottish *Colkelbie Sow* would fill a small book, and the lyrics represented by titles and snatches in numerous other long works from Gerald of Wales to Robert Fabyan would increase the collection considerably. The meager interest of learned men in popular song is typified by Dunbar's animadversion on the minstrels of Edinburgh: "Your commone menstrallis hes no tone, / Bot 'Now the day dawis,' and 'Into Joun'."[3] A contemporary, Gavin Douglas, is more circumstantial about the songs and dances which he reports among the recreations of Scottish maidens, but he too quotes only snatches of the actual songs:

> Sum sing sangis, dansis ledys, and rovndis,
> Wyth vocis schill, quhill all the daill resovndis;
> Quharso thai walk into thar caraling,
> For amorus lays doith all the rochis ryng.
> Ane sang, *The schip salis our the salt fame,*
> *Will bring thir merchandis and my lemman hame,*
> Sum other singis, *I wil be blyth and lycht,*
> *Myne hart is lent apon sa gudly wycht.*[4]

These were not necessarily folk songs; indeed, the stanza which Robert Fabyan records in the *New Chronicles* as sung by maidens of Scotland after Bannockburn[5] has a semilearned appearance, somewhat reminiscent of Minot. But there is little doubt that the lost dance songs were a great deal more popular than most of the lyrics which remain for study.

For all the ecclesiastical coloring, the fifteenth-century carol[6] is generally regarded as a late development from dance song, the *chanson de carole*. This genre, defined by Greene as "a song on any subject, composed of uniform stanzas and provided with a burden,"[7] is in England intimately associated with religion and by Chambers' reckoning especially with Christmas.[8] Fewer than a hundred carols of nearly five hundred written before 1550 may be accounted secular; about half of those from before 1500 have been handed down in two manuscripts—Sloane 2593 and Bodleian Eng. poet. e.1. Though the former collection was once regarded as minstrel work, its substantial Latin content points to a learned origin. The manuscript is demonstrably heterogeneous, and its parts unquestionably derive from diverse sources. Since several Sloane lyrics are incompatible with proper religious attitudes, it is altogether probable that the collector included some minstrelsy in his book.

As far as the Church was concerned, the secular carol was an unwanted mutation, a throwback calling to mind the obnoxious themes and associations of dance song, which men of religion had endeavored to suppress under an overlay of pious sentiment. The "Godlification" of the old genre was part of a well-conceived plan to substitute devotional song for profane and thus promote religiosity with the Devil's own merry instrument. It is little wonder that by the fifteenth century only the refrain (or burden) suggests dance origins. Nothing remains of the *fêtes de mai*. Though the amorous carols occasionally reflect ancient folk practices surviving in the late Middle Ages, they are not on that account of high antiquity and probably not even in direct descent from the tradition represented by two carol-like songs of the early fourteenth century, *Ichot a burde in boure bryht*, of Harley 2253, and the *pastourelle, Als i me rod this ender dai*, of Hale 135, both of which Greene includes in his collection. The exact role of clerks in the making of secular carols cannot be determined, since the authors are largely unidentified; but such composers as are known, Thomas Ryman, a Franciscan, who is charged with about one third of the corpus of early English carols, and the Augustinian John Audelay, were indisputably holy men. Since the carol is merely a form, which might be imitated by anyone, the Church need not be convicted of gross secularity, if not depravity, on circumstantial evidence. Chambers considers at least two indecent specimens to be the work of minstrels,[9] and still others which lack Latin phrases may be of the same class.

The Church may sometimes be apprehended in the act of adaptation. Spread among the Latin hymns of the *Red Book of Ossory* are snatches of eight secular lyrics, which were designed to signify the musical settings of the pious songs which followed.[10] That the author, presumably Richard de Ledrede, Bishop of Ossory from 1317 to 1360, found this arrangement practicable is certain proof that the secular songs so employed were widely known in Kilkenny and vicinity.[11] The fragments suggest simple love songs on the order of the Rawlinson scraps. Another instance of wholesale adaptation is the *Gude and Godlie Ballatis*,[12] which the three Wedderburn brothers of Dundee composed in part from "prophaine sanges" in the middle of the sixteenth century. The New Kirk was no less active than the old Established Church in combatting secular singing, and various evangelical persuasions have continued to regard nonreligious song with suspicion.[13] Detached instances of this process are common: occasionally both the secular original and pious adaptation are extant, as the *Notbrowne Mayde* and the *New Notbroune Mayd upon the Passion of Cryste*.[14] On the other hand, the process was often reversed. The mingling of piety with secularity in the English carols has sufficient precedent in numerous Latin and French poems of parodical intent. Snatches of the hymns, proses, and antiphons were on the tongues of all, and it was inevitable that their use would be occasionally perverted, though a scurrilous parody of the Paternoster in a sixteenth-century carol is extreme.

The surviving poetry of the fifteenth century, as that of the entire Middle Ages, is predominantly religious or didactic. Whether this circumstance is a true index to the taste of the times is debatable. Robbins has maintained that if secular song had been widely esteemed it too would have been preserved.[15] This supposition has the support of manuscript collections of lyrics, but it is hard to believe that religious verse was preferred to secular in a century noted for its roistering yeomanry and uncouth middle class. Extant minstrel song would not keep a singer busy more than an hour, and it stands to reason that those named in royal accounts and paid in the minted coin of the realm were not mute. This is not to say, however, that the lost songs of the minstrels were necessarily superior to the religious lyrics which have survived.

One effect of the old fracture of the singing lyric was to establish as poets of a reluctant kind individuals who were primarily musicians. A high percentage of the carols are so deficient in spirit and sentiment as to be utterly worthless for any purpose save that of supporting melody; the highly esteemed *Agincourt* carol is not excepted from this invidious observation, though numerous others fare worse. This is, indeed, a predictable consequence of the perfection of vocal and instrumental music. Accordingly a song which has a substantial lyric content or a lyric which goes rather melodiously though unprovided with music is exceptional.

The rash of poems in the fifteenth century on the power of money is significant of the increased importance of hard money and of the trading interests which were coming to displace the enfeebled baronage as the authors of English prosperity. Everywhere money was in demand: by day laborers wandering from farm to farm in search of employment, by the fat burgesses of the growing towns, by the exporting merchant class. The businessman of the period— shrewd, practical, middle-class—was, like Chaucer's Merchant, "Sownynge alwey th'encrees of his wynnyng." Still, the poems on money are not the work of a disdainful aristocracy satirizing bourgeois worship of money nor yet the admonitions of the clergy against Mammon. The effete nobility lacked the insight exhibited in the lyrics on Sir Peny, and the secularized clergy was much too taken up with his worship to criticize his practice. The authors of these lyrics were doubtless men in ordinary circumstances who saw the main tendency of the times. Pounds brought power. The humblest peasant's son by the acquisition of wealth could defy the stigma of his birth and ignore the Statutes of Apparel, thus assuming a role reserved in the past for his betters. While aristocracy warred, England's middle class gained ground, despite the perils of internecine strife and the impediments imposed by Lancastrian and Yorkist autocrats. If the new class is raw and vulgar, unleavened by sweet culture, it is at least vigorous. To its unidentified members must be ascribed that little poetry of the period standing free of the fatal clasp of preciosity and abstractness.

Gold personified is the omnipotent actor in many a poem written during the Middle Ages and after, some humorous, others lamely satirical, but all attesting the thriving condition of what tilting religious attacked as *avaritia*. Joseph Ritson regarded a fabliau, *De Dom Argent,* as the source of the numerous poems on money preserved in Latin and European vernaculars,[16] though Wright later expressed the opinion that *De Cruce Denarii* and *De Nummo,* both set down in English manuscript (Reg. 8 B. VI), were the "foundation of a class of ballads" dealing with money.[17] In addition to these two poems, which Wright associated with the work attributed to Walter Mapes, there is yet another Latin exercise, *Versus de Nummo,*[18] probably from the twelfth century. *De dan Denier,*[19] from a thirteenth-century French collection, is an unexceptional specimen, perhaps imitated from the Latin, though in the phrase *dan denier* (literally, Lord Penny) a connection with the English *Sir Peny* is struck. Whatever the source of these poems on money, all have some antiquarian and sociological interest, if no conspicuous literary merit.

In the English poems, no derogatory connotation adheres to the penny on account of its worth. Indeed, the penny (or *denier*) was in the Middle Ages a coin of considerable purchasing power. As late as the fifteenth century, Kendal cloth cost 4½d. per yard and shoes 6d.[20] In Chaucer's time, a small quantity of money, by modern reckoning, purchased a sumptuous feast, for prepared roast pig cost only 8d., a roast goose 7d., a pullet 2½d., and ten eggs could be had, surprisingly enough, for a single penny.[21] The forlorn wayfarer of *London Lickpenny* purchased a pint of wine in Cornhill for 1d.

Perhaps the most notable of the vernacular poems on money is *Sir Peny*, a fourteenth-century piece in *rime couée*. Hazlitt's edition,[22] a composite of the versions in MSS. Caius Cambridge 174 and Cotton Galba E.ix, is for most purposes satisfactory. At the outset the author echoes the Latin poem *Versus de Nummo*:

> In erth there ys a lityll thyng,
> That reynes as a grete kyng
>   There he is knowen in londe;
> Sir Peny is hys name callydde,
> Ffor he makyth both yong and olde
>   To bowe unto hys hande.   st. 1

In the second stanza, the poet avers that all serve Peny— pope, king, emperor, bishop, abbot, prior, parson, priest, knight, duke, earl, and baron. The Latin is more economical, if less spirited:

> In terris summus rex est hoc tempore nummus,
> Nummum mirantur reges et ei famulantur;
> Nummo venalis favet ordo pontificalis;
> Nummus in abbatum cameris retinet dominatum;
> Nummum nigrorum veneratur turba priorum.[23]

Trans. At this time money is the greatest king in the land.
Kings admire money and serve it. The venal class
of priests favors money. Money in the chambers of
abbots holds dominion. The crowd of degraded
priors venerates money.

"That lytyll roende swayn" requires obedience and reverence
from all, the English writer continues. There is none so
strong that he will oppose Sir Peny, because the little knight
makes the arrogant meek by his miraculous power. He
rules everywhere by his unexampled puissance—"in burgh
and in cete, / In castell and in towre." Right avails not at
all against him:

> He makyth the fals to be soende,
> And ryght puttys to the grounde
> And fals lawys ryse.

A carol of Sloane 2593, *Peny is an hardy knyght*, com-
presses the principal ideas into five stanzas, to which a rol-
licking refrain is joined: "Go bet, Peny, go bet, go, / For
thou mat makyn bothe frynd and fo."[24] A version in eight-
line stanzas reposes in the Bannatyne Manuscript,[25] the work
no doubt of a contemporary of Henryson and Dunbar. Little
that is new appears in the piece, but like so much else that
the Middle Scots "makaris" set hand to it is slyly indirect,
whimsical, and pleasantly ironic. The last stanza is ex-
cellent:

> Sir Penny now is maid ane owle;
> Thay wirk him mekle tray and tene;
> Thay hald him in quhill he hair-mowle,
> And makis him blind of baith his ene.
> Thairowt he is but seyndill sene,
> So fast thairein they can him steik,
> That pure commownis can nocht obtene
> Ane day to byd with him to speik.

The power of money is the subject of a piece in nine qua-
trains, *Man upon mold, whatsoever thou be*,[26] and a swing-

ing carol, *Aboue all thing thow arte a kyng,* in which the
poet avows in conclusion that money makes the man.

Once Lydgate was credited with authorship of a con-
summate handling of the ancient didactic motif, but *London
Lickpenny* has for the past century been denied him,[27]
despite the testimony of Stow's *Survey of London.* This
plain, serious poem, incredibly good for the period comes
down in two defective manuscripts, Harley 367 and 542,
of which, in Miss Hammond's opinion, the language of the
latter recension is the older.[28]   Holthausen took some lib-
erties with Harley 367 to make the lines consistently deca-
syllabic,[29] though emendation seems hardly justified in the
light of metrical waywardness in the fifteenth century.

The fiction of *London Lickpenny* is simple enough. A
Kentish farmer comes to town seeking legal redress for a
grievance not clearly specified. He proceeds from court to
court—King's Bench, Common Pleas, Exchequer, and Chan-
cery[30]—without finding a "man of lawe" who will handle
his affairs. In Chancery, clerks read over his evidence and
tell him what he finds to be universally true: "they seyde,
trewer things might there not be, / but for lacke of money
I myght not spede." As the poor husbandman turns again
home, he is assailed on every side by chapmen hawking
their wares—Flemish hats, ribs of beef, "hot pescodes,"
pepper, saffron, and clove. In Cheapside, velvet, silk, and
lawn are offered him, but he must look in vain, for lack of
money. Among "stolen gere" commonly sold in Cornhill,
he perceived his own hood, but had not the money to re-
claim it. His only penny went for a pint of wine. "Sore
a-hungred," the Kentishman bade farewell to "London
lykke-peny" (that is, lick up the pennies) and went to
Billingsgate to procure passage over the Thames:

> Then I conveyede me into Kent,
> for of the law would I medle no more;
> by-caus no man to me would take entent,
> I dight me to the plowe, even as before.

This fifteenth-century Langland resists the temptation to moralize, to complain profusely over social injustice, and contents himself with the poignant refrain: "for lacke of money I mighte not spede." For all this, *London Lickpenny* is nonetheless effective social commentary, being the un-adorned record of a poor man's futile progress through the law courts of medieval London, a London which had for-gotten the Peasants' Revolt of 1381 and John Ball's disquiet-ing couplet, "When Adam delved and Eve span, / Who was then the gentleman?" Beyond the implicit indictment of English justice and the materialistic bent of the century, *London Lickpenny* is realistic description, a series of val-uable vignettes by a rough and grim artist who had no wish to make the city appear other than it was. Hence, the shouting drapers of Candlewick street come alive, and the aroma of "Hot shepes fete!" sizzling on the griddle blends with the stench of melwell and mackerel.

By comparison with the vapid ballades or the jingoistic political songs of the previous century, *London Lickpenny* is carefully controlled poetry, avoiding most of the faults which dog the verse of the period. If it is deficient in figurative language and metrical grace, it counts as un-qualified gains the vividness of its description and the vig-orous and idiomatic phrasing of its verses. There is none of the superficiality of the court poet or the uncritical ortho-doxy of the clerical carol-maker in the work. The poet, if at times grimly humorous, is nevertheless devoted to a serious purpose. He intends commentary, and this he achieves by skillful indirection. Beneath the plain surface of the poem operates a wise, analytical mind, whose power-ful emotion is implied in the terse refrain.

Political carols show no such independence as *London Lickpenny* and with hardly an exception are undistinguished. Despite Henry's injunction that no ditties be made on Agincourt, a specimen described by Greene as a "stirring song" and the "best-known carol in English not concerned with the Nativity" was written on the forbidden subject.[31] John Audelay himself celebrated the victory in a carol composed for the coronation of ten-year-old Henry VI in 1429. Though Greene is undoubtedly correct in declaring this song superior to two ceremonial poems on the same subject, "blind Awdlay" gains nothing by the comparison.[32] For fear or favor, carol writers eschewed the controversial and avoided the appearance of dissent; the effort vitiated what little inspiration the mediocre versifiers possessed in the first place. The mere curiosities of the period are intrinsically more interesting than the servile songs to royalty.

Human delight in ambiguity expresses itself on unsophisticated cultural levels in the riddle and among the privileged in *double entendre* and complex metaphor, of the last of which allegory is merely a radical extension. Middle English affords a few specimens of the simple riddle, and these are usually epigrammatic snatches bound up with more serious matter. Riddles, however, were susceptible to literary treatment, as Child's riddling ballads[33] and the durable *Riddle Song*[34] attest. The ballad is essentially dramatic and requires no discussion here, but the song, for its amazing history, deserves more than a passing glance. Cecil J. Sharp, the famous folk-song authority, recorded three versions of the *Riddle Song* in as many counties of Kentucky during a rapid tour in 1917,[35] and a popular ballad singer at the present time carries the piece in his repertoire. Oral tradition has little altered the song since it was set down five hundred years ago in MS. Sloane 2593—an introductory couplet dropped, a gift or two changed, but the central idea is faithfully preserved. The Sloane song begins,

> I have a yong suster fer beyondyn the se,
> Many be the drowryis that che sente me.
> Che sente me the cherye withoutyn ony ston;
> And so che dede the dowe withoutyn ony bon;
> Sche sente me the brere withoutyn ony rynde;
> Sche bad me love my lemman withoute longgyng.

The riddles are solved in the concluding two couplets:

> Quan the cherye was a flour, than hadde it non ston;
> Quan the dowe was an ey, than hadde it non bon;
> Quan the brere was onbred, than hadde it non rynd;
> Quan the maydyn hast that che lovit, che is without
> longyng.

Having a plain structure, each part of which suggests the others, the *Riddle Song* like a ballad hangs on in the folk memory. This curiosity recognizes a past so remote as to make the average carol seem modern by comparison.

Ancient customs enter prominently into the carols of the *Boar's Head* and *Holly and Ivy*, although the form in which they are preserved probably does not antedate the fifteenth century. The meaning of the boar's head ceremony is now completely lost and may have been unknown to those who sang at Yuletide the festive burden:

> Caput apri refero,
> Resonens laudes Domino.

Trans. I bear the head of the boar, singing praises to God.

following the leader's request in the opening stanza:

> The boris hed in hondis I brynge
> With garlondis gay & byrdis syngynge,
> I pray you all, helpe me to synge,
> Qui estis in conviuio.

Trans. Who are at the feast.

The head is regularly served with mustard *(cum sinapio)* and by tradition departs the board on Twelfth Day.[36]   One ecclesiastic recognized the symbolic character of the proceedings and tried to supply an explanation: "The borys hede, that we bryng here, / Betokeneth a prince [Christ] withowte pere."[37]   According to a version yet sung at Queen's College, Oxford, the steward provides the boar's head in honor of Christ. There remains, of course, the possibility that the adapters, knowing the significance of the ancient custom, invested the ritual with a religious motif in the interest of Christian doctrine.

Somewhat more may be deduced from the carols of *Holly and Ivy.* Greene takes the exclusion of Ivy and her partisans from the hall to be a reflection of the curious superstition about "first-footing." According to tradition in some British communities, for a woman to be the first to enter a house on Christmas was extremely unfortunate, and precautions were taken to prevent such an occurrence.[38] The symbolism is sexual—that is clear; but the logical basis appears to have been obscured by accretions of irrelevant matter. The key to the problem may lie in the diœcious nature of *Ilex aquifolium,* the English holly. If this hypothesis be correct, Chambers errs somewhat in attributing the popularity of holly to striking fruiting habits.[39] The reason is not so much that the plant, with glossy leaves and red berries, is conspicuous, but that it perfectly symbolizes the division of the sexes.[40] Monœcious ivy counts for nothing in this connection and may be an intrusive element of relatively late date.

There is no denying, however, the close association of holly and ivy at the time that the carol writers dipped into the current of folk custom. Holly with his merry men symbolizes the masculine element dominating Ivy and her maidens during the Christmas season. The writers praise Holly extravagantly and link "him" with the joyous spirit of Christmas. Instead of dancing and singing, Ivy and her partisans weep and wring their hands. Birds of good omen consort with Holly, but the sorry owl perches on Ivy, who is compelled to stand outside. The female element is clearly inferior in this sex contention, though not in others.[41]

The association of holly with ivy was not inevitable in medieval lore; the two plants figure alone in some ceremonies. In Derbyshire three kinds of holly—prickly, smooth, and variegated[42]—were commonly brought into the house to ensure a prosperous New Year.[43] If the "smooth" holly were carried across the threshold first, according to tradition, the wife would rule the house for the following year; if the prickly, the man.[44] Further proof that the division of sexes in holly was recognized at an early date comes from Gascoigne's *The Princely Pleasures of Kenelworth Castle,* which Greene cites: "Mary there are two kinds of Holly, that is to say, he Holly, and she Holly. Nowe some will say that the she Holly hath no prickes, but thereof I entermeddle not."[45] Gascoigne was only partially correct: sex cannot be determined until the holly blooms. Nevertheless, holly was known to be diœcious, and that is the important point. This fact accounts for the use of holly to represent the sexes; it points ultimately perhaps to fertilization rites, in which the male and female kinds of holly were used symbolically.

Ivy was in all likelihood joined with holly somewhat late, probably after most people had forgotten or had chosen to ignore the basic significance of the ceremony. In any case, the holly with red berries, which acts the masculine part in the carol, would be the female kind and on that account inappropriate. Obviously, once the symbolism was obscured, the fruited sorts of holly and ivy would be esteemed for decorative purposes. But, it is remarkable that clericals would anthologize such a carol, since evergreens, traditionally associated with heathen practices, were regarded with suspicion and kept out of the church.[46]

Another autochthonous type widespread in Europe during the Middle Ages and afterward was the so-called "lying-song," the *Lügenlied* of German popular tradition. Less poetic than curious, it is altogether popular.[47] Like the *Riddle Song,* it depends upon ambiguity, achieving its effect through the rapid accumulation of impossible conditions, which by their very weight carry conviction to the shaky thesis—normally the faithlessness of womankind. The only specimen of consequence before 1500 is a carol:

> When nettuls in wynter bryng forth rosys red;
> And al maner of thorn trys ber fygys naturally;
> And ges ber perles in every med;
> And laurell ber cherys abundantly;

and so on throughout seven seven-line stanzas. The burden in this instance applies the "lying-song" to women: "Whane thes thynges foloyng be done to owr intent, / Than put women in trust and confydent." The Bannatyne Manuscript has numerous examples, all probably written after 1500.[48] The consummate handling is unquestionably John Donne's *Go and catch a falling star*. Two prophecies on the battle of Bannockburn bear witness to the flexible character of the formula and tend to show that the association with antifeminism may be a late development. The fiction of the prophecy from MS. Harley 2253 has the Countess of Dunbar asking Thomas of Erceldoune "quant la guere descoce prendreit fyn." His ambiguous reply (or that attributed to the protean Thomas) recalls the "lying-song":

> When man as mad a kyng of a capped man;
> When mon is leuere other mones thyng then is owen;
> When londyon ys forest, ant forest ys felde . . .[49]

A lyrical type poorly represented in Middle English is the drinking song. Though medieval men were fabulous topers from all accounts, serious scribes have conspired to deny posterity more than a whiff of vernacular *potatoriae*—as if the times could thus be made to appear less secular than truth allows. If the manufacturers of liquors had not yet learned to fortify their products by distillation (whisky, brandy, and gin were unknown), they compensated for the lack of this technique by providing an abundance of ale and wine for a people who regarded water with outright distrust. Though the pale English sun encouraged cereals rather than grapes, the wool surplus repaired nature's oversight; and ships laden with the fermented wealth of France, Germany, and Spain plied the waters between England and the Continent.[50] Under these circumstances, the tavern figured prominently in the daily life of the Isles, but little musical evidence of conviviality has endured. As early as 1200, wassailers were singing an Anglo-Norman *quête* song, *Seignors, or entendez a nus*,[51] which was merely an oblique request for wine by wandering revelers of the Yuletide. There must have been dozens of well-known drinking songs in English, but before the beginning of printing the type is hardly to be found.

One of the Rawlinson fragments appears to be a drinking song, though little can be made of the wretched text. A prohibitionist carol of Bodleian MS. Eng. poet. e.1. may take its lively refrain from some popular song of the tavern, "Doll thi ale, doll, doll thi ale, dole." Another piece from the same Bodleian collection is the only good drinking song set down in English before 1500:

> Bryng us in no browne bred, fore that is mad of brane,
> Nor bryng us in no whyt bred, fore therin is no game.
> But bryng us in good ale.

The refrain affirms in the same undulating measure the drinkers' desire for nothing except ale. Though the longest version has only eight stanzas, the song, like the *Old Chisholm Trail*, is susceptible to infinite expansion—just as long as the revelers can think of something they do not want.

The English songs, including most of the Tudor specimens, are nevertheless small beer beside the old Goliardic *potatoriae*, one of which is luckily deposited in that precious repository of antique treasures, Sloane 2593.[52] Little the worse for wear, an immortal passage from the *Confessio* of the Archpoet—"Meum est propositum in taberna mori"[53]—has come down from the twelfth century. This disgraceful sentiment together with the accompanying verses has been relished by students for another five centuries, and few could but wish that the prayer of the sinful old *vagus* be answered, "Deus sit propitius huic potatori." The Sloane song offers besides fellowship the novel excuse that wine makes friends speak good Latin. Though English affords the like neither of this nor of *Potatores exquisiti*[54] of the *Carmina Burana*, it has *Back and Sides*,[55] which is in its English way inimitable.

Innocuous misogyny is doubtless endemic in most cultures present and past, betraying its existence in oblique references and bawdy jests of masculine authorship, though seldom developing into a gush of satires on women such as the twelfth century brought forth. Whatever the origins of antifeminism, the Latin satires of Marbod of Rennes, Hildebert of Tours, Bernard of Morlas, Alexander Neckham, and Walter Mapes[56] betray an intimate association with the purposes of the Church and are clearly intended to dissuade from matrimony. These malicious treatises overlay, as do many patristic writings, the strong conviction that woman is inferior to man and, by extension, of a baser nature. Antifeminism does not, of course, originate with these satires, any more than with the Pauline Epistles. Lately, Utley has cautioned against seeking the source of misogynous attitudes in any particular place or among any special group of people,[57] and it is perfectly obvious that the attacks on women in Latin and vernacular letters spring from motives as diverse as a desire to preserve the monastic ideal and a masculine wish to achieve revenge for a feminine slight. Nevertheless, the Latin satires bequeathed to vernacular letters carefully phrased indictments and effective formulas and in effect codified sporadic and disconnected sentiments. The tradition bore its first important vernacular fruit between 1266 and 1277, when Jean de Meun completed *Le Roman de la Rose*. This encyclopedic continuation of the chivalric allegory of Guillaume de Lorris contains among other things a mass of satire of women,[58] taken generally from the tradition, but especially indebted to *Adversus Jovinianum* of Jerome of Stridon and the satires of Juvenal.[59] It was the *Rose* which provoked *L'Epistre au Dieu d'Amours* of Christine de Pisan and Jean Gerson's *Sermo Contra Luxuria* in 1399, thus touching off the "querelle des femmes."[60]

The beginnings of vernacular satire—with ecclesiastical coloring—are virtually coeval with the *Canterbury Tales,* which writers found to be a small compendium of anti-feminism extracted from Jerome, Meun, Deschamps, and Mapes. It is not literally true, of course, that formal satire was unknown in Middle English before Chaucer; *The Thrush and the Nightingale*[61] of MS. Digby 86 were sufficient to show that the tradition so abundantly represented in Latin had been translated to the vernacular by the end of the thirteenth century. A defense, *Praise of Women,* translated from a French lyric of the Harleian manuscript also dates from this period.[62] These early examples, however, do not alter the fact that Chaucer was the first in England to employ such satirical matter extensively, or that, as Utley remarks, his poetry influenced most of the satires of his time and the early fifteenth century. The *Envoy to Bukton* is a jesting warning against marriage, the *Clerk's Envoy* a mock defense, *Against Women Unconstant* a conventional attack, and the *Wife of Bath's Prologue* a miscellany of dissuasive matter prepared for the Pardoner's edification.[63]

Lydgate had to his credit both satires and defenses, which he cultivated with equal enthusiasm and merit. There is no consistency in his approach to the "querelle," and no seriousness either, and it is for these reasons, quite apart from the monk's friendship with high-born ladies of the land, that it would be unfair to accuse him of harboring invidious sentiments. In the *Troy Book* he rebuts the charges of Guido della Colonna[64] and in the *Fall of Princes* qualifies the antifeminism of Boccaccio's *De Casibus Virorum Illustrium*.[65] Lydgate, it must be admitted, did translate the infamous *De Conjuge non Ducenda*,[66] associated with the mythical Golias, and composed several short satires. In *Examples Against Women,* he calls the roll of men injured by women—Solomon, Holofernes, Samson—and comments on the unstable nature of the sex. *Beware of Doublenesse* is ironic praise, and *Horns Away* a conventional satire of the forked headdresses affected by women in his time and before.[67] But this verse, as indeed all of Lydgate's satire on women, is polemical and discursive and merits little attention as lyric.

About 150 poems of satire and defense have been indexed by Utley for the Middle English period. Some categories, such as instructions to women and single revolts against the tyranny of love, bespeak a mild contempt or a momentary revulsion, but hardly the deep and abiding indignation which ecclesiastical polemics show at every step. These marginal types were hardly regarded in the Middle Ages as especially hurtful to women. The clerical bias figures most conspicuously in debates, ironic defenses, warnings against wedlock, and general treatises in verse, and far less in the so-called *mal marié* songs and the lyrics of a popular character, notably the secular carols, which are seldom free of humorous coloring.

Fifteenth-century antifeminism is partly an echo of Chaucer and partly a sympathetic reaction to the conflict in France. In degree of intensity it is a mere prelude to the outbreak in the Renaissance. As far as the record goes, the first seventy-five years of the sixteenth century produced far more satires of women than Middle English affords during three centuries.[68] The curious taste of George Bannatyne was mainly responsible for the preservation of a large number of pieces composed before 1568, when he put his notable manuscript together.[69] Increased activity at the end of the fifteenth century augured the widespread interest in the tradition manifest after printing had commenced. Henryson wrote the *Testament of Cresseid,* and Dunbar the *Tua Mariit Wemen and the Wedo,* neither of which is lyrical. From MS. Cambridge Ff.5.48 comes the *Misogynic Nightingale,*[70] a debate between a clerk and a nightingale over the merits of women, which recalls the late thirteenth-century poem *The Thrush and the Nightingale* of MS. Digby 86, except that in the former the nightingale argues against women. The clerk is himself a lover and stoutly defends the sex, whereas the bird cites the usual examples and insists that "on gode [woman] is not in londe." Ecclesiastical bias distinguishes two Bannatyne satires which are regarded by Brown and Robbins as products of the fifteenth century. Some phrasal resemblances exist between *O wicket wemen wilfull and variable* and *Devyce proves and eik humilitie,* which stand together in the Scottish collection.[71] The former is an extravagantly alliterated accumulation of abusive epithets, and the latter a conventional treatise poem leveling conventional charges at women and calling up the usual witnesses. To the Middle English period belongs also an undistinguished Bannatyne defense in rhyme royal.[72] MS. Trinity College, Cambridge, 599, of the last half of the century, affords two satirical descriptions of women[73] and a general attack,[74] all traditionally associated with and clearly indebted to Chaucer. Multiplying the instances of satire of women avails nothing in the discussion of lyric developments; antifeminism pervades Middle English literature, finding expression not only in art lyric, but also in sermons, proverbs, and plays.

Classical or ecclesiastical sources need not be sought for the antifeminism implicit in several secular carols. There are here few traces of external influences and fewer examples

of outright indebtedness to the heavy-handed Latin treatises
or the diffuse court lyrics. Nor need one attribute the de-
lightful jesting over shrews and gossips to "ce fond de ran-
cune," which Bédier alleged, "l'homme a toujours eu contre
la femme."[75] The popular songs about women were un-
questionably relished for their entertainment value and
hardly sprang from motives so serious as to involve monas-
tic ideals or bourgeois reactions against *amour courtois*.
The broad humor of these secular carols recalls the anti-
feminist ballads—*Our Goodman*, the *Wife Wrapped in
Wether's Skin*, and the *Farmer's Curst Wife*. It is not that
the arrangement and phrasing of the carols are not obviously
indebted to the Church; it is that so few of the satirical
formulas are carried over.

Yet, an exceptional carol from MS. Bodley Eng. poet.
e.1.—*Dayly in Englond mervels be found*—is an arresting
compound of learned and popular elements. The poet's
complaint is succinctly expressed in the second line of
the burden: "The moste mayster of the hows weryth no
brych." Instead of a "fight for the britches," the poet dis-
cusses the refractory character of women. In the first
stanza, he observes that "Ne pene cane scribull the totall
declaracyon" of the trouble married people endure, which
may be an echo of the widely used "pen and ink" formula.[76]
Elsewhere, Adam, Eve, Hercules, Samson, and David are
introduced for the commonplace purpose of exemplification.
Whether the phrase "Ye maryd men" is to be taken as an
indication that the author was unmarried (and possibly in
orders) does not appear, though the handling of the trite
theme in this carol points to the singer's familiarity with
the traditional attacks on women. This is exceptional, how-
ever, and it is vain to look for the antifeminist apparatus in
other carols. Greene finds in *Yyng men, I red that ye bewar*
slight traces of the influence of the Latin satire, *De Conjuge
non Ducenda*;[77] it is an altogether trivial piece warning

young men to avoid the snare of matrimony. Of the learned sort there is slight evidence, perhaps for the reason that the arguments of satires of women can be but badly managed in song.

Humor is instinct in the laments of henpecked husbands, and these are better than the average. The author of a delightful Sloane carol cites his own experiences to dissuade young men from taking old wives. Like other lyrics from the collection, this has an authentic popular ring:

> Quan I cum fro the plow at non,
> In a reven dych myn mete is don,
> I dar not askyn our dame a spon;
> I dar nat seyn quan sche seyght 'Pes!'

Whatever his request, physical misfortune awaits him. The husbandman of a Bodleian carol is indeed a Milquetoast who must struggle to satisfy the prodigious appetite of his strapping wife:

> All that I may swynk or swet,
> My wyfe it wyll both drynk and ete,
> And I sey ought, she wyl me bete;
> Carful ys my hart therfor.

The sage warnings and rueful testimonies are the more attractive songs of this class, whatever the recommendation may be worth. Satires of women, in any event, are further illustrations of the strange perversion of taste during the transition, and not one shows exceptional spirit or originality.

If the noncourtly amorous song of the century pays woman no superlative compliments, it at least avoids the unreality of *amour courtois* and the extremes of revulsion which produced the hysterical satires of the sex. For all the weakness which popular song exhibits as lyric, it generally comes off better than the polished effusions of the courtiers and deals with the subject in a direct, if crude, manner. The authorship of these lyrics is unknown, but the clergy, become rather careless of their vows, are likely candidates. The Latinity of the amorous carols as a whole points to ecclesiastical authorship, and other traces of learning rule out purely popular composers. Thus, the parodical *As I went on Yol Day in owre prosessyon* mixes the liturgy with the amorous perambulations of a clerk who sings the mass. The impropriety of the burden is obvious: "Kyrie, so kyrie, Jankyn syngut merie, / with aleyson." Churchmen are clearly involved in the sordid actions of several other carols, including the infamous parody of the Paternoster in a sixteenth-century collection printed by Richard Kele, which concerns the improper behavior of a friar with a nun.

Further evidence of learning in the secular carols comes from a group of atypical specimens which express a courtly attitude toward love. An illustration is *Some tyme y loved, as ye may see*, of MS. Cambridge Univ. Ff.I.6, a late fifteenth-century miscellany notable for several courtly lyrics in four-stress lines with eccentric rhymes. This is the lament of a rejected lover:

> Butt well y wote y hadde nat done
> Hur to displese, but in grete mone;
> She hath me left and ys agone;
> For sorwe my hert doth blede.[78]

Somtyme y lovid, so do y yit,[79] of the same manuscript, is a comparable lyric,[80] having an identical structure and some phrasal resemblances. Greene conjectures that the speaker is a woman[81] happy to be free of love in general and of a "wyckid creature" in particular. But "danger" in the first stanza may be the antecedent of "He,"

> Grete payne for nought y dide endur,
> Al for that wyckid creature,
> He and no mo y you ensure
> Overthrew al my matere.

If so, "I am escapid from his band" in the fourth stanza is to be explained as the lover's escape from "Dangier," the personification of the lady's conventional indifference in courtly poetry. Among the curiosities is another rebellion against love, which Greene found in MS. Gonville and Caius, Cambridge 383. It is an antiphrastic parody of the usual complaint. One other carol merits notice among the learned sort, and that an abominable exercise in *traductio* from a collection of letters in Canterbury Cathedral. The play on "heart" rivals the worst examples of Elizabethan punning.

The thinness of sentiment already noted as an unfortunate characteristic of the carol is sometimes offset by a jaunty burden which strongly implies an excellent tune. A maid's rather insignificant praise of serving men in MS. Sloane 1584 is supported by a rollicking "Troly, loley" repeated phrase. A thin appreciation of a lady's beauty in MS. Harley 7578 is somewhat enlivened by the burden, "My lady is a prety on, a prety, prety, prety on; / My lady is a prety on as Ever I saw."[82] The carol of pretty little Mopse from the Christ Church Letters of Canterbury Cathedral, however, not only has a merry burden, but also a delightful debate of the most trivial sort. The subject, which is a kiss, is at last resolved in no unexpected manner.

Two otherwise trivial seduction carols are important for the light they throw on heathen survivals. That clerks are involved in both is no compliment to the Church, even if the circumstances strongly suggest secular authorship. The first of these, from MS. Camb. Univ. Lib. Ff.5.48, affords a brief glimpse of a forbidden ablution rite. Thomas Wright observed in connection with *The last tyme I the wel woke* that many traces of the worship of wells remained in modern observances and further declared, "The fairs, or wakes, in our country villages, often originated from the custom of 'waking the well'."[83] Greene remarks that despite Church prohibitions well-wakes survived until modern times.[84]   The association of well-waking with St. John's Eve connects the observance to the complex of traditions entering into Midsummer festivals, of which bathing in the sea, spring, or river was regarded as spiritual ablution.[85] The festival had always been a mating period, and considerable license was no doubt permitted in European celebrations.   The purpose for which the girl sought the well in this instance is not made clear, for the wake is interrupted by "Ser John," doubtless a priest, who peremptorily seduces her.

A carol of MS. Gonville and Caius College, Cambridge—*Ladd Y the daunce a Myssomur Day*—has its setting in a Midsummer Day celebration.   From time immemorial the summer solstice had been an occasion for festivities; even the slaves and plebeians of ancient Rome had enjoyed unwonted liberty for the day.[86]   The Church had masked the pagan rites by associating them with John the Baptist, but a great deal of heathenism remained in the perambulations of fertility symbols.   By the fifteenth century much of the original significance of the festival had unquestionably been lost, and the period was given over to games, dancing, and revelry little different from May Day and Whitsuntide celebrations of later date.[87]   The young girl, whose confession the carol is, had gone off to lead a ring dance.   The dancers probably sang a traditional *carole,* though there is no mention of it.   Jack, the "holy-water" clerk, lures the girl away, and the song ends on an indecent note.   Chambers, as previously noted, rejects Greene's supposition that this is folk song.   The plain diction and realistic statements contrast favorably with the decorative verse of the times, but simplicity does not alone make a folk song.   There seems to be no very good reason for thinking this and the preceding piece of a separate class from other loose carols.

Few secular songs not in carol form have survived, and those few can give but a slight notion of the popular lyric of the century. The Sloane manuscript affords a scurrilous piece closely resembling the *Riddle Song* in form. The *double entendre* upon which the song turns is of a sort to delight a Mercutio:

> I have a newe gardyn, and newe is begunne;
> Swych another gardyn know I not under sunne.
> In the myddis of my gardyn is a peryr set,
> And it wele non pere bern, but a pere jenet.[88]

The seduced maid has a witty reply in conclusion on the fruit of the tree, "Che said it was a pere robert, but non pere jonet." This recalls a carol from the same manuscript, *We bern abowtyn non cattes skynnys*, in which a chapman draws an evil analogy based on his wares.[89]   Richard Hill's Commonplace Book has a merry song employing one motif of the *Miller's Tale*, but is not indebted to Chaucer for the widespread jest.   Whatever the merit of the piece as lyric, it has a jaunty movement.   The first stanza bears quoting:

> Hogyn cam to bowers dore,
> Hogyn cam to bowers dore,
> He tryld vpon the pyn for love,
> Hum, ha, trill go bell!
> He tryld vpon the pyn for love,
> Hum, ha, trill go bell![90]

This is unquestionably popular song.   The piece was designed for singing before an audience who would relish the strong rhythm, the merry repetitive elements, and the rowdy conclusion.   Moreover, the phrasing is instinct with melody, which must have been, however, held in a position subordinate to the meaningful narrative.   Another trivial love song of the end of the century, beginning *masteres anne, I ame your man*, has a different though nonetheless rhythmical movement.   This snatch from Trinity Cambridge 597 has been represented in the discussion of the *Notbrowne Mayde*, which in point of meter it resembles.

If amorous ditties about Hogyn and his girl, carols of Midsummer revelry and henpecked husbands, and lyrics of secular and divine love-longing have small place in the golden treasuries of literature, the *Notbrowne Mayde* and *Robene and Makyne* claim exception from the derogative judgments conventionally passed on fifteenth-century poetry and demand the serious attention of literary criticism. The conspicuous excellence of these spirited dialogues seems well-nigh impossible in a period rarely possessed of genuine lyric inspiration; and, as a consequence, determined efforts have been made to hand over both poems to foreign influences. Until Continental sources are actually discovered, however, Henryson and the unknown author of the *Mayde* should be given full credit for the dramatic lyrics. There are in truth no creditable grounds for denying Britain either of these authentic gems shining in the debris of the transition.

The *Notbrowne Mayde*, intercalated by Richard Arnold in the *Customs of London* (*ca.* 1502),[91] resists comparison with the extant verse of the fifteenth century, avoiding both the tedious preciosity of *vers de société* and the boisterous directness of popular song. No doubt, as a consequence of this circumstance, rather diverse views of the origin of the lively dialogue have been expressed. Francis Douce, who reprinted the work in 1811, conjectured that the source was German,[92] but a European original has yet to be discovered. Thomas Percy included the *Mayde* in the *Reliques of Ancient English Poetry* (1765),[93] although, as Gummere remarked,[94] it "has not the faintest claim" to classification as popular verse. The resemblance of the poem to the "testing" ballads *Child Waters* and the *Fair Flower of Northumberland* implies no direct relation; the Griselda motif is commonplace. More recently, the *Mayde* has been described by Berdan as "an epitome of Medieval Latin influence,"[95] largely on the basis of its unusual metrical arrangement, for which there is some Latin precedent. This hypothesis, however, neither establishes a likely connection nor disposes of antecedent Middle English verse which accounts in a general way for the form and matter of the *Notbrowne Mayde.*

For Berdan, physical resemblances are presumptive evidence of the dependence of much transition poetry upon medieval Latin metrical patterns:

"When the forms used by the English poets between Lydgate and Wyatt are examined, these same characteristics [as exhibited by Latin verse] are to be found. Aside from the rime-royal, the 'Monk's Tale' stanza and the heroic couplet, . . . poetic forms are marked by short lines and simple rime-schemes. While all these are not necessarily borrowed from the Medieval Latin [as represented in *I trattati medievali di ritmica latina,* which is Berdan's chief authority], it is worthy of notice that the majority are to be found discussed in the Medieval Latin treatises. Of these in the English the popular forms are aab-ccb, aab-ccd, aaab-cccb, and aaab-cccd for lyrics. . . . To illustrate the extent to which the English stanza-forms are taken from the Medieval Latin . . ."[96]

The arrangement of the *Notbrowne Mayde* is, then, according to medieval poetic, "iambic dimeters, iambic trimeter differentia," with the "differentiae" four times rhymed;[97] but for the practicing poet of the fifteenth century, the stanza was hardly more than modified common measure. Whatever the merits of the general theory which explains late Middle English versification in terms of Latin models, the *Mayde* at least appears to be the culmination of a prosodic tendency manifest in English verse no later than the first decade of the fourteenth century, possibly even earlier.

Whether a further development of *rime couée,*[98] a "fourteener" split in the octosyllabic section by rhyme,[99] or even

a direct borrowing from Latin, the metrical arrangement
of the *Notbrowne Mayde* was by no means new at the be-
ginning of the sixteenth century. The possibility of indebt-
edness to the Latin is not strong, although a comparable pat-
tern was noticed by Schipper in a thirteenth-century col-
lection:

> O Fortuna, velut luna
> statu variabilis,
> semper crescis aut decrescis;
> vita detestabilis . . .[100]

Little need be made of the resemblance of the Latin pat-
tern to that of the *Mayde:*

> Be it right or wrong, these men among
> 　　On women do complaine,
> Affermyng this how that it is
> 　　A labour spent in vaine
> To loue them wele for neuer a dele
> 　　They loue a man agayne:
> For lete a man do what he can
> 　　Ther fauour to attayne
> Yet yf a newe to them pursue
> 　　Ther furst trew louer than
> Laboureth for nought and from her thought
> 　　He is a bannisshed man.[101]　　st. 1.

A clear demonstration of tripartite segmentation of the
septenary appears in a lyric of MS. Harley 2253. The first
stanza of *De Clerico et Puella* has, moreover, two instances
of internal rhyme, which in the *Mayde* is a metrical prin-
ciple:

> My deth y loue, my lyf ich hate,
> 　　for a leuedy shene,
> heo is briht so daies liht,
> 　　that is on me wel sene;
> al y falewe so doth the lef
> 　　in somer when hit is grene;

> yef mi thoht helpeth me noht,
> to wham shal y me mene?

One of the first fully developed examples of internal rhyme, the *Moral Poem*,[102] notable for its curious "E.I.O." refrain, has virtually the same stanza pattern as the *Mayde*. As Saintsbury suggests,[103] this religious lyric may be considerably older than the Thornton MS. (*ca.* 1440), in which it appears. Each stanza is composed of six septenaries rhyming aaaabb, with the octosyllabic portion of the long line divided by rhyme. This poem then clearly establishes the fact that the author of the *Notbrowne Mayde* had been anticipated by more than half a century. Internal rhyme as a metrical principle, moreover, had been used in the fourteenth century by Chaucer,[104] as Saintsbury remarks, and by the composer of a carol in MS. Advocates 18.7.21,[105] and throughout the fifteenth and early sixteenth centuries by authors of carols.[106] Of course, not all of these examples are to be accounted for by the fracture of the septenary, but they do prove that a poet in 1500 had no need to seek models in the textbooks of poetics.

Even in or around 1500, when the *Mayde* was probably composed, internally rhymed poems were being written. Dunbar further complicates the scheme by rhyming the octosyllables of the *Lady Solistaris at Court:*

> Thir ladyis fair, That makis repair,
> And in the court ar kend,
> Thre dayis thair, Thay will do mair,
> Ane mater for till end . . .[107]

The Scot was a Latinist who might have recalled the metrical prescriptions of his schoolbooks in this instance. No such suspicion attaches to a popular song written on a flyleaf of MS. Trinity Cambridge 597 at about the same time:

> masteres anne, I ame your man,
> as you may well espye;

> if you will be content with me,
> I am merrie, [say I].[108]   st. 1.

Further proof that the scheme was occasionally cultivated
by popular poets may be taken, with some hesitation, from
the ballads, which have been fairly trustworthy guardians
of ancient conventions. Isolated quatrains, such as the
following from *Johnie Cock*,

> O bows of yew, if ye be true,
> In London, where ye were bought,
> Fingers five, get up belive,
> Manhuid shall fail me nought.[109]   A.st.18

are not uncommon; but the most striking specimen is the
Grey Cock, which, with the exception of one stanza, depends
upon the three-part septenary:

> It's now ten at night, and the stars gie nae light,
> And the bells they ring ding, dang;
> He's met wi some delay that causeth him to stay,
> But he will be here ere lang.[110]   st. 2

These examples do not suggest a continuous tradition;
rather they should be regarded as the products of a natural
prosodic tendency, which any poet using common measure
may hit upon. Hence, the internally rhymed refrain of
the *Ballad of Jesse James*[111] need not be traced to medieval
Latin treatises.

The subject of the *Notbrowne Mayde* is the worth of
womankind, and the form a debate. That it was designed
as a dramatic representation before a polite audience ap-
pears from the third stanza, and Chambers conjectures that
it may "have been recited by two minstrels in a baronial
hall, as a kind of *estrif*."[112] Berdan describes the dialogue
as a *conflictus*,[113] but this term might better be reserved for
encounters involving abstractions,[114] like the debates be-
tween the body and the soul, the heart and the eye, the
wine and the water, summer and winter, which are repre-

sented both in Latin and in the European vernaculars.[115] The preliminary agreement of the interlocutors to adjudge of the integrity of women through a rehearsal of the experiences of the "Nutbroune maide" is an unusual though nonetheless effective introductory device; otherwise, the poem agrees in outline with the general type. Two Middle English debates must be accounted precursors of Arnold's poem, though these had no more influence on the *Mayde* than the "testing" ballads. The thirteenth-century debate, *The Thrush and the Nightingale*,[116] of MS. Digby 86, deals with the woman question, and in the end the thrush is won over to the feminist point of view by the nightingale. A comparable handling of the familiar theme is the *Misogynic Nightingale*,[117] a fifteenth-century debate; in this instance the antifeminist bird unequivocally rejects the arguments of his opposite, a clerk.

In view of the universality of the debate and the widespread interest in the "querelle des femmes,"[118] it seems quite unnecessary to seek foreign or learned sources for form and content any more than for prosody. As for the spirit of the *Notbrowne Mayde,* responsibility rests with a very English mind who happily avoided the worst literary faults of the transition.

Although the *Mayde* avoids aureate terms and other stylistic frills, it is somewhat deficient in intensity and concreteness. The constant maiden and the presumptuous earl's son are dimly characterized and too obviously serve a purpose external to the dramatic proceedings. The conclusion is anticipated by the preliminary arrangements. To the Squire's charge that women are faithless, the Puella cites the constancy of the "Nutbroune maide." Her opposite then proposes a debate and calls upon the audience to pay attention, "Wherfore ye that present be / I pray you geue an eare." The verdict is more or less directed by the Puella's prelude:

And I your wylle for to fulfylle
In this wyl not refuse
Trusting to shewe in wordis fewe,
That men haue an ille vse
To ther owne shame wymen to blame
And causeles them accuse:
Therefore to you I answere now . . .

The strong initial emphasis upon the didactic motif invests the drama with the tone of a morality, and the Griselda-like submissiveness of the maid vitiates the illusion of a true-to-life representation. As a consequence, the tension which is fundamental to a situation in which lovers prepare to undertake a hazardous course of action is inadequately sustained. Instead of an impassioned dialogue, the *Notbrowne Mayde* is a series of thrusts and counterthrusts over the worth of womankind. The situation is so patently synthetic that it possibly did not strongly engage the sympathies of the genteel audience for which the poem was written. On the other hand, the poet was primarily concerned with vindicating the honor of women, and in this abstract purpose he succeeded quite well. Moreover, the vivacious spirit, lively measure, and happy ending provoke a warm response even in modern readers. For the deficiencies, which are closely identified with the literary ideals of the courtly society, the poet is not wholly responsible; and he had no way of knowing that four centuries later the conveyance would be valued far more highly than the thesis. The *Notbrowne Mayde* was one of the more or less popular remains with which Bishop Percy fattened the book of the *Folio,* and since the late eighteenth century the poem has wasted no breath on the desert air for lack of admirers.

In contrast, *Robene and Makyne* has been infrequently reprinted and little noticed south of the Tweed, although it is in point of balance, economy of expression, and subtle management the superior of the English poem. If neglect were not injury enough, early French lyric has been given on the flimsiest of grounds a large share in the creation of the dialogue in the mind of the whimsical schoolmaster of Dunfermline, Robert Henryson.

Forty years ago, Gregory Smith theorized that the inimitable *estrif d'amour* of the author of the *Testament of Cresseid* owed a considerable debt to French *pastourelles*.[119] Smith's conjecture has, by repetition, taken on the appearance of demonstrated fact, so that the distinguished authors of a recent book have been led to write, "*Robene and Makyne* is . . . a French *pastourelle* translated[120] to the 'holtes hair' of Scotland . . . A little masterpiece, French in its grace, Scottish in its astringent moral."[121] Yet, there is no tradition that Henryson was acquainted with this numerous Continental genre, and his lyrico-dramatic poem is essentially different from the strict *pastourelle*. Indeed, the Middle Scots lyric makes scant use of the conventions which distinguished this variety of *chanson d'aventure* from other types of medieval lyric. *Robene and Makyne* has certain superficial resemblances to both *pastourelle* and ballad, but it is uncritical to describe it as either. A better tag, if one be required, is pastoral or pastoral ballad.[122] However labeled, the poem should be left in the undisputed possession of Scotland.

In the Scottish Text Society edition of Henryson's works, Gregory Smith called the poem a "disputoison" of the pastoral type, perhaps suggested by a French *pastourelle,* and compared it with *Li Gieus de Robin et de Marion*[123] of Adan de la Halle. He was careful to observe, however, that there was no proof of Henryson's indebtedness and then added the further qualification, "it may well be doubted whether he has availed himself of more than a poet's right to work on a familiar theme."[124] In 1931, W. P. Jones, with some misgivings, proposed as the source a *pastourelle* by Baudes de la Kakerie, a thirteenth-century French poet, arguing that the situations were similar in both poems and that the "spirit and the setting . . . [were] the same."[125] The objections to this conjecture are numerous. It cannot be shown that Henryson knew any *pastourelles,* much less one by an obscure trouvère who flourished two centuries earlier. There are no phrasal resemblances between the two poems. The similarity of situation, upon which the hypothesis mainly rests, does not alone constitute proof; and, for that matter, the incidents are far from identical.[126]

Henryson's poem resembles the typical *pastourelle* in that the setting is rural and the characters answer to the names of Robene and Makyne. Robin, at least, is very often the name of the shepherd swain[127] who loves the shepherdess, usually called Marion, or variants thereof. But further, the comparison cannot legitimately be extended. Even the piece by Baudes de la Kakerie, which is not typical, agrees at the outset with prescribed form. A *chevalier*—the poet— rides forth at the break of day in a thoughtful mood, customarily induced by love-longing. In a meadow or beside a road, he encounters a maiden plaiting a chaplet of flowers or singing a song. He importunes her in the conventional manner. Thereafter, the poet may manage the action as he sees fit, and the outcome of the adventure varies from poem to poem,[128] though success usually attends his solicitations.

Instead of the "riding out" introduction, with the vestigial *reverdie,* the Scots poem uses, "Robene sat on gud grene hill,"[129] which calls to memory the ballad *Lord Thomas and Fair Annet* (No. 73A); "Lord Thomas and Fair Annet / Sate a' day on a hill,"[130] rather than a *pastourelle.* Makyne confesses her devotion and predicts death will result if Robene does not relieve her distress. But Robene is an unimaginative rustic who admits that he knows nothing of love. Makyne offers him an "a b c" if he will learn it. A formal "a b c"[131] for courtly lovers is not forthcoming,

though, as Smith remarked, her prescription recalls Perte-
lote's charge to Chauntecleer:

> be heynd, courtass, and fair of feir,
> Wyse, hardy, and fre;
> So that no denger do the deir,
> quhat dule in dern thow dre;
> preiss the with pane at all poweir,
> be patient and previe.[132]   ll. 19-24

Robene is unchanged. Later, "sum pairte of mawkynis
aill" crept into his heart, whereupon he rushed back to dis-
close the change suddenly wrought in him. Her proverbial
reply is the theme of the little poem:

> Robene, thow hes hard soung & say,
> In gestis and storeis auld,
> The man that will nocht quhen he may
> sall haif nocht quhen he wald.   ll. 89-92

Why Smith imagined that this motif "may have been sug-
gested by French models"[133] is not clear. Though the
theme of lost opportunity is implicit in several *pastourelles,*
it is by no means the exclusive property of France. The
proverb itself would appear to be traditional in Britain,
to judge from a stanza of the *Baffled Knight* (112D):

> There is a gude auld proverb,
> I've often heard it told,
> He that would not when he might,
> He should not when he would.[134]   st. 14

The ballad is certainly not to be regarded as the source of
the poem; not only are the incidents dissimilar, but the old-
est recorded version of the *Baffled Knight* belongs to the
early seventeenth century. Yet, Henryson would know a
"gude auld proverb" as well as a ballad-maker, and not
necessarily from reading thirteenth-century *pastourelles.*
   The influence of the ballad on the form of *Robene and*

Makyne has long been recognized. Each stanza is composed of two quatrains linked by rhyme, or simply eight lines rhyming abababab. The alliterative formulas are commonplaces of northern poetry.[135]

What remains needs no explication in terms of trouvère lyric. The quiet humor and tough idiom are Henryson's own. Such characteristics as the Scottish poem shares with the *pastourelle*—especially the irony of lost opportunity—are universal. Missing from *Robene and Makyne* are the gay abandon and frequent pruriency of the French genre, together with the strong seduction motif and element of class distinction sustained by the *chevalier*. There are no elements in the Scots poem not readily explained by reference to traditions certainly known to the poet.

The perfection of *Robene and Makyne* is owing in large part to Henryson's careful management of a wholly credible situation, in which two very real personages act out a commonplace but nonetheless interesting drama. The action is compressed into 128 lines, two tense scenes and three or four stanzas of continuity and terse observation. Neither rhetorical flourishes nor irrelevant commentaries are permitted to relax the tension of the frame, though the poet himself skillfully shifts the focus of the struggle when Robene's obstinacy provokes a compensating reaction in Makyne. Within the tight, unified structure, Henryson deftly lays out a green hillside, grazing sheep, and man with maid in impassioned conversation. The turn comes abruptly when Robene rushes back to accept the golden opportunity. Makyne's aphoristic rejoinder hastens the conclusion and underlines the moral. The proverb is not an excrescence, because Robene's rude behavior places the poet under obligation to teach him a lesson. That the lesson is universally applicable in no way invests the poem with a didactic bias. It is well to insist upon the organic nature of the moral which this poem inculcates, since Henryson is characteristically didactic; indeed, the *Abbey Walk*, the *Garmont of Gude Ladeis, In Prais of Aige*, and the *Bludy Serk* are tediously so. In this respect, *Robene and Makyne* has also a signal advantage over the *Notbrowne Mayde*, where the love adventure is an instrument rather than a slice of life.

Without the tough idiom of the Lowlands dialect, a strong illusion of reality could be maintained only with difficulty, even when the circumstances are segments of everyday experience. Yet, this diction, studded with phonological and orthographical thistles, constitutes an encumbrance under which Middle Scots poetry has labored for recognition these past four centuries and a half. But *Robene and Makyne* succeeds in communicating a poignant drama of rural society precisely because Henryson wrote in this instance much as he talked, and the natural language of the schoolmaster was not substantially different from that of country folk dwelling in the vicinity of Dunfermline. The reluctant shepherd and his eager maid speak as expected, and their language lends conviction to the spectacle of rustic lovers vigorously contending as the sun sets below green Scottish hills. Realistic and jesting, the poem is throughout in good taste and implicitly expresses Henryson's own gentle humor, homely wisdom, and honest sympathy. The priceless lines of the conclusion communicate the poet's personal solicitude for the lovers, and the reader has some hope of alteration in Makyne, who, free of love, "went hame blyth annewche," leaving the shepherd,

> In dolour & in cair,
> Kepand his hird vnder a huche,
> amangis the holtis hair.

By modern, if not contemporary, standards, *Robene and Makyne* is the finest jewel in the debris of the fifteenth century. The pastoral is a miraculous hybrid: a ballad plot interfused with the whimsical sensibility of a good poet. Scores of sentimental ballads from later periods suggest the difficulty of the experiment and by contrast emphasize Henryson's achievement.

CHAPTER SEVEN

WILLIAM DUNBAR

THE CONVENTIONAL PORTRAIT OF WILLIAM DUNBAR as a Scottish Chaucerian is unfortunate in that it tends to obscure his original lyrical talent. Studied in relation to Chaucer and Lydgate, the sardonic pensioner[1] at the court of James IV is a derivative if brilliant author of satires and allegories, admirable alike for felicitous phrasing and trenchant wit. The satires are often diverting, though only the *Tua Mariit Wemen and the Wedo*[1] is truly extraordinary. The allegories, like *The Thrissil and the Rois* and the *Goldyn Targe*, doubtless possess some merit, but by the beginning of the sixteenth century rather too many poems had already been fitted out with the ornate imagery and capering personifications of *Le Roman de la Rose*.[2] In the main, the longer poems disclose a striking pictorial quality and considerable vigor, but neither remarkable narrative nor dramatic power. As an allegorist, Dunbar is an accomplished decorator; as a lyric poet, he is frequently competent, occasionally inspired. His talent if anything is lyrical.

G. Gregory Smith's criticism, "Of lyrical . . . excellence, there is little in Dunbar,"[3] ignores the fact that the Scot was the best lyric poet between Chaucer and Wyatt. This hasty judgment, moreover, takes no account of five or six short poems in which Dunbar deviates markedly from the fifteenth-century norm—by unity of expression and intimacy of style advancing the technique of lyric art to a point not realized in English since the Anglo-Saxon *Wife's Lament*. Though not a humanist in the strict sense,[4] Dunbar, in contrast to most of his predecessors, did conceive of

lyric as a proper genre for purely individual expression, and
some of his best short poems exhibit the fully developed
egoism which is conspicuous in much post-medieval verse.

As a matter of fact, the able Middle Scots poet was him-
self a supreme and melancholic egoist, who, like the dean
of St. Patrick's two centuries later, snarled at the society of
his times for real and imaginary grievances. If he lacked
Swift's deep moral sense and social conscience, he shared
with him a keen insight into the world's ills, as well as a
strong propensity to relieve his indignation with virulent
satire. The pure lyric impulse had then to contend with
a satirical urge in the mind of the poet, as a consequence
of which an excessive number of the ninety-odd poems
attributed to Dunbar are occupied with petty quarrels. It
is therefore certain that he was far from happy during
his long residence at the Scottish court, although the cir-
cumstances are now so obscure that the poet's most recent
editor has been able to state in five and a half pages vir-
tually all that is known about his life and a great deal more
that is merely conjectured.[5] He may have been that Wil-
liam Dunbar who took a Master of Arts at St. Andrews in
1479. *How Dumbar wes desyrd to be ane Freir* gives rise
to the belief that he was at one time a Franciscan novice,
in which role he seems not to have been exemplary. From
the same poem, it appears that he went to France in the
habit of a friar:

> In freiris weid full fairly haif I fleichit,
> In it haif I in pulpet gon and preichit
> In Derntoun kirk, and eik in Canterberry;
> In it I past at Dover our the ferry
> Throw Piccardy, and thair the peple teichit.

On other evidence, it is thought that he visited the Conti-
nent on diplomatic missions.[6] By 1500, Dunbar was on the
government payroll, there to stay until a benefice should be

provided him. Whether he got it is not known. He dis-
appears from the records in 1513, leaving a sheaf of poetry
rather unequal in quality.

Against the Middle Scots poet it may be alleged that he
was not consistently aware of the respectable uses of lyric
and that a majority of his short poems are little better than
the average for the period. On the other hand, his bom-
bastic petitions and addresses to the court, tedious didactic
and religious musings of doubtful inspiration, and truculent
attacks on little-known personages indicate the effect of a
decadent literary heritage on a talented poet, and by con-
trast emphasize the effectiveness of *To a Ladye, Medita-
tioun in Wyntir, My heid did yak yesternicht,* and the
Petition of the Gray Horse, Auld Dunbar, for which poems
the period offered negligible precedent. In truth, Dunbar's
literary background was singularly deficient in the type of
poetry which he was by temperament best qualified to man-
age. There were few useful models for the service of a
mind which instinctively sought the *bon mot,* the well-
turned epigrammatic phrase in short, compressed flights.
The greater number of his lyrical poems is, accordingly, of
a sort esteemed by the effete aristocracy and conservative
clergy, in whose keeping literature remained during the
melancholy transition to the Renaissance. On this account,
censure of Dunbar for writing secular and religious lyrics
after the conventional manner need not be harsh. It should
be recalled that Chaucer, as a lyric poet, never freed him-
self entirely of French influences. Indeed, it was the mas-
ter, with some assistance from Gower,[7] who translated to
England the spirit and form of the artificial genres culti-
vated in the school of Guillaume de Machaut. The influence
of Chaucer's ballades, roundels, and complaints, all in the
French style, must have been considerable in court circles
during the fifteenth century.

The worthlessness of the available models taken into

account, Dunbar's achievements are by no means slight. He worked of necessity within the medieval tradition, but rebelled frequently against the standards of *vers de société*. With the lugubrious pose of the humble lover, the Scot had no patience, and he abhorred the slovenly rhetorical and metrical habits of the period. What has come from his pen is characterized by concise and logical statement; he wrote little effusive verse and nothing that is completely shoddy. In all likelihood, due recognition has been withheld, because, in the first place, the overshadowing connection with Chaucer emphasizes the longer allegorical and satirical pieces, and, in the second, scholars have been reluctant to differentiate between the uninspired work and the lyric with some originality.[8]

For experimentation with metrical forms if for no other reason, Dunbar merits close attention. Chaucerian monuments imposed couplets, *Monk's Tale* octaves, and rhyme royal on Hoccleve, Lydgate, and other courtly versifiers; out of lethargy or respect, they did not often depart from the established patterns, unless it was to shorten the decasyllabic line by a foot. Dunbar, on the other hand, used these staves in less than one third of his extant poems, obviously preferring four- and five-line octosyllabic stanzas with rhyme schemes of aabb and aabab. The Scot varied the type-aabab with both octosyllabic and decasyllabic stanzas in aabba, of which the latter is that of the *Cuckoo and the Nightingale*.[9] Besides various irregular stanzas, Dunbar used alliteration as a metrical principle in the *Tua Mariit Wemen and the Wedo*, a scintillating exhibition of technical skill. Inevitably, the poet's facile pen attempted the impossible. In *Ane Ballat of Our Lady* internal rhyme and aureate diction reach an abominable limit:

> Haile, sterne superne! Haile, in eterne,
>   In Godis sicht to schyne!
> Lucerne in derne, for to discerne

> Be glory and grace devyne;
> Hodiern, modern, sempitern . . .

The angry *Complaint to the King Aganis Mure* is a measure of Dunbar's concern with versification:

> That fulle dismemberit hes my meter,
> And poysound it with strang salpeter,
> With rycht defamowss speiche off lordis,
> Quhilk with my collouris all discordis:

For a transition poet, this meticulousness is unusual. Such liberties as acephalous lines and anapestic substitutions, which occur occasionally in his work, are undoubtedly intentional, certainly not the result of "metering" in Lydgate's irresponsible manner. Saintsbury regarded this prosodic fastidiousness as added proof that Dunbar was merely at school to the English poets and had not learned to use permissible variations.[10] Yet the English Chaucerians, born and bred to the staple dialect, made only chaos of metrical form.

The diction of the Scot's verse exhibits unusual variety, which is probably to be explained by the circumstance that no Northern dialect was wholly acceptable as a literary language. There are poems in Lowland Scots, like the *Flyting of Dunbar and Kennedie*, filled with vigorous and picturesque phrases, but the characteristic expression of Middle Scots is artificial. Yet, a number of the didactic pieces, including the *Lament for the Makaris*, are strikingly free of both aureate and dialectal terms. These poems in the plain style, interestingly enough, often recall the homely, intimate moralizing of Burns. By the critical opinion of the period, however, poetic diction was the proper medium. Dunbar suggests his own standards when he evaluates Chaucer, Gower, and Lydgate in the *Goldyn Targe:*

O reuerend Chaucere, rose of rethoris all,

. . . .

Thy fresch anamalit termes celicall
    This mater coud illumynit haue full brycht:

. . . .

O morall Gower, and Ludgate laureate,
Your sugurit lippis and tongis aureate . . .

He of course underestimated his own aureate powers, for
not one of the three excelled him in the gentle art of flour-
ishing.[11]   The pictorial extravagance of the fifth stanza of
the *Goldyn Targe* is unequalled in Middle English:

The cristall air, the sapher firmament,
The ruby skyes of the orient,
    Kest beriall bemes on emerant bewis grene;
The rosy garth depaynt and redolent,
With purpur, azure, gold, and goulis gent
    Arayed was, by Dame Fflora the quene,
    So nobily, that ioy was for to sene;
The roch agayn the rywir resplendent
As low enlumynit all the leues schene.

Such stuff makes the ultimate concession to contemporary
taste for decorative verse and marks the culmination of a
sorry tendency begun before Chaucer and unfortunately
encouraged by *Troilus and Criseyde*.[12]   The learned poets
of the fifteenth century were the eager victims of the heresy
of form, which early killed off lyric and had ultimately to
extinguish all poetry.   Without the support of rhetorical
amplification and imported Latinisms, poets of the caliber
of Lydgate would have remained silent for lacking the
means to stretch their meager ideas; but Dunbar deserved
a more enduring medium.   Fortunately, aureate forms
plague the lyrics less than the allegories.

Smith called attention to the obvious fact that Dunbar's
"love poems are few and, taken as a whole, undistin-
guished,"[13] but from this invidious generalization he failed

to except *To a Ladye,* a compact, witty statement such as no other identified poet of the transition was capable of shaping. The tight organization of this amorous complaint is presumptive evidence that Dunbar recognized the need for careful articulation of the component parts of a lyric in order to produce a unified effect. If the unity of this poem is intentional (the alternative view is scarcely credible), then the Scottish poet clearly apprehended a principle which appears to have counted for little with his fifteenth-century precursors. For medieval *vers de société* characteristically effects dilatation by expository means, that is, the accumulation, normally haphazard, of related ideas around a theme. Since Lydgate, Hoccleve, and a host of unidentified versifiers were usually satisfied to combine generalities and conventional ornaments without much consideration for logical arrangement, their lyrical verse is inevitably deficient in unity and concreteness. In contrast, Dunbar's lyrics frequently have a wealth of detail and a respectable basis of organization.

In *To a Ladye,* Dunbar has forced conventional praise and ornate imagery into organic harmony with his central purpose, which is a subtle statement of love-longing. By devious means he intends to communicate to the lady the notion that her coolness toward him is out of keeping with a gracious manner. Trite floral metaphors appear at the outset to be no more than conventional baggage, but their real use becomes obvious when Dunbar objectifies the lady's virtues in a real garden:

> Sweit roiss of vertew and of gentilnes,
> Delytsum lyllie of everie lustynes,
> Richest in bontie, and in bewtie cleir,
> And everie vertew that is held most deir,
> Except onlie that ye ar mercyless.

The lily and the rose which are virtues are also connotatively red lips and cheeks and throat white as swan by association with the stock similes of medieval love song. These metaphorical flowers are objectified primarily in the garden, secondarily in the features of the lady. *Mercyless,* in the fifth line, though not a virtue, has a direct bearing on *rew:*

> In to your garthe this day I did persew,
> Thair saw I flowris that fresche wer of hew;
> Baithe quhyte and reid moist lusty wer to seyne,
> And halsum herbis vpone stalkis grene;
> Yit leif nor flour fynd could I nane of rew.

Though without floral counterpart, *mercyless* is nevertheless hardened by contrast with rue, both quality and plant. The absence of rue from the garden is logically paralleled by the lady's lack of regard for the poet. But rue, the perennial evergreen shrub, is doubly rich in meaning, since its bitter, pungent leaves have medicinal virtue. In the last stanza, Dunbar proposes to replant the shrub:

> I dout that Merche, with his cauld blastis keyne,
> Hes slane this gentill herbe, that I of mene;
> Quhois petewous deithe dois to my hart sic pane
> That I wald mak to plant his rute agane,
> So confortand his levis vnto me bene.

This statement is intentionally elliptical, for the desired revival in the woman of rue, the virtue, is an inescapable inference. The "cauld blastis keyne" of March are indifference, which has dissipated her natural kindness. Replanting rue in the garden, a symbolic act, makes known the poet's need. This "gentill herbe" is curative by tradition, though, like rue, meaning sorrow, repentance, and regret, it is characterized by bitterness. And this secondary factor adds pungency to the compassion which he would revive in her. It is the rue of the heart, then, not that of the garden, which will prove his cure, though the excellent pun signifies virtue in either case.

A century later, Thomas Campion re-created the antique image somewhat more economically and perhaps less meaningfully:

> There is a garden in her face,
> Where roses and white lilies grow;
> A heav'nly paradise is that place,
> Wherein all pleasant fruits do flow.

The Elizabethan garden has, besides an obvious lushness, sharper detail and in the first four lines, at least, extraordinary melody. If the poet-musician does not again blend off-beat feet so effectively with iambs, the tune nonetheless persists. The result is that the reader, carried away by the rhythm as well as by the rich imagery, overlooks the inanity of such lines of the poem as, "Those cherries fairly do enclose / Of orient pearl a double row," which is an excessively conceited way of describing lips and teeth. If Dunbar's complaint lacks the music of Campion's song, it is surely a more careful performance. Within narrow physical limits, the Scot has sustained a fairly complex analogy and in the end fused the two kinds of rue in a subtle declaration of his own longing. He was doubtless unaware of the exceptionalness of *To a Ladye*, but later poets would have valued the expanded metaphor, compressed wit, and unified sensibility, clearly recognizing the contrast between this perfected organism and the uncontrolled lyric of the fifteenth century.

That Dunbar wrote few poems of serious love is not surprising. Even had he not developed a fundamental distaste for the driveling, supplicatory tone of contemporary complaints, his religious affiliations doubtless would have constituted an impediment of some consequence, notwithstanding the licentious climate of pre-Reformation Edinburgh. Although some evidence of a chivalrous youth appears in *Of Lufe Erdly and Divine*, the experience left him cynical:

> I haif experience by my sell;
> In luvis court anis did I dwell,
> Bot quhair I of a joy cowth tell,
> I culd of truble tell fyftene:

Like Lydgate, he assumed two extreme attitudes toward
women: the monastic, traditionally hostile; and the courtly,
devoid of carnal implications. But as many another celibate,
Dunbar found praise of the sex less congenial than satire.
Quhone he list to feyne, an effective parody of the typical
complaint, reveals the poet's contempt for the artificial style.
The first stanza is an extended address to "My hartis
tresure, and swete assured fo," paralleled *ad infinitum et
nauseam* in courtly verse at the end of the Middle Ages.
In the fifth stanza, Dunbar describes himself so ludicrously
as to destroy completely the transparent disguise main-
tained to this point:

> Behald my deidlie passioun dolorous!
> Behald my hiddows hew and wo, allace!
> Behald my mayne, and mwrning merwalous,
> Withe sorrowfull teris falling frome my face!

However titillating, this risible portrait states the cynical
view of love which prevented Dunbar from properly using
the best part of personal experience, that part which has
inspired the vast majority of great lyrics. But if he can
seldom treat of love chivalrously, the Scotsman does very
well in a mildly satirical vein.

The *Twa Cummeris,* like the *Tua Mariit Wemen and the
Wedo,* recalls the *chanson de mal mariée* of twelfth- and
thirteenth-century France, without the resemblance presum-
ing actual connection, however. Although there is little
intrinsic merit in the account of two gossips on Ash Wed-
nesday lamenting the privations of the Lenten season, the
vignette has an intimate style and piquant realism. Quite
as much as the portraits of these voluptuaries, the rare

personality who created them attracts notice; if this sardonic poet speaks with less humanity than Chaucer, his incisive understanding is not inferior to the master's. The larger of the women sits before the fire, pretending to be too feeble to rise. Dunbar exclaims with feigned ignorance, "God wait gif scho wes grit and fatt." The other "cummer" with perfect sincerity observes,

> Ye tak that nigirtness of your muder;
> All wyne to test scho wald disdane
> Bot mavasy . . .

Having decided to let their husbands endure the fast, they have good reason to think "That Lenterne swld nocht mak thame lene." The same ironic pose threads the *Lady Solistaris at Court,* which for all its racy rhythm is inferior to the *Twa Cummeris.* *Of ane Blak-Moir* purposes humor, but is needlessly scurrilous. *Of a Dance in the Quenis Chalmer* is a series of invidious portraits of real persons, including the author; the tart humor is reinforced by the arch refrain, "A mirrear Dance mycht na man see." *The Tod and the Lamb* is a transparent allegory probably based on an amorous encounter of the king, and *A Brash of Wooing* is an indelicate dialogue stuffed with baby talk. Although the lyrical quality of these jocular pieces is low, the spontaneity is gratifying.

The personality of the poet is more clearly defined in the trivial lyric *My heid did yak yesternicht* than in any of the poems of love, satirical or serious. As in few medieval lyrics, the attitude of the author counts for everything. There is no substantial narrative core, no peerless fair, no profound concept, but only the brief statement of a poet that his headache has rendered him incapable of even the most routine activities. The poem is obviously of insufficient magnitude in a period which seldom dealt with subjects less weighty than devotion to God or worship of a lady. The poet himself, moreover, claims the exclusive interest of the reader, the headache counting for nothing save in its effect. This assertion of the private emotion unattached to a person or idea of prominence represents a significant deviation from the norm. Even in the most subjective complaints, the lover is forced to share the canvas with the object of his adoration. Usually, the complaining lover is a mere automaton uttering sentiments which were commonplace when Chrétien de Troyes sang chansons of devotion at the court of Marie de Champagne three centuries before Dunbar's time. The individualized sense of pain in the Scottish poem is an egregious affront to the medieval principle of self-effacement.

In contrast to much Middle English lyric which is dilated by narration and description or the accumulation of general ideas, *My heid did yak yesternicht* expands largely by objective, non-narrative means. In the first stanza, the headache is resembled to an arrow piercing the brain:

> My heid did yak yesternicht,
> This day to mak that I na micht,
> 　So sair the magryme dois me menyie,
> 　Perseing my brow as ony ganyie,
> 　That scant I luik may on the licht.

Desiring to write, the poet discovers that the "sentence" is lodged tightly in the back of his head:

> And now, schir, laitlie, eftir mess,
> To dyt, thocht I begowthe to dress,
> 　The sentence lay full evill till find,
> 　Vnsleipit in my heid behind,
> 　Dullit in dulness and distres.

Another notable metaphor (probably not then trite) describes the melancholic state into which the "magryme" has cast him:

Full oft at morrow I wpryse,
Quhen that my curage sleipeing lyis,
For mirth, for menstrallie and play,
For din, nor danceing, nor deray,
It will nocht walkin me no wise.

Dunbar set out to describe a headache, and this he has
done in language metaphorical and concrete, not affective.
The migraine pierces his head like an arrow; the pain is so
intense that he cannot write. Not even minstrelsy and
revelry arouse his drooping spirits. Although the headache
is particularized and the mind of the poet clearly mirrored,
the emotion proper is attached to nothing peculiarly me-
dieval, but to a universal experience. The referents, more-
over, have lost nothing of their original meaningfulness. The
historical interest of the poem rests on the assertion of
purely personal emotion as fitting matter for poetry, the
choice of a subject altogether trivial, and the expansion of
theme by objective, non-narrative methods. Though of
little intrinsic merit, *My heid did yak yesternicht* is never-
theless a radical departure from the normal transition lyric
and a promising fissure in the hopelessly decayed structure
of poetic principle at the end of the Middle Ages.

A poem of sensibility, *Meditatioun in Wyntir*, reflects
Dunbar's dread of the wintertime.[14] For the poetic imagina-
tion of the Middle Ages, the harsher manifestations of
nature—frost and snow, ice and rain—had no appeal; wild
nature was not until the eighteenth century in England a
proper object of esthetic contemplation. Habitually, then,
before modern times, poetry associated spring and summer
with joy, winter with sorrow. The first stanza, a shuddering
picturization of damp autumn, establishes the equation be-
tween mood and season:

In to thir dirk and drublie dayis,
Quhone sabill all the hewin arrayis,
    With mystie vapouris, cluddis, and skyis,

>Nature all curage me denyis
>Off sangis, ballattis, and of playis.

The second and third stanzas are legitimate variations on
the winter-melancholy theme, expressed affectively. In an
effort to restore a measure of concreteness to the poem,
Dunbar introduces an allegorical exhibition, in which the
abstractions Despair, Patience, Hope, Truth, Prudence, Age,
and Death prey upon his imagination. The maneuver suc-
ceeds indifferently until the eighth stanza, where quasi-
concreteness is achieved with a startling representation of
one of the most fearful concepts ever created by the me-
dieval superstitious fancy:

>Syne Deid castis up his yettis wyd,
>Saying, "Thair oppin sall ye abyd;
>   Albeid that thow were never sa stout,
>   Vndir this lyntall sall thow lowt:
>Thair is nane vther way besyd."

The abiding fear of passing the gates of death is relaxed in
the final stanza, as the poet takes courage in the thought
that a happier season lies ahead:

>Yit, quhone the nycht begynnis to schort,
>It dois my spreit sum part confort,
>   Off thocht oppressit with the schouris.
>   Cum, lustie symmer! with thy flouris,
>That I may leif in sum disport.

The allegory is here less intrusive than at first appears. If
not actually concrete by modern reckoning, these personi-
fied abstractions were more or less animated to the medieval
intelligence. In the five stanzas of allegory, moreover, the
poet has an opportunity to show fairly objectively the
operation of a brooding mind, attacked successively by
conflicting impulses. Though scarcely extraordinary, the
Meditatioun is a consistent expansion of the winter-mel-

ancholy motif and a competent analysis of the state of despondency.

Another poem of serious purpose, the *Lament for the Makaris*, though better known, is a great deal less successful than the *Meditatioun*. As good as the average medieval poem utilizing the *ubi sunt* motif, it is demonstrably far short of Villon's haunting *Ballade des Dames du Temps Jadis*. The sharp differences between these poems should have cried caution long ago to those who uncritically gave Villon credit for influencing Dunbar.[15] Buttressed by the liturgical refrain, "Timor mortis conturbat me,"[16] the *Lament* expands by fits of moralizing and a catalogue of little-known personages. Nothing in it suggests the painful nostalgia of the Parisian's rhetorical question, "Mais où sont les neiges d'antan," which has not often been heard in Europe since the passing of the *vagantes*. The contrast need not be pressed: Dunbar's is not the pure if overripe lyric note of the lone, corrupted soul of Paris, who had withal a broad humanity mingled with his unsuppressed despair. The Scot of course knew the art of thickening his matter, but the *Lament for the Makaris* is a rather bare and discursive longing after departed friends—far short of the *Wanderer*. Dunbar's failure with the elegiac mood underscores his inability to manage wholly serious topics; his religious and didactic poetry, if sometimes sincere, is nevertheless pale and flat. Satire is an inseparable element of the poet's lyrical talent, and those poems threaded with a jest are usually the best.

The extended comparison of the poet to an old horse in the *Petition of the Gray Horse, Auld Dunbar*, for example, is on the surface pleasantly droll. Although a trivial jest is no part of Dunbar's main intention, it establishes a key in which the author writes extremely well, and perhaps more importantly provides a disguise of sorts for the ironic undertone. The coloring, then, at some variance with the

serious purpose, throws an attractive light over what other-
wise would be an intolerable complaint. It is well to
emphasize the successful management of this occasional
poem, because the petitions of Dunbar to the court are
usually shrill, discursive requests for money or preferment.
By resembling himself to a broken-down horse, Dunbar is
enabled to describe his own condition the more poignantly,
and to give the sharpest kind of edge to his sense of de-
feated expectation.

A means of objectifying his dejection was doubtless sug-
gested to the poet by a dialect expression, "Yuillis yald"
(literally, Yule's mare), applied derogatively to one not
so fortunate as to procure new clothing at Christmas.[17]
From this local usage, the "old mare" too poor to purchase
clothing ties in with the "gray horse" exhausted from service
at court and likewise unable to live comfortably. The re-
frain, in which this connection is established, gives the
poem a sense of immediacy. Dunbar unquestionably in-
tended that the pathetic recital confer an immediate
benefit:

> Thocht in the stall I be nocht clappit,
> As cursouris that in silk beine trappit,
> With ane new houss I wald be happit,
> Aganis this Crysthinmes for the cald.
> Schir, lett it nevir in town be tald,
> That I sould be ane Yuillis yald!

Obtaining new clothing is however of secondary interest—
merely an excuse to sketch analogically a career which
seems to Dunbar to have been quite unsuccessful. In the
figure of the horse, he elaborates the pathetic theme: I have
served the king faithfully and deserve some reward; in-
stead, I am put aside in my old age. The cruel imagery of
the sixth stanza provides a desolate background for this
statement:

> I am ane auld horss, as ye knaw,
> That evir in duill dois drug and draw;

> Great court horss puttis me fra the staw,
> To fang the fog be firthe and fald.

The powerful fourth line comprehends all the misery of the damp cold and disheartening somberness of the northern winter and intensifies the plight of old Dunbar in the winter of life turned loose to scrabble for a living.

The major cause of the poet's dissatisfaction in this and several other poems is failure to find preferment in the Church.[18] Whether specifically stated or not, his own sense of unrewarded merit lies behind his vicious attacks on the clergy. Presumably, he had been led to believe from an early age that high ecclesiastical station awaited him: "I wes in yowth on nureiss kne, / Dandely, bischop, dandely." When urged by St. Francis in the vision, *How Dumbar wes desyrd to be ane Freir*, to accept the habit of a mendicant, the poet replied impudently: "Quhairfoir ga bring to me ane bischopis weid, / Gife evir thow wald my saule gaid vnto Hevin." Far from translating Dunbar to a bishopric, the Church seems to have denied him even a modest benefice. Since the poet nowhere states the source of hierarchical prejudice against him, the merits of the case cannot be judged. Otherwise, the poet did not fare so shabbily: in 1510, he began receiving annually from the crown the handsome sum of 80 pounds, and royal accounts for other years disclose substantial payments.[19] This is not to say that he was not frequently pressed for money, or even that his complaints were not in the main quite just. Whether for sufficient cause or not, Dunbar was consumed with a sense of unappreciated merit, and this attitude colors much of his poetry. Although this bitterness of spirit is characteristically expressed in indignant accusations and invidious comparisons, in the *Petition of the Gray Horse* the tartness has gone out of his address. He appears sincerely humble, if not cowed by evil circumstance: "The court hes done my curage cuill, / And maid me ane forriddin muill."

Whether the *Petition of the Gray Horse* is a work of old age does not appear,[20] though the point of view is retrospective. Dunbar informs the king, "My mane is turned in to quhyt," and in the seventh stanza he testifies to a life of deprivation:

> I haif run lang furth in the feild,
> On pastouris that ar plane and peild;
> I mycht be now tein in for eild,
> My beikis ar spruning he and bauld.

Comparing himself to a horse with protruding corner teeth (a mark of age) may be an exaggeration. If so, it is not surprising, for begging songs traditionally incorporated a great deal of overstatement. Similarly, the lines in which he calls upon the king to keep his skin from the cobblers are hardly to be taken as an indication that the poet had premonitions of an early death: "Latt nevir the soutteris have my skin, / With uglie gumes to be gnawin." Exaggerated or not, this ugly image stamps the meaning of death on the imagination as a plain statement could not. By implication, it accuses the court of shameless ingratitude and pleads for some manifestation of favor before that other faithful servant, old Dunbar, suffers comparable degradation. The immediacy of death, then, lends a sense of urgency to the poet's desire "to weir trappouris at this Yuill," which is on the surface the motivating factor behind the poem. In an epilogue, Dunbar represents the king as favorably disposed. The addition is anticlimactic, though possibly necessary to his purpose.

That Dunbar expended a great deal of art in the construction of the involved analogy of the *Petition* is some indication that the utilitarian aspect was to him of minor significance. For polished formulas were ready at hand in the *Complaint of Chaucer to His Purse* and Lydgate's *Letter to Gloucester* to draw a smile and therewith a pittance from a prince of the blood. Incorporating the general complaint with the specific request for apparel was convenient, because the term "Yuillis yald," applicable during the Christmas season, was an excellent means of validating the assumed resemblance of a neglected poet to a super-annuated horse. This equine metaphor, a familiar Lowland Scots usage, imposed no strain upon the imagination and was therefore an efficient fulcrum upon which to balance an enlarged comparison. Dunbar maintains the equilibrium of the equation with rare skill. Perhaps only the image of the cobblers softening the hide with their teeth clearly outrages credibility, and in this instance the poet felt the need of a startling conclusion to convince the king of his penury. The poem could hardly have failed to touch James IV. He unquestionably knew Dunbar well enough to recognize that the humorous gloss was a mere disguise for a serious purpose and that the poet in his own dejection had imaginatively achieved an intimate identification of his own career with that of the horse. For all its spontaneity, the *Petition* is a carefully organized lyric, revolved logically on the theme of disappointed hope. The reader, moreover, is never permitted to forget that the conspicuous referent, the gray horse, is actually a horse, yet Dunbar too. As a consequence of this tight control, the poem is a unified exposition such as the period seldom affords. Fortunately, the poet used dialect instead of literary Scots, since the harsh, writhing phrases, which carry conviction to the theme, could not be fashioned in the artificial style.

The intimacy of style which characterizes much of Dunbar's best verse and indeed much of Middle Scots[21] vitiates the objectivity even of narrative canvasses. In that delightful nonsense poem, *Kynd Kittok*, usually attributed to Dunbar, the grinning author stands beside the reader, asking his approval of the carefully controlled sacrilege:

> My Gudame wes a gay wif, bot scho wes rycht gend,
>   Scho duelt furth fer in to France, apon
>   Falkland fellis;
> Thay callit her Kynd Kittok, quhasa hir weill kend:
>   Scho wes like a caldrone cruke cler vnder kellis;
> Thay threpit that scho deit of thrist, et maid
>   a gud end.

En route to Heaven she passed by "ane elriche well" and there procured a ride on a snail. Riding an inch behind its tail, the crone arrived at her night's lodging in an ale-house. Like George III in Byron's *The Vision of Judgment*, she slipped past St. Peter, all of which made God "lewch his hert sair." But the "aill of hevin wes sour," and seven years later Kynd Kittok went out for a fresh drink. Denied re-admission to Heaven, she returned, perhaps not unhappily, to the alehouse, the "pycharis to pour." At the conclusion, the Scot steps forward to make a request which for all its facetiousness provokes a warm regard not only for the sinful old woman, who comes vividly alive, but also for the poet, who invests the poem with his own delightful whimsy:

> Frendis, I pray you hertfully,
>   Gif ye be thristy or dry,
>   Drink with my Guddame, as ye ga by,
>   Anys for my saik.

The intrusion of the poet into the narrative frame of *Kynd Kittok* illustrates a tendency previously noted. Dunbar has nothing of the steady detachment necessary to the accomplishment of extensive narrative; he is most effective when roaming the interior of a short poem in his own person.

The lyrical verse of the gifted Middle Scots poet is unequal in conception, not in execution; the most fastidious of craftsmen, he polished all that he wrote. Possessed of a good ear for rhythm and a prominent flair for sharp, bold phrasing, the Scot was as often as not occupied more with "termis" than with "sentence." An artist with vast technical power, Dunbar unfortunately lacked the capacity to interpret his age or to give the eternal truths brilliant restatement. When he attempts profundity in religious and didactic lyric, he is merely tedious. But then, a mind cast in the medieval mold had no message for a world at the threshold of a new era. Save in his individualism, the northern poet has little of the spirit of the Renaissance. Nevertheless, Dunbar, as many learned men of his day, felt an increasing tension, the conflict of old and new, although he did not resolve the struggle within himself. Devoted to the material world "Off sangis, ballattis, and of playis," he was yet acutely aware that this life is "A fre chois gevin to Paradice or Hell."

Dunbar anticipates the Renaissance, then, not as a seer, but as a poet, the wholly self-conscious artist risen after three centuries of experimentation with lyric form and style. If courtly lyric in the insipid manner is abundantly represented in the extant work, the reason is simply that he could not consistently ignore his literary inheritance, sterile though it was; the atypical poems are symptomatic of rebellion. The poetry of generalized experience, diffuse and often insincere, contrasts sharply with the lyrics which confess an emergent sensibility. *All Erdly Joy Returnis in Pane*, for example, belongs to the medieval world of selfless contemplation of Heaven:

> Sen erdly joy abydis nevir,
> Wirk for the joy that lestis evir;
> For vder joy is all bot vane:
> All erdly joy returnis in pane.

As certainly, *My heid did yak yesternicht* is occupied with a particular man and his ills in the material world. *To a Ladye*, though provided with conventional garden imagery, differs from polite complaints in form and spirit, having a hard, witty core and a tight organization. These less conventional poems of Dunbar illustrate his developing concept of lyric as a medium for wholly personal expression, for the assertion of the intrinsic interest and importance of the poet's own experience. Thus, the *Petition of the Gray Horse* traces the growth of an attitude, complex and unique. Not a general exposition of "man's inhumanity to man," it deals with the reaction of an individual. Dunbar has then the true lyric urge to report the world with respect to himself, not objectively. It is probably correct to say that his lyric succeeds in proportion as this impulse is unfettered.

Rebel and conformist by turns, Dunbar completes a cycle in which form triumphs over spirit, at the same time expressing discontent with the abominable practices of a century of formalized art. If not a great poet, the Scot is historically important as a transition figure, in whose work the blossoming of modern lyric is foreshadowed. His poetry as a whole may justify Ker's description of him as "one of the first modern light horsemen, the lyrical journalists of the passing day."[22] On the other hand, Dunbar at his worst is never inferior to the average poet of the fifteenth century; at his best, he is unquestionably superior to most of those poets of the sixteenth century whose verse is represented in Tottel's *Songs and Sonnets*. With the sardonic Scot, medieval lyric may make an honorable, if not a distinguished, end.

NOTES

NOTES FOR CHAPTER ONE

LYRIC DEVELOPMENT

1 *The Form of Perfect Living,* ed. C. Horstman, *Yorkshire Writers* (London and New York, 1895-96), I, 22 f.

2 Cæsarius, a sixth-century bishop of Arles, exclaimed, "Quam multi rustici, quam multae rusticae mulieres cantica diabolica, amatoria et turpia ore decantant." Karl Voretzsch, *Introduction to the Study of Old French Literature,* trans. F. M. Du Mont (New York, 1931), pp. 58 f., conveniently assembles early strictures on dance song and secular entertainments in religious houses.

3 F. J. Furnivall (ed.), *The Minor Poems of the Vernon MS.* (Pt. II), EETS, CXVII, London, 1901, p. 762.

4 F. E. Schelling, *The English Lyric* (Boston and New York, 1913), p. 1.

5 E. B. Reed, *English Lyrical Poetry* (New Haven, 1912), p. 10.

6 Ernest Rhys, *Lyric Poetry* (New York and London, 1913), p. vi.

7 John Erskine, *The Elizabethan Lyric* (New York, 1903), p. 15.

8 See U. T. Holmes Jr., *A History of Old French Literature* (New York, 1937), p. 193.

9 *The Golden Treasury,* ed. Herbert Bates (New York, 1915), p. iv.

10 J. G. Frazer, *The Golden Bough* (3d ed.; New York, 1935), II, 66 f., cites in this connection the *Anatomie of Abuses* (1583) of Phillip Stubbes, who wrote that on the evenings before Whitsuntide, May Day, and other festivals, rural folk were accustomed to go into the woods seeking the "may," and to return the following day with a Maypole and greenery, for the celebration.

11 Robert of Brunne, *Handlyng Synne,* ed. F. J. Furnivall, EETS, CXIX, London, 1901, p. 156.

12 E. K. Chambers, *The Medieval Stage* (Oxford, 1903), I, 119 f.

13 Robert of Brunne, EETS, CXXIII, 1903, p. 283.

14 Alois Brandl and Otto Zippel (eds.), *Mittelenglische Sprach- und Literaturproben* (2d ed.; Berlin, 1927), pp. 254 f. See also *Romania,* XXV (1896), 341.

15 James Cranstoun (ed.), *The Poems of Alexander Scott,* STS, XXXVI, Edinburgh and London, 1896, pp. 23-25, 130-37.

16 Bele Aeliz is a well-known personage of the *caroles,* usually represented as rising in the morning and going out to pick flowers. What happens to her is never learned, although Joseph Bédier, "Les plus anciennes danses françaises," *Revue des Deux Mondes,* XXXI (1906), 414 f., conjectured that the Bele Aeliz fragment was merely a stereotyped introduction for dramatic dance song which could otherwise vary to suit the inclinations of the composers.

[17] Paul Meyer, "Les Manuscrits français de Cambridge," *Romania*, XXXVI (1907), 501 f. See also Louis Petit de Julleville (ed.), *Histoire de la langue et de la littérature française* (Paris, 1896-99), II, 240, and R. L. Greene (ed.), *The Early English Carols* (Oxford, 1935), pp. cxiv f.

[18] Matt. 12:36. The author uses the Latin of the Vulgate, of course.

[19] Max Förster, "Kleinere mittelenglische Texte," *Anglia*, XLII (1918), 152-54.

[20] Cf. the European custom of casting sticks and stones at the effigy of the vegetation spirit on Midsummer Day. Frazer, *Golden Bough*, IV, 264.

[21] Leroux de Lincy (ed.), *Recueil de chants historiques français* (Paris, 1841), I, i f., printed a Latin translation of a song celebrating the victory of Clotaire II over the Saxons in 625. According to the translator, Hildegaire, bishop of Meaux under Charles the Bald, this inoffensive song was danced to by women.

[22] *Le Roman de la Rose ou de Guillaume de Dole*, ed. G. Servois, SATF, Paris, 1893, pp. 162 f.

[23] EETS, CXIX, 156.

[24] Helen Waddell, *The Wandering Scholars* (Boston and New York, 1927), p. 208; App. E (pp. 244-70) contains the judgments of councils from the fourth to the fourteenth century on the extraecclesiastical activities of worldly clerks. See also J. M. Manly, "Familia Goliae," *MP*, V (1907-08), 201-09, J. H. Hanford, "The Progenitors of Golias," *Speculum*, I (1926), 38-58, and F. J. E. Raby, *A History of Secular Latin Poetry in the Middle Ages* (London, 1934), II, 338 ff.

[25] A. W. Haddan and William Stubbs, *Councils and Ecclesiastical Documents Relating to Great Britain and Ireland* (Oxford, 1869-78), III, 133.

[26] Chambers, *Med. Stage*, I, 31-41, and Edmond Faral, *Les Jongleurs en France au Moyen Age* (Paris, 1910), pp. 272-327, together print the most significant passages from medieval documents which have to do with minstrelsy.

[27] Chambers, I, 59-62; II, 262. Cf. the *Minstrel's Farewell*, which has a pronounced religious tone, in Brandl-Zippel, pp. 144 f. See also Langland, *Piers the Plowman*, ed. W. W. Skeat, EETS, XXXVIII, London, 1869, p. 2, B. 31-34, and the discussion of E. T. Donaldson, *Piers Plowman: the C-Text and Its Poet* (New Haven, Conn., 1949), pp. 136-52.

[28] Faral, p. 2, uses *jongleur* as a general term to designate "tous ceux qui faisaient profession de divertir les hommes."

[29] Chambers, I, 54 f.

[30] A. F. Leach, *The Schools of Medieval England* (New York, 1915), p. 167.

[31] J. J. Jusserand, *English Wayfaring Life in the Middle Ages (XIVth Century)*, trans. L. T. Smith (rev. ed.; New York, 1929), pp. 201 f.

[32] *CT.*, F. 77-78.

[33] *CT.*, F. 268-71.

[34] *HF.*, 1216-26.

[35] *CT.*, I. 445.

[36] This problem is studied at length in Chapter IV.

[37] Gaston Paris, Review of Jeanroy's *Les Origines de la poésie lyrique en France au Moyen Age, Journal des Savants*, July, 1892, p. 427.

[38] H. E. Wooldridge, *The Oxford History of Music* (Oxford, 1905), II (Pt. II), 22 f. For further discussion of troubadour music, see Gustave Reese, *Music in the Middle Ages* (New York, 1940), pp. 198 ff.

[39] In 1324, Machaut composed a motet for the archbishop of Rheims, Guillaume de Trie. *Oeuvres*, ed. Ernest Hœpffner, SATF, Paris, 1908-21, I, xv.

[40] Wooldridge, p. 23.

[41] For lists of instruments mentioned in contemporary documents, see C. C. Olson, "Chaucer and the Music of the Fourteenth Century," *Speculum*, XVI (1941), 66 f.

[42] See Carleton Brown and R. H. Robbins, *The Index of Middle English Verse* (New York, 1943), pp. 737-39.

[43] Chambers, *Med. Stage*, II, 234-58.

[44] Lord Raglan, "The Origin of Folk-Culture [Presidential Address, 1947]," *Folk-Lore*, LVIII (1947), 259.

[45] Barbara Smythe (trans.), *Trobador Poets* (London and New York, 1911), p. xiii; H. J. Chaytor, *The Troubadours* (Cambridge, 1912), p. 22.

[46] Holmes, *Hist. OF Lit.*, pp. 3, 198.

[47] Brown-Robbins, *Index*, pp. 742 f.

[48] W. Heuser, "Fragmente von unbekannten Spielmannsliedern des 14. Jahrhunderts, aus MS. Rawl. D. 913," *Anglia*, XXX (1907), 173-79, strives commendably to reconstruct the scraps, but deterioration has been beforehand.

[49] St. John D. Seymour, *Anglo-Irish Literature* (Cambridge, 1929), pp. 97 f., prints the fragments with commentary.

[50] J. A. H. Murray (ed.), *The Complaynt of Scotland*, EETSES, XVII-XVIII, London, 1872-73, pp. 64 f.

[51] F. J. Child (ed.), *The English and Scottish Popular Ballads* (Boston and New York, 1882-98), Nos. 162, 163.

[52] David Laing (ed.), *Select Remains of the Ancient Popular and Romance Poetry of Scotland*, re-ed. John Small (Edinburgh and London, 1885), pp. 247-50.

[53] There are only three Middle English *pastourelles; Crow and Pie* of MS. Rawlinson C. 813 (*ca.* 1500) is traditionally grouped with the ballads. The characteristic introduction is echoed—often very faintly—by about one hundred Middle English poems, the great majority of which show no other resemblance to the French type.

[54] See Gaston Paris (ed.), *Chansons du XVᵉ siècle*, SATF, Paris, 1935, Nos. VI, XXIV, XXIX, LX.

[55] H. E. Sandison, *The "Chanson d'Aventure" in Middle English* (Bryn Mawr, Pa., 1913), pp. 3 ff., considers these distinctions.

[56] E. K. Chambers and Frank Sidgwick (eds.), *Early English Lyrics* (London, 1926), p. 266.

[57] Cf. *Twa Corbies, Wee Wee Man, Carnal and the Crane, Bonny Bee Hom, Christopher White, King James and Brown, Archie O Cawfield, Willie's Fatal Visit, John of Hazelgreen, Erlinton C, Sir Lionel D,* and *Duke of Athole's Nurse* C, D, F.

[58] *Sweet William's Ghost* C, D, E; *Lady Isabel and the Elf Knight* A, *Burd Ellen, Hind Etin* A, B; *King's Dochter Lady Jean, Lady Alice* A, *Young Benjie* A, *Prince Heathen,* and *Child Owlet.* Cf. *Lord Thomas and Fair Margaret* A9.

[59] E. K. Chambers, *English Literature at the Close of the Middle Ages* (Oxford, 1945), p. 184.

[60] W. P. Ker, *Collected Essays,* ed. Charles Whibley (London, 1925), II, 101.

[61] The Norman character is generally described as practical and utilitarian; there is not much reason to think that secular lyric flourished among the immediate followers of William I. See Emanuel Walberg, *Quelques aspects de la littérature anglo-normande* (Paris, 1936), p. 36.

[62] Karl Bartsch (ed.), *Altfranzösische Romanzen und Pastourellen* (Leipzig, 1870), p. 10.

[63] Louise Pound, *Poetic Origins and the Ballad* (New York, 1921), pp. 1-27, protests the assumption of the older generation of ballad scholars that communal composition preceded individual and cites numerous personal songs from primitive cultures.

[64] Frances Densmore, *Pawnee Music* (Smithsonian Institution, Bur. of Amer. Ethnology, Bull. 93; Washington, D. C., 1929), p. 64.

[65] Densmore, *Chippewa Music* (Smithsonian Institution, Bur. of Amer. Ethnology, Bull. 45; Washington, D. C., 1910), p. 151, also prints musical notation and Chippewa text.

[66] My informant was unfortunately unable to render the Papuan into Malayan, the commercial language of the area, and I have no knowledge of the Biak dialect. Many traditional songs of the southwestern Pacific, however, are no longer understood by those who sing them.

[67] *Guillaume de Dole,* p. 72.

[68] Heuser, *Anglia,* XXX, 175.

[69] Densmore, *Chippewa Music,* pp. 192 f.

[70] Pound, pp. 85 f., maintains that dance song is of no greater antiquity than other sorts. The matter has been of no consequence save to the communalists, who were concerned with ballads, not with primitive lyric as such.

[71] *Early Bodleian Music,* ed. John Stainer (London and New York, 1901), II, 5, has the music. On the date see Carleton Brown (ed.), *English Lyrics of the XIIIth Century* (Oxford, 1932), p. 169.

[72] See *Early Bodleian Music,* II, 10, for the notation.

[73] The mode is Dorian, according to William Chappell, *Popular Music of the Olden Time* (London, [1855-59]), I, 57 f.

[74] *NED, small,* III, 10 *q.v.*

[75] *Carmina Burana,* ed. J. A. Schmeller (4th ed.; Breslau, 1904), p. 185.

[76] *Early Bodleian Music,* II, 61 f.

[77] *Ibid.,* II, 68-70.

[78] See Edmond Faral, *Les Arts poétiques du XIIᵉ et du XIIIᵉ siècle* (Paris, 1924), pp. 61 ff.

[79] Thomas Wright (ed.), *Anecdota Literaria* (London, 1844), p. 96.

[80] Cf. *Love's Madness,* Brown, *Lyrics XIIIth Cent.,* p. 14, and the notes on pp. 169 f., 208-09; Leroux de Lincy, *op. cit.,* I, xlviii; Alfred Jeanroy and Arthur Långfors (eds.), *Chansons satiriques et bachiques du XIIIᵉ siècle* (Paris, 1921), pp. 29-31; *Carm. Bur.,* pp. 150 f.; and see the discussions of R. M. Wilson, *Early Middle English Literature* (London, 1939), p. 262, and H. J. Chaytor, *The Troubadours and England* (Cambridge, 1923), pp. 117 f. Sixteenth-century poets also used the artifice without spectacular success.

NOTES FOR CHAPTER TWO

THE HARLEIAN LOVE LYRICS

[1] Otto Heider, *Untersuchungen zur mittelenglischen erotischen Lyrik (1250-1300)* (Halle a. S., 1905), p. 6, takes the period to extend from 1250 to 1300. The manuscript was made *ca.* 1320. See J. E. Wells, *A Manual of the Writings in Middle English* (New Haven, Conn., 1926), pp. 487-89, for dates of other early collections of lyrics.

[2] Chambers, *EELyrics,* p. 276, seeks the impulse in the thirteenth-century or bourgeois phase of trouvère poetry.

[3] Fifty-odd *chansonniers* put together in the thirteenth and fourteenth centuries contain the bulk of the early song, according to Holmes, *Hist. OF Lit.,* p. 198.

[4] Brown, *Lyrics XIIIth Cent.,* pp. xxxvi f. Chambers' statement, *EELyrics,* p. 276, "It was with the Adans de le Hale . . . that our monk was in touch during the *wanderjahre* in which he first heard the songs that he afterwards wrote down . . ." should probably not be taken as representing this scholar's real view; there is no evidence whatsoever that the Herefordshire religious turned into English a sheaf of exquisite lyrics got on a tour of northern France.

[5] Heider, pp. 55-57. Nevertheless, there is little evidence of Goliardic activity at the beginning of the fourteenth century in England.

[6] See G. R. Owst, *Literature and Pulpit in Medieval England* (Cambridge, 1933), pp. 217 ff.

[7] Heider, p. 35.

[8] For a list of Anglo-Norman secular lyrics, see Johan Vising, *Anglo-Norman Language and Literature* (London, 1923), pp. 61-63, 72.

[9] Paul Meyer, "Les Manuscrits français de Cambridge," *Romania,* XV (1886), 248-55.

[10] Arthur Långfors, "Mélanges de poésie lyrique française," *Romania*, LII (1926), 422.

[11] Cf. Ballade No. 220, *Poésies lyriques*, ed. V. Chickemaref (Paris, 1909), I, 198 f.

[12] Karl Bartsch and Leo Wiese (eds.), *Chrestomathie de l'ancien Français* (12th ed.; Leipzig, 1927), p. 247.

[13] Thomas Wright, *Specimens of Lyric Poetry*, Percy Soc., IV, London, 1842, pp. 63 f.

[14] Chaytor, *Troubs. and Eng.*, pp. 20 f.; Elinor Rees, "Provençal Elements in the English Vernacular Lyrics of Manuscript Harley 2253," *Stanford Studies in Language and Literature* (Stanford University, Calif., 1941), pp. 81-95. Jean Audiau, *Les Troubadours et l'Angleterre* (new ed.; Paris, 1927), presses the case for direct influence without sufficient justification.

[15] Rees, p. 95, locates Provençal rhyme schemes for twenty Harleian lyrics.

[16] Paris, *JS*, July, 1892, p. 427.

[17] *Ibid.*, p. 424.

[18] For this identification, see Holmes, *Hist. OF Lit.*, p. 269.

[19] *Guillaume de Dole*, p. 125.

[20] Paris, *Chansons*, p. 47.

[21] Paris, *JS*, July, 1892, pp. 426 f.

[22] The numerous theories pertaining to the origin of French lyrical poetry are conveniently summarized by Voretzsch, *Intro. OF Lit.*, pp. 146-56.

[23] Karl Bartsch (ed.), *Altfranzösische Romanzen und Pastourellen* (Leipzig, 1870), pp. 22 f.

[24] Gace Brulé, *Chansons*, ed. Gédéon Huet, SATF, Paris, 1902, p. 1.

[25] P. S. Allen, "Mediaeval Latin Lyrics," *MP*, VI (1908-09), 138-41. Paris, *JS*, July, 1892, p. 416, declared that the spring songs of the manuscript, German as well as Latin, were ultimately of French origin.

[26] The evidence for this dating has been summarized by Brown, *Lyrics XIIIth Cent.*, pp. 168 f.

[27] M. F. Bukofzer, *Sumer is icumen in: A Revision* (Univ. of Calif. Publications in Music, Vol. II, No. 2; Berkeley and Los Angeles, 1944), pp. 92 f.

[28] Among others, the development of the rota out of motet, *conductus*, and *rondellus;* the use of the term *pes* for tenor; the frequency of sixth-chords.

[29] George Saintsbury, *A History of English Prosody* (2d ed.; London, 1923), I, 120, shrewdly guessed that the lyric was too good for a period earlier than the late thirteenth century.

[30] A. J. Ellis, *Early English Pronunciation*, EETSES, VII, London, 1869, pp. 423-25, discusses the phonology and orthography of the song.

[31] C. R. Baskervill, "Dramatic Aspects of Medieval Folk Festivals in England," *SP*, XVII (1920), 43, maintains that it "was almost certainly composed for processions in such inductions of summer" as Robert Grosse-teste, Bishop of Lincoln, mentions in his complaint against clerks who make

"ludos quos vocant miracula; et alios ludos quos vocant Inductionem Maii sive Autumni."

[32] See *Carm. Bur.*, Nos. 51, 100, 106, 107, 121, 122, 140.

[33] Brown, *Lyrics XIIIth Cent.*, pp. xv f.

[34] Giraldus Cambrensis, *Opera*, Rolls Series, XXI, London, 1868, vi, 189-90, Lib. I, cap. xiii.

[35] Wilson, *Early ME Lit.*, p. 260.

[36] Chambers, *EELyrics*, p. 273, regards it with considerable justice as a "learned composer's adaptation of a *reverdie*."

[37] For the lack of an unequivocal term for the springtime, Middle English poets were compelled to use *somer* to comprehend the interval between the vernal and the autumnal equinoxes. This usage corresponds to the medieval Latin *aestas*, which in several songs of the *Carmina Burana* (cf. Nos. 51, 106, 107, 122) obviously signifies spring. Since the Julian calendar had fallen nearly two weeks behind by the fourteenth century, the season was well advanced in April; the Harleian poet who wrote "Lef & gras & blosme springes in aueryl" was unquestionably correct. The cuckoo arrives on the southern coast of England about the second week of April *(Encyl. Brit.*, 14th ed., *cuckoo, q.v.*), or, by Julian computation, some twelve days earlier. According to medieval reckoning, then, the circumstances fit April rather better than May.

[38] Many times edited. A facsimile of the song is printed as the frontispiece of the first volume of Chappell's *Popular Music of the Olden Time*.

[39] The older anthologists sometimes made ludicrous attempts to gloss "bucke uerteth" in a way tolerable to Victorian sensibilities. Most recent editors have recognized what every farm boy knows—that quadrupeds disport themselves in the spring precisely as the poet has said. To the fourteenth century, the idea was probably inoffensive.

[40] Cf. ll. 2049-56, 911-20, 6998-7004, 2901-06, ed. Henry Weber, *Metrical Romances of the Thirteenth, Fourteenth, and Fifteenth Centuries* (Edinburgh, 1810), I, 89, 43-44, 287, 122. *King Alisaundre* may have been composed in Kentish as early as the thirteenth century, but the earliest recension has been dated *ca.* 1400, according to Wells, *Manual*, p. 100. Cf. *Arthour and Merlin*, ll. 1716-19, ed. J. W. Hales and F. J. Furnivall, *Bishop Percy's Folio Manuscript* (London, 1868), I, 475; *Sowdone of Babylone*, ll. 963-78, ed. Emil Hausknecht, EETSES, XXXVIII, London, 1881, pp. 28 f.; *Sir Orfeo*, ll. 55-66, ed. W. H. French and C. B. Hale, *Middle English Metrical Romances* (New York, 1930), p. 325.

[41] Weber, II, 149 f.

[42] All of the amatory lyrics of Harley 2253 have been edited by Wright, *SLPoetry* and Karl Böddeker, *Altenglische Dichtungen des MS. Harl. 2253* (Berlin, 1878), and nearly all by Brown, *Lyrics XIIIth Cent.* A new edition of the religious and love lyrics, ed. G. L. Brook, *The Harley Lyrics* (Manchester, 1948), appeared after the completion of this study. Valuable emendations have been suggested by Kemp Malone, "Notes on Middle

English Lyrics," *ELH*, II (1935), 58-65; R. J. Menner, "Notes on Middle English Lyrics," *MLN*, LV (1940), 243-49; and Howard Meroney, "Line-Notes on the Early English Lyric," *MLN*, LXII (1947), 184-87.

43 The phraseology of the couplet suggests a French model: cf. "Or vienent pasques les beles en avril," Bartsch, *Rom. u. Past.*, p. 17; *Chansons et descorts de Gautier de Dargies*, ed. Gédéon Huet, SATF, Paris, 1912, p. 22; *Les plus anciens chansonniers français*, ed. Jules Brakelmann (Paris, 1870-91), p. 123. But see the *Menologium* (ll. 75-95), ed. E. V. Dobbie, *The Anglo-Saxon Poetic Records* (New York, 1942), VI, 51.

44 Cf. Brown, *Lyrics XIIIth Cent.*, p. 101.

45 *Ibid.*, p. 207.

46 *Encyl. Brit.*, 11th ed., *nightingale, q.v.*; W. W. Skeat (ed.), *Chaucerian and Other Pieces* (Oxford, 1897), p. 526.

47 For full development of the nature prelude in *pastourelles*, cf. Bartsch, *Chrest.*, pp. 216 f.

48 Competently reconstructed by W. W. Skeat, "Fragment of a Middle English Poem," *MLR*, V (1910), 104 f.

49 Böddeker, *AEDicht.*, pp. 158-60.

50 Brandl-Zippel, *ME Spr. u. Literaturproben*, p. 128.

51 Sandison, *Chanson d'Aventure*, p. 45, thinks the cultivation of the religious and didactic *chanson d'aventure* was due to the fact that in England literature was so largely in the hands of the clergy.

52 Arthur Långfors, "Mélanges de poésie lyrique française," *Romania*, LIII (1927), 475-77.

53 *Ibid.*, pp. 513-15; but cf. chansons, pp. 481-538 *passim*, and Alfred Jeanroy, *Les Origines de la poésie lyrique en France au Moyen Age* (2d ed.; Paris, 1904), pp. 480-91.

54 Böddeker, *AEDicht.*, pp. 216 f.

55 *Ibid.*, pp. 218 f.

56 *Ibid.*, p. 61. Cf. "Bi a wode as I gon ryde," Brown (ed.), *Religious Lyrics of the XIVth Century* (Oxford, 1924), p. 196.

57 Brown, *Lyrics XIIIth Cent.*, pp. 161-63.

58 Brown (ed.), *Religious Lyrics of the XVth Century* (Oxford, 1939), pp. 76 f., *Lyrics XIIIth Cent.*, pp. 111, 118; F. A. Patterson, *The Middle English Penitential Lyric* (New York, 1911), pp. 153-55.

59 Cf. Greene, *Carols*, Nos. 145, 146, 149, 151, 164, 175, 183, 184, 234.

60 Paris, *JS*, Dec., 1891, pp. 729-32.

61 *Ibid.*, pp. 740 f.

62 Jeanroy, *Origines*, pp. 19-23.

63 See *L'autrier jost' una sebissa*, ed. Karl Bartsch, *Chrestomathie provençale* (4th ed.; Elberfeld, 1880), pp. 51-54.

64 Edmond Faral, "La Pastourelle," *Romania*, XLIX (1923), 259.

65 W. P. Jones, *The Pastourelle* (Cambridge, Mass., 1931), p. 32.

66 Holmes, *Hist. OF Lit.*, p. 196, puts the number at 150; Bartsch, *Rom. u. Past.*, prints 182 lyrics as *pastourelles*.

67 Julleville, *Histoire*, I, 356.

68 Wilson, *Early ME Lit.*, p. 263, suggests the resemblance of this poem to a popular *carole*.

69 Sandison, *Chanson d'Aventure*, pp. 47 f.

70 Böddeker, *AEDicht.*, p. 158.

71 Bartsch, *Rom. u. Past.*, p. 193.

72 Cf. *Crow and Pie*, Child, *Ballads*, No. 111.

73 M. P. Medary, "Stanza-Linking in Middle English Verse," *RR*, VII (1916), 270, regards linking as of popular origin and confined to northern poetry; but A. C. L. Brown, "On the Origin of Stanza-Linking in English Alliterative Verse," *RR*, VII (1916), 283, refers it to Welsh origins.

74 Cf. Bartsch, *Chrest.*, p. 217, "dorenlot, alez avant, ja ne me troverez fole!"

75 Child, *Ballads*, No. 112.

76 C. J. Sharp (ed.), *English Folk Songs from the Southern Appalachians*, re-ed. Maud Karpeles (Oxford, 1932), Nos. 59, 82, 98, 127, 143, 145, 155, 157, 180.

77 This poem is regarded as an example of the dialect of the northeast Midland, where the nightingale is a frequent visitor.

78 The Châtelain de Coucy suggests the impact which the nightingale had on the poetic imagination of the Middle Ages, "La douce voiz del rosignol sauvage, / k'oi nuit et jor contoier et tentir, / me radoucist mon cuer et rassouage," Bartsch, *Chrest.*, pp. 165 f.

79 This belief was an old one, though the troubadours gave it currency in Romance love lyric. Cf. Chaytor, *Troubs. and Eng.*, p. 110; an Anglo-Norman chanson (late thirteenth century), "Si amur m'ad d'un dart enpeynt," Meyer, "Les Manuscrits français de Cambridge," *Romania*, XV (1886), 251; the Harleian lyric, *A wayle whyt ase whalles bon*, "Hyre heye haueth wounded me ywisse," Böddeker, *AEDicht.*, p. 162; *Carm. Bur.*, No. 51, "Venus me telo vulneravit aureo, quod cor penetravit," and further see P. S. Allen, "Mediaeval Latin Lyrics," *MP*, VI (1908-09), 166; Thibaut de Champagne, "Amors, qui en moi s'est mise, / Bien m'a droit son dart geté," *Les Chansons*, ed. Axel Wallensköld, SATF, Paris, 1925, p. 83.

80 Bartsch, *Chrest.*, pp. 112 f. See also *Amors tençon et bataille*, ed. Jules Brakelmann, *Les plus anciens chansonniers français* (Paris, 1870-91), pp. 44-46.

81 Holmes, *Hist. OF Lit.*, pp. 313 f., says that the French poet of the thirteenth century, having forgotten the meaning of courtly love, employed the forms conventionally.

82 Bartsch, *Rom. u. Past.*, p. 321. Cf. Froissart's other *pastourelles*, *ibid.*, pp. 321-37.

83 Chambers, *EELyrics*, p. 274.

84 Occasional stanza-linking and the Burns measure, presumably here first used in English. For Provençal examples of this stanza, see two lyrics of Guillaume IX, ed. Carl Appel, *Provenzalische Chrestomathie* (6th ed.; Leipzig, 1930), pp. 80, 95.

85 Child, *Ballads*, No. 78.

[86] Chambers-Sidgwick, *EELyrics*, p. 277. Wilson, *Early ME Lit.*, p. 261, likewise regards the refrain of this lyric as folk song.

[87] Böddeker, *AEDicht.*, pp. 154 f. Brown, *Lyrics XIIIth Cent.*, pp. xxxix f., has tabulated the parallels, which are certainly striking.

[88] "brudes bryht" (Böddeker, p. 153), "ledies . . . bryht in bour" (Böddeker, p. 166), "bricht in bure" (Brown, *Lyrics XIIIth Cent.*, p. 118), "bryht in bour" (Böddeker, p. 213), "bryht berde yn boure" (*Sir Launfal*, l. 548).

[89] "semly on syht" (Böddeker, p. 145), "that semly forte se" (Böddeker, p. 149), "semlier to min sithe" (Brandl-Zippel, p. 128), "semyle was of syhte" (*Sir Launfal*, l. 285).

[90] "for beste of bon and blod" (*Early Bodleian Music*, II, 10).

[91] Brown, p. 231, compares this stanza with a series of gems in MS. Bodley 86, employed metaphorically in praise of the Virgin. This artificiality is the product of the medieval love of catalogues (of gems, flowers, trees, musical instruments) and the influence of rhetoric. Cf. Thomas Wright and J. O. Halliwell-[Phillipps] (eds.), *Reliquiae Antiquae* (London, 1841-43), II, 222; Eustache Deschamps, *Oeuvres complètes*, ed. Le Marquis de Queux de Saint-Hilaire and Gaston Raynaud, SATF, Paris, 1878-1903, III, 278 f., 287 f.

[92] Cf. Chaucer's *Complaint of Venus*, ed. F. N. Robinson, *The Complete Works of Geoffrey Chaucer* (Boston and New York, 1933), pp. 633 f., which is paraphrased from three ballades of Otes de Granson; and Deschamps' Ballade No. 537, *Invocation à l'Amour, Oeuvres*, III, 377 f. In the latter, Amour oppresses the lover with "Doulx Regart, Penser et Souvenir."

[93] Wilson, *Early ME Lit.*, p. 261, conjectures that *Alysoun* is a literary development of a *carole* of the popular type. H. J. Chaytor, *The Troubadours* (Cambridge, 1912), p. 137, notices that the rhyme scheme was used by Gaucelm Faidit, a poet of Provence. The wonderment of Rhys, *Lyric Poetry*, p. 40, that this lyric could be written at a time when Norman-French "was threatening to break . . . the native idiom and turn for melody" is misplaced. There is every sign that English poets of the Harleian circle had effected a fairly satisfactory synthesis.

[94] Cf. the Anglo-Norman chanson, *Quant le tens se renovele*, *Romania*, XV, 253-55.

[95] Sandison, *Chanson d'Aventure*, p. 64.

[96] See W. C. Curry, *The Middle English Ideal of Personal Beauty* (Baltimore, 1916), p. 3; and my article, "The Eyen Greye of Chaucer's Prioress," *PQ*, XXVI (1947), 307-12. Deschamps' Ballade No. 960, *Oeuvres*, V, 186 f., has one of the fullest catalogues of conventionalized charms. See also Bartsch, *Rom. u. Past.*, p. 25.

[97] Joseph Bédier (ed.), *Les Chansons de Colin Muset* (Paris, 1938), p. 34.

[98] Bernhard Ten Brink, *History of English Literature*, trans. H. M. Kennedy, L. D. Schmitz, and W. C. Robinson (New York, 1883-96), I, 306, thought the same poet wrote *When the nyhtegale singes*. There are obvious structural similarities, and both are in the northeast Midland dialect.

⁹⁹ The *clericus* earlier had become a contender with the *chevalier* in love pursuits. *Melior and Ydoine*, a thirteenth-century debate with a *chanson dramatique* introduction, turns on the question, "quel vaut meuz a amer gentil clerc ou chivaler." Paul Meyer, "Notice du MS. 25970 de la Bibliothèque Phillipps," *Romania*, XXXVII (1908), 236 ff. Cf. *Geste of Blancheflour and Florence, ibid.*, pp. 221-23; and *Exiit diluculo, Carm. Bur.*, No. 63, a pastoral in which a clerk acts the part of a knight.

¹⁰⁰ Böddeker, *AEDicht.*, p. 165, conjectures on the basis of metrical similarity that the author also wrote *Lenten ys come with loue to toune.*

¹⁰¹ Brown, *Lyrics XIIIth Cent.*, pp. 235 f., discusses its relationship to a religious poem in the same manuscript and to another in Egerton 613.

¹⁰² Associated with several religious poems; see W. Heuser, "With an O and an I," *Anglia*, XXVII (1904), 300 ff.

¹⁰³ Brown, *Lyrics XIIIth Cent.*, pp. 228 f.; F. L. Utley, *The Crooked Rib* (Columbus, Ohio, 1944), p. 287.

¹⁰⁴ Böddeker, *AEDicht.*, pp. 455 f.; Brown, *Lyrics XIIIth Cent.*, p. 229, argues against the identification.

¹⁰⁵ For fully developed anadiplosis, see Jakob Schipper, *Englische Metrik* (Bonn, 1881-88), I, 317.

NOTES FOR CHAPTER THREE

SONGS OF SATIRE AND PROTEST

¹ The re-establishment of English as the prevailing literary language is thoroughly investigated by A. C. Baugh, *A History of the English Language* (New York and London, c. 1935), pp. 155-92.

² Thomas Wright (ed.), *The Political Songs of England*, Camden Soc., VI, London, 1839, pp. 3-6, 36-41, prints a *sirvente* against King John and two against Henry III, but these satires deal with the monarchs in their capacity as rulers of Continental territories. The influence of the genre cannot be traced in England, although S. M. Tucker, *Verse Satire in England Before the Renaissance* (New York, 1908), p. 36, declared, for reasons not clearly stated, that the English gleeman inherited from troubadours and trouvères the tradition of satirical song.

³ Brown, *Lyrics XIIIth Cent.*, pp. 222-24, documents the historical allusions with appropriate citations from contemporary accounts of the Barons' War.

⁴ Wright, *Pol. Songs*, pp. 59-63, 63-68, prints two French poems, *The Song of the Barons* and the *Song of the Peace with England*, and the long Latin piece, the *Battle of Lewes*, pp. 72-121. Further see Leroux de Lincy (ed.), *Recueil de chants historiques français* (Paris, 1841), I, 192-210. Simon was proclaimed martyr and saint after his death and even compared

with Thomas à Becket. Wright, *Pol. Songs*, p. 124, prints a hymn written in his honor.

5 Brown-Robbins, *Index*, lists about seventy-three such preludes, few of which suggest minstrel authorship, however.

6 T. F. Tout, *The History of England from the Accession of Henry III to the Death of Edward III* (London and New York, 1905), pp. 109-12, notes that Henry secured a papal bull from Alexander IV excusing him from his oath and on a later occasion obtained a favorable decision when Louis IX of France, called upon to arbitrate the dispute, sustained the papal decree setting aside the Provisions.

7 See the articles on Bigod and Warenne in the *DNB*.

8 The non-amatory lyrics of Harley 2253 were first edited by Thomas Wright for the Camden Society in 1839 and later by Karl Böddeker.

9 C. W. Previté-Orton, *Political Satire in English Poetry* (Cambridge, 1910), pp. 13 f., considers the treatment unjust, preferring the nobler Latin poem, the *Battle of Lewes*. The two pieces, however, are not comparable; the English is a song, the Latin a long narrative and polemical treatment of the events and issues of the Barons' War.

10 The prince had fallen away from Simon after first showing a strong interest in his cause, but nevertheless revealed the good effects of the earl's tutelage when he came to rule as Edward I. See Tout, p. 128.

11 Hilda Johnstone, "France: The Last Capetians," *Cambridge Mediaeval History*, VII, 322 f.

12 Böddeker, *AEDicht.*, p. 115, so regards him, and nothing contradicts this supposition.

13 C. R. Baskervill, "Dramatic Aspects of Medieval Folk Festivals in England," *SP*, XVII (1920), 53-55.

14 Böddeker, *AEDicht.*, pp. 140-43, 453-55, prints both the translation and the original.

15 *Ibid.*, p. 139.

16 Thomas Wright (ed.), *Political Poems and Songs*, Rolls Series, XIV, London, 1859-61, I, 215-18.

17 G. R. Owst, *Literature and Pulpit in Medieval England* (Cambridge, 1933), pp. 68-76, studies this "nautical simile" closely and concludes that the author, who may himself have been a homilist, drew the figure directly out of sermon literature, which affords examples as early as the eleventh century. See further, Greene, *Carols*, p. 441; Deschamps, *Oeuvres*, I, 256 f.

18 See Wright, *Pol. Songs*, *Poem on the Evil Times of Edward II* (pp. 323-45), *On the King's Breaking His Confirmation of Magna Charta* (pp. 253-58), *Song on the Times* (pp. 251 f.).

19 H. D. Traill and J. S. Mann (eds.), *Social England* (illus. ed.; New York and London, 1902), II, 142.

20 W. H. R. Curtler, *The Enclosure and Redistribution of Our Land* (Oxford, 1920), p. 22, distinguishes between the hayward and the haward (or hedgekeeper), whose duty it was to maintain the fences.

21 See *Social England*, II, 133 f., for further discussion of manor officials.

[22] Curtler, p. 19.

[23] As energetic yeomen came into possession of several virgates, they had to hire for wages the free laboring class detached from the manor during this period.

[24] Böddeker, p. 102. Owst, pp. 214-27, regards the satirical and political matter of Harley 2253 and other pre-Chaucerian collections as the work of the clergy and especially of the mendicants, who sympathized with the peasantry.

[25] J. P. Oakden and E. R. Innes, *Alliterative Poetry in Middle English: A Survey of the Traditions* (Manchester, 1935), p. 10.

[26] W. W. Capes, *The English Church in the Fourteenth and Fifteenth Centuries* (London, 1920), p. 240, observes that the archdeacons were notoriously corrupt.

[27] W. R. W. Stephens, *The English Church from the Norman Conquest to the Accession of Edward I* (London, 1929), pp. 49 f., 164-66.

[28] *Ibid.*, p. 165.

[29] G. M. Trevelyan, *England in the Age of Wycliffe* (2d ed.; New York, 1899), p. 117.

[30] Trevelyan, p. 113, maintains that the ecclesiastical courts were no worse than the civil. Whatever the comparison is worth, it in no way lessens the venality of consistory.

[31] Wright, *Pol. Poems*, I, 263-70.

[32] Even Augustus Jessopp, *The Coming of the Friars and Other Historic Essays* (London, 1908), p. 50, concedes that Minorites, Dominicans, and their imitators had by the fourteenth century lost the pristine holiness which characterized the begging friars who first came to England more than a century before.

[33] Joseph Hall (ed.), *The Poems of Laurence Minot* (Oxford, 1887), has in this and subsequent editions collected all the extant material bearing on Minot's verse, including sketches of Edward's military operations.

[34] But see Ten Brink, *Hist. Eng. Lit.*, I, 322: "Minot seems to have been only a glee-man, though one about to become a minstrel; that is, to find permanent employment in the household of some nobleman."

[35] Hall, p. 21. Cf. the headlink to the following poem, p. 27.

[36] *Ibid.*, p. 73.

[37] Rhys, *Lyric Poetry*, p. 104.

[38] Hall, p. 85.

[39] *Ibid.*, p. 45.

[40] Rhys, p. 106, suspects that Minot's lyrics were sung.

[41] See the discussion of G. H. McKnight (ed.), *Middle English Humorous Tales in Verse* (Boston and London, 1913), pp. ix-xxi.

[42] Numbers 15:32-6.

[43] O. F. Emerson, "Legends of Cain, Especially in Old and Middle English," *PMLA*, XXI (1906), 841-45. See also Sabine Baring-Gould, *Curious Myths of the Middle Ages* (new ed.; New York, 1897), pp. 190-208.

44 See R. J. Menner, "The Man in the Moon and Hedging," *JEGP*, XLVIII (1949), 7-11.

45 Seymour, *A-ILit.*, p. 109. The verse is from Harley 913, a miscellaneous collection associated with Ireland.

46 Wright-Halliwell, *Rel. Ant.*, II, 175.

47 Cf. a fragmentary poem probably by Richart de Semilli (late twelfth century), in which each stanza begins with a prayer to a saint, edited by Alfred Jeanroy, "Notes sur le tournoiement des dames," *Romania*, XXVIII (1899), 237.

48 The manuscript has been thought to be the work of a Friar Michael of Kildare, but Seymour, p. 52, regards only the religious poem *Sweet Jesus* as his.

49 Wright-Halliwell, *Rel. Ant.*, I, 240. Kenneth Sisam (ed.), *Fourteenth Century Verse & Prose* (Oxford, 1921), p. 169, dates the poem 1425-50, but Wells, *Manual*, p. 235, notes that the poem is written on a fourteenth-century leaf of MS. Arundel 292.

50 E. P. Kuhl, "Daun Gerveys," *MLN*, XXIX (1914), 156.

51 Wells, p. 235.

52 Those who clothe horses (in armor) and burn water (that is, temper the metal by dipping in cold water).

NOTES FOR CHAPTER FOUR

ART LYRIC: A PRELIMINARY

1 Saintsbury, *Prosody*, I, 45.

2 Sisam, *XIVth Cent. Verse & Prose*, p. xvii, finds the reason for meager lyric remains in the fact that French influence was little felt in the North.

3 Saintsbury, I, 114-20.

4 *Ibid.*, I, 381-87.

5 T. S. Omond, *English Metrists* (Oxford, 1921), p. 251, comments on Saintsbury's unwillingness to recognize quantities.

6 Richard Morris (ed.), *An Old English Miscellany*, EETS, XLIX, London, 1872, p. 94.

7 Saintsbury's *History of English Prosody* and Jakob Schipper's *Englische Metrik* (Bonn, 1881-88) remain the standard works. The latter has been conveniently translated into English in an abridged form, *A History of English Versification* (Oxford, 1910).

8 See J. M. Berdan, "The Influence of the Medieval Latin Rhetorics on the English Writers of the Early Renaissance," *RR*, VII (1916), 305-06; C. S. Lewis, "The Fifteenth-Century Heroic Line," *Essays and Studies by Members of the English Association*, XXIV (1938), 28; C. F. Babcock, "A Study of the Metrical Use of the Inflectional *E* in Middle English, with Particular Reference to Chaucer and Lydgate," *PMLA*, XXIX (1914), 92;

E. P. Hammond, *English Verse Between Chaucer and Surrey* (Durham, N. C., 1927), pp. 17-24.

⁹ Schipper, *A History of English Versification*, p. 98.

¹⁰ Morris, p. 158.

¹¹ Wright, *SLPoetry*, p. 93.

¹² See Guillaume de Machaut, *Poésies lyriques*, ed. V. Chickemaref (Paris, 1909), 2 vols., for numerous ballades and *chansons balladées* set to music by the author. The editor does not print the notation.

¹³ *Lay*, here, is not to be confused with the romances, such as the *lais* of Marie de France, or with the genre described by Deschamps, *L'Art de dictier, Oeuvres*, VII, 287 f. The term could be applied to any lyric; cf. "thou leue vpon mi lay," from a lyric in MS. Harley 2253, ed. Brown, *Lyrics XIIIth Cent.*, p. 140; and the opening couplet of a chanson of Thibaut de Champagne, "Conmencerai / A fere un lai," *Chansons*, p. 216.

¹⁴ *LGW Prol.* F., 422-23. Cf. *CT.*, F. 947-48; Machaut, *Le Remède de Fortune, Oeuvres*, II, ll. 401-06. Deschamps, VII, 274 ff., describes these genres in detail.

¹⁵ *HF.*, 620-23.

¹⁶ Gower, *The English Works*, ed. G. C. Macaulay, EETSES, LXXXII, London, 1901, Bk. VIII, ll. 2941-46.

¹⁷ Robinson, *Chaucer's Comp. Wks.*, p. 330.

¹⁸ Lydgate, *Fall of Princes*, ed. Henry Bergen, EETSES, CXXI, London, 1924, Bk. I, ll. 351-53. Cf. *LGW Prol.* F., 422-23, and *CT.*, F. 947-48.

¹⁹ Ten Brink, *Hist. Eng. Lit.*, II (Pt. 1), 191.

²⁰ T. R. Lounsbury, *Studies in Chaucer* (New York, 1892), I, 357 ff.

²¹ Robinson, p. 612.

²² J. M. Manly (ed.), *Canterbury Tales* (New York, 1928), p. 503, thought it likely that Chaucer composed music, though more recently C. C. Olson, "Chaucer and the Music of the Fourteenth Century," *Speculum*, XVI (1941), 73, has found no real proof of Chaucer's technical knowledge of the subject.

²³ Robinson, p. 612.

²⁴ Aage Brusendorff, *The Chaucer Tradition* (London, 1925), pp. 432 f.

²⁵ Machaut, *Oeuvres*, II, ll. 2857-92, 3013-36, 431-680, 905-1480, 1985-2032, 3451-96, 4107-14.

²⁶ It was the author's intention to incorporate the *chansons de toile* and other twelfth-century genres so cleverly into the romance that only the court society could perceive them. *Guillaume de Dole*, pp. lxxxix ff. See my article, "Chaucer's Use of Lyric As an Ornament of Style," *CL*, III (1951), 32-46.

²⁷ *Guillaume de Dole*, p. xc.

²⁸ The seventy-nine known lyrics—ballades, rondeaux, and virelayes—of Wenceslas de Bohême, duke of Luxembourg and Brabant, were intercalated in Froissart's romance *Méliador*, ed. Auguste Longnon, SATF, Paris, 1895-99, 3 vols.

²⁹ For the musical setting, see Machaut, *Oeuvres*, II, 1-27 (appendix).

30 *An ABC, Complaint unto Pity, Complaint to His Lady, Complaint of Mars, To Rosemounde, Womanly Noblesse, Adam Scriveyn, Former Age, Fortune, Truth, Gentilesse, Lak of Stedfastnesse, Complaint of Venus, Lenvoy de Chaucer a Scogan, Lenvoy de Chaucer a Bukton, Complaint of Chaucer to His Purse, Against Women Unconstant, Complaynt d'Amours, Merciles Beaute,* and *Balade of Complaint.*

31 *PF.*, 680-92. Perhaps the envoy of the *Clerk's Tale* (*CT.*, E. 1177-1212) should be included.

32 *LGW Prol.* F., 249-69, G. 203-23. The ballade seems inappropriate for the use to which it is put: Chaucer (G. 200-01) observes that the ladies danced as they sang, "as it were in carole-wyse."

33 *BD.*, 475-86, 1175-80.

34 *TC.*, II. 827-75. Robinson's notes refer to the individual studies on the sources of this and other lyrics of the *Troilus.*

35 *TC.*, I. 400-20.

36 *TC.*, III. 1744-71.

37 *TC.*, V. 638-44.

38 *TC.*, V. 1317-1421, 1590-1631.

39 *TC.*, III. 1422-42, 1450-63, 1702-08.

40 C. R. Baskervill, "English Songs on the Night Visit," *PMLA*, XXXVI (1921), 594, considers these songs in relation to the whole tradition.

41 Bartsch, *Chrest.,* p. 168.

42 Child, *Ballads,* IV, 390.

43 The roundel "Now welcome, somer, with thy sonne softe" and another Valentine poem, the *Complaynt d'Amours,* satisfy the conditions rather well.

44 What Chambers has said recently about the fifteenth century in *Eng. Lit.,* p. 122, applies equally well to the last half of the fourteenth: "In the fifteenth century we must be content to take as lyric, besides the carols, for which there is clear evidence of choric singing, most of those pieces which have the more elaborate stanza forms, and in particular those which have refrains; and as narrative those which . . . are, as a rule, in simpler couplet or septenar metres."

45 Cf. *CT.,* F. 77-78, F. 268-71, B². 845-50, E. 271; *LGW,* 2615-17. The professional minstrel, it should be noted, is not one of the company going down to Canterbury. For an excellent discussion of the decadent state of English minstrelsy in Chaucer's time, see Chambers, *Med. Stage,* I, 42-86.

46 Cf. *HF.,* 1197-1226. Further see Olson, pp. 67 f.

47 Holmes, *Intro. OF Lit.,* p. 193.

48 H. L. Cohen, *The Ballade* (New York, 1915), p. 50.

49 See M. F. Bukofzer, "An Unknown Chansonnier of the 15th Century," *Musical Quarterly,* XXVIII (1942), 24 ff.

50 *CT.,* A. 672.

51 *CT.,* A. 237.

52 *CT.,* A. 3216-17.

53 *CT.,* A. 3257.

54 *CT.,* A. 3361-62.

55 W. W. Skeat, "Chanticleer's Song," *Athenaeum,* Oct. 24, 1896, 566.

56 *CT.,* B². 2879.

57 *PF.,* 680-92. Chaucer surely means what he says, "The note, I trowe, imaked was in Fraunce" (l. 677).

58 *CT.,* A. 1510-12.

59 That Chaucer does not distinguish between song and literary lyric is doubtless the fault of the language, as no general term existed for the short poem not designed for singing. The word *lyric* seems not to have been introduced much before 1581, the date of the earliest quotation in the *NED.* His followers use "song" no less loosely. Thomas Hoccleve calls his three roundels "trois chaunceons" and refers to the last, *Humorous Praise of His Lady,* as "our song," *Works,* ed. Israel Gollancz, EETSES, LXXIII, London, 1924, pp. 35, 38. Lydgate completes *A Lover's New Year's Gift* with the injunction "Go forthe in hast, thou lytel songe," *Minor Poems* (Pt. II), ed. H. N. MacCracken, EETS, CXCII, London, 1934, p. 427.

60 J. S. P. Tatlock, "The Epilog of Chaucer's 'Troilus'," *MP,* XVIII (1920-21), 627-31, traces this convention to Ovid, and briefly discusses its use in medieval narrative and lyric poetry, including that of Provence and northern France.

61 Bartsch, *Rom. u. Past.,* p. 55. Cf. Bartsch, p. 15, in which the poet closes on a personal note, "et je, qui ceste chancon fis / sor la rive de mer pansis / comanz a deu bele Aelis."

62 Thibaut de Champagne, *Chansons,* p. 19; cf. Nos. 5 and 14. Cf. Gace Brulé, *Chansons,* p. 98, "Chançons, di li que cil n'a d'amors cure."

63 Wright, *SLPoetry,* p. 63. Cf. the macaronic quatrain, "Scripsi haec carmina in tabulis . . ." *Ibid.,* p. 65.

64 In the opinion of Emile Legouis, *Geoffrey Chaucer,* trans, L. Lailavoix (London and New York, 1913), p. 55, the best of trouvère art had disappeared before Chaucer's time, and *chansons de toile* and *pastourelles* of all descriptions seem to have gone out of style. There is no evidence that would indicate the poet's familiarity with English lyrics on the order of those in the Harleian manuscript.

65 Julleville, *Histoire,* II, 336, observes that the fourteenth century considered trouvère lyric much too free and rustic.

66 Machaut, *Oeuvres,* II, 71.

67 *Ibid.,* p. 110.

68 Deschamps, *Oeuvres,* III, 368.

69 *Ibid.,* p. 390.

70 The theory of Deschamps, VII, 270 f., throws considerable light on the courtly lyric in France and England: "L'autre musique est appellée *naturele* pour ce qu'elle ne puet estre aprinse a nul, se son propre couraige naturelment ne s'i applique, et est une musique de bouche en proferant paroules metrifiées, aucunefoiz en *laiz,* autrefoiz en *balades,* autrefoiz en

rondeaulx cengles et *doubles,* et en *chançons baladées,* qui sont ainsi appellées pour ce que le refrain d'une *balade* sert tousjours par maniere de rubriche a la fin de chascune couple d'icelle, et la *chançon baladée* de trois vers doubles a tousjours, par difference des *balades,* son refrain et rebriche au commencement, que aucuns appellent du temps present *virelays.* Et ja soit ce que ceste musique naturele se face de volunté amoureuse a la louenge des dames, et en autres manieres, selon les materes et le sentement de ceuls qui en ceste musique s'appliquent, et que les faiseurs d'icelle ne saichent pas communement la musique artificiele ne donner chant par art de notes a ce qu'ilz font, toutesvoies est appellée musique ceste science naturele, pour ce que les diz et chançons par eulx faiz ou les livres metrifiez se lisent de bouche, et proferent par voix non pas chantable, tant que les douces paroles ainsis faictes et recordées par voix plaisent aux escoutans qui les oyent, si que au *Puy d'amours* anciennement et encores est acoustumez en pluseurs villes et citez des pais et royaumes du monde."

71 *Ibid.,* VII, 270.

72 *Ibid.,* p. 271.

73 *Ibid.,* I, 248 f.

74 *Ibid.,* II, 140.

75 Dunbar, *Poems,* ed. John Small, STS, II, IV, XVI, XXI, XXIX, Edinburgh and London, 1884-93, II, 10, l. 257.

76 Lydgate, *Fall of Princes,* Bk. I, l. 278.

77 *TC.,* V. 1797-98. Cf. *TC.,* III. 1814.

78 W. W. Skeat (ed.), *The Complete Works of Geoffrey Chaucer* (2d ed.; Oxford, 1894-1900), II, 504, first suggested that "songe" here meant reciting in an intoned voice. Of course, Old English *sang* must be taken occasionally as *poem* without musical implication (*NED, song, q.v.*).

79 *BD.,* 471-74. Cf. the Clerk's statement of his intention just before the envoy, "I wol with lusty herte, fressh and grene, / Seyn yow a song to glade yow, I wene." *CT.,* E. 1173-74.

80 H. J. Chaytor, *The Troubadours* (Cambridge, 1912), p. 22.

81 There are upwards of fifty schemes.

82 Cohen, *Ballade,* p. 222.

83 An otherwise unidentified Quixley of York translated the eighteen ballades of Gower's sequence *Un Traitié selonc les auctours pour essampler les amantz marietz;* see Cohen, pp. 264-66.

84 R. H. Robbins, "The Burden in Carols," *MLN,* LVII (1942), 20, counts twelve Middle English roundels, including four each by Chaucer and Hoccleve and excluding, of course, 102 attributed to Orléans.

85 Deschamps, *Oeuvres,* VII, 274-81. Miss Cohen, pp. 208-21, summarizes the theories of ballade development and codifies allowable variations.

86 H. N. MacCracken, "An English Friend of Charles of Orléans," *PMLA,* XXVI (1911), 179 f.

87 Cohen, pp. 225 ff., documents this laxity in Middle English. Dunbar, it should be added, speaks regularly of "ballattis," by which term he means

neither ballades nor ballads. Proof of this statement comes out in the second poem on James Dog, the queen's wardrober, where the poet refers to the first as a "ballet." Both poems are in octosyllabic quatrains rhyming aabb, with the fourth line a constant refrain.

88 Faral, *Arts poétiques*, p. xiii. Besides Faral, see for general surveys, C. S. Baldwin, *Medieval Rhetoric and Poetic* (New York, 1928), and J. W. H. Atkins, *English Literary Criticism: The Medieval Phase* (New York and Cambridge, 1943).

89 J. M. Manly, "Chaucer and the Rhetoricians," *Proceedings of the British Academy*, XII (1926), 99.

90 *Ibid.*, p. 104.

91 Chaucer's influence figures mightily in the adherence to rhetorical principles, as the fifteenth-century allusions to his stylistic accomplishments clearly indicate.

92 Faral, p. 59.

93 *Ibid.*, pp. 61 ff.

94 For lists of "colours" and tropes, see Faral, pp. 52-54, and Baldwin, pp. 304 f.

95 Manly, p. 95.

96 *CT.*, B². 3347-54.

97 Robinson, *Chaucer's Comp. Wks.*, p. 861.

98 Cf. Faral, p. 208.

99 Manly, p. 110.

100 Alexander Chalmers, *The Works of the English Poets* (London, 1810), I, 558-60.

101 Cf. Faral, p. 59.

102 Apostrophe in medieval usage consisted of an address to any person or thing, whether, by the reckoning of the Ancients, actually apostrophe or merely *exclamatio*. Faral, p. 71.

103 The third stanza alone affords examples of *exclamatio, pronominatio, dissolutio, repetitio,* and *translatio*.

104 J. C. Mendenhall, *Aureate Terms* (Lancaster, Pa., 1919), p. 10.

105 *Ibid.*, p. 13.

106 The extent to which Chaucer introduced new words remains in doubt. See Joseph Mersand, *Chaucer's Romance Vocabulary* (Brooklyn, 1937), and the dissenting opinion of J. R. Hulbert, *PQ*, XXVI (1947), 302-06.

NOTES FOR CHAPTER FIVE

THE CHAUCERIAN LYRIC MODE

1 The *canso* passed over intact to northern France, where Chrétien de Troyes composed *Amors tençon et bataille* and *D'amor qui m'a tolu a moi* in the Provençal style before 1180. See Voretzsch, *Intro. OF Lit.*, pp. 290 f., 327.

236   NOTES FOR CHAPTER V

2 G. C. Macaulay (ed.), *The Complete Works of John Gower* (Oxford, 1899-1902), I, lxxii f., argues for a late date, that is, the several years prior to 1399 when the poet seems to have lost his sight.

3 Jeanroy, *Origines*, p. xviii, maintained that until the end of the twelfth century in northern France the poets addressed the whole population, not just the court.

4 *PF.*, 225-26.

5 Machaut, *Oeuvres*, II, 72.

6 Cf. the rubrics of Deschamps' Ballades Nos. 1279-87 (*Oeuvres*, VII): "L'amour n'existe pas sans jalousie," "Il est toujours bon de se nantir d'un gage," "Les arts mécaniques procèdent des arts libéraux," "Du mariage d'Anthoine, filz de monseigneur de Bourgogne," "Des bonnes gens du temps ancien," "Dieu nous punit de nos fautes," "Les clercs échappent à la justice séculière," "Comment Rome fut imperial monarchie . . . ," "Comment l'auteur maudit cellui qui le requerra de combatre."

7 Robinson, *Chaucer's Comp. Wks.*, p. 974.

8 Hammond, *Eng. Verse*, pp. 4-6.

9 History takes a bleak view of Hoccleve's versified denunciation of Sir John Oldcastle for entertaining heretical beliefs; the poem is a melancholy commentary on fifteenth-century religious intolerance.

10 Hoccleve, *Works*, ed. F. J. Furnivall, EETSES, LXI, London, 1892, pp. 25-39; this volume also contains the life records.

11 Hoccleve, *Works*, EETSES, LXI, ix ff.

12 EETSES, LXXII, London, 1897, p. 75.

13 EETSES, LXI, xxxiv f.

14 Cf. the oblique attack on Oldcastle in a poem on Lollardry by an unknown author of the period. Wright, *Pol. Poems*, II, 243-47.

15 EETSES, LXI, 59-64.

16 Cf. Colin Muset's *Sire cuens, j'ai vielé*, ed. Joseph Bédier, *Les Chansons* (Paris, 1938), pp. 9-10, which rather demands than requests; Rutebeuf's address to Louis IX, ed. Achille Jubinal, *Oeuvres complètes* (Paris, 1874), I, 1-4; and the cringing petition of a *clericus vagans*, *Carm. Bur.*, p. 50.

17 EETSES, LXXIII, 35-37.

18 EETSES, LXI, 62.

19 EETSES, LXXIII, 37. Utley, *Crooked Rib*, pp. 218 f., 213, briefly discusses the type. For other invidious portraits of the fifteenth century, see *I haue a lady where so she bee* and *O mossie quince hanging by your stalke*, Chalmers, *Eng. Poets*, I, 563 f.; *Vnto you most froward this lettre I write* and *O fresch floure most plesant of pryse*, ed. R. H. Robbins, "Two Middle English Satiric Love Epistles," *MLR*, XXXVII (1942), 416 f.

20 George Saintsbury, "The English Chaucerians," *CHEL*, II, 225 f.

21 "Voluminous, prosaic, and drivelling monk," quoted from Saintsbury, p. 234.

22 Mendenhall, *Aureate Terms*, p. 46.

23 Lydgate, *Minor Poems II*, p. 417.

24 Robert Steele (ed.), *Lydgate and Burgh's Secrees of Old Philisoffres*, EETSES, LXVI, London, 1894, pp. xxxi f.

25 *A Selection from the Minor Poems of Dan John Lydgate*, Percy Soc., II, London, 1840.

26 Hammond, *Eng. Verse*, pp. 237, 208 f., presents the arguments against these attributions. See also Hammond, "London Lickpenny," *Anglia*, XX (1898), 409, and MacCracken's discussion of the Lydgate canon, *Minor Poems* (Pt. I), EETSES, CVII, London, 1911, p. xlvii.

27 *CHEL*, II, 232.

28 For a contemporary English account of the battle and capture of Orléans, see the ragged narrative poem printed by Wright, *Pol. Poems*, II, 125-27.

29 Robert Steele (ed.), *The English Poems of Charles of Orleans*, EETS, CCXV, London, 1941, p. xxi.

30 *Ibid.*, pp. xxvi ff.

31 *Ibid.*, pp. xxxiv f.

32 Cf. Ballades 57-65. Steele, pp. xxix f., tentatively dates these ballades in 1436-37.

33 Steele, p. xli.

34 *Ibid.*, p. xl.

35 See Robert Steele and Mabel Day, *The English Poems of Charles of Orleans* (Pt. II), EETS, CCXX, London, 1946, p. 43.

36 Cf. Gaston Raynaud (ed.), *Rondeaux et autres poésies du XVᵉ siècle*, SATF, Paris, 1889, p. 25.

37 Both Chaucer and Deschamps were interested in this convention. See G. L. Kittredge, "Chaucer and Some of His Friends," *MP*, I (1903-04), 1-7, and G. L. Marsh, "Sources and Analogues of 'The Flower and the Leaf'," *MP*, IV (1906-07), 121-67, 281-327.

38 See W. A. Neilson, *The Origins and Sources of the Court of Love* (Boston, 1899), pp. 200 f.

39 By the insistence of the Church upon the wickedness of carnal love, orthodox poets had been reduced to speaking of the flesh in very general terms. See C. S. Lewis, *The Allegory of Love* (Oxford, 1936), p. 17.

40 Cohen, *Ballade*, p. 48, observes that on one occasion the circle composed ballades on the theme of a given refrain, the paradoxical, "Je meurs de soif auprès de la fontaine." For further examples of this inane practice, notice the several lyrics composed on a common first line: "En la forest de Longue Atente," "En la montaigne de Tristesse," and "Pour acquerir honneur et pris." Raynaud, pp. 30-131 *passim*.

41 H. N. MacCracken, "An English Friend of Charles of Orléans," *PMLA*, XXVI (1911), 142-80, edits the verse and discusses the relationships. For evidence that Suffolk was not the author of the English poems, see M. M. Crow, "John of Angoulême and His Chaucer Manuscript," *Speculum*, XVII (1942), 89.

42 *DNB, Pole, William de la, q.v.*

⁴³ Cf. "This Fox at Bury slowe oure grete gandere [Gloucester]," *On the Arrest of the Duke of Suffolk*, Wright, *Pol. Poems*, II, 224; and the wooden elegy on Gloucester's death, ed. F. J. Furnivall, *The Babees Book*, EETS, XXXII, London, 1868, pp. cxix f.

⁴⁴ Frederic Madden, "Political Poems of the Reigns of Henry VI and Edward IV," *Archaeologia*, XXIX (1842), 320. Cf. Dunbar's *Dregy* and Skelton's *Philip Sparrow*.

⁴⁵ Wright, *Pol. Poems*, II, 224 f. From the same manuscript comes the most elaborate specimen of the period (*ibid.*, pp. 221-23), in which the political situation during the troubled 1440's is concisely represented, and the participants identified by means of conspicuous features of their coats-of-arms. A contemporary gloss supplies the identifications.

⁴⁶ Hardin Craig (ed.), *Two Coventry Corpus Christi Plays*, EETSES, LXXXVII, London, 1902, pp. 110-14.

⁴⁷ M. D. Harris (ed.), *The Coventry Leet Book* (Pt. II), EETS, CXXXV, London, 1908, pp. 391-93.

⁴⁸ Harris, *The Coventry Leet Book* (Pt. III), EETS, CXXXVIII, London, 1909, pp. 589-91.

⁴⁹ James Raine (ed.), *A Volume of English Miscellanies*, Surtees Soc., LXXXV, London, 1890, pp. 54-57.

⁵⁰ Cf. Hoccleve's addresses, EETSES, LXI, 39-62 *passim*.

⁵¹ *Minor Poems* II, p. 625. Cf. the aureate address of Charles d'Orléans to Cupid, EETS, CCXV, 100.

⁵² Cohen, *Ballade*, p. 46. Cf. Chaucer's *Fortune, Lak of Stedfastnesse*, and *Complaint of Venus*.

⁵³ R. H. Robbins, "Two Middle English Satiric Love Epistles," *MLR*, XXXVII (1942), 420.

⁵⁴ F. M. Padelford, "The Songs in Manuscript Rawlinson C. 813," *Anglia*, XXXI (1908), 341-46.

⁵⁵ *Ibid.*, pp. 368 f.

⁵⁶ *Ibid.*, pp. 356 f.

⁵⁷ *Ibid.*, pp. 357 f. The author of No. 37 (pp. 370 f.) calls his work successively "byll," "queare," and "letter."

⁵⁸ F. J. Furnivall (ed.), *Political, Religious, and Love Poems* (rev. ed.), EETS, XV, London, 1903, pp. 71 f. This lyric, however, is indexed under *Epistles* by Brown-Robbins, *Index*, p. 753. Another lyric in the same manuscript, *Iuellis pricious cane y none fynde to Sell* (Furnivall, pp. 66 f.), has a complimentary close and was perhaps intended as a letter.

⁵⁹ Nevertheless, *letter* and *bill* are intimately associated. Cf. John Myrc, *Instructions for Parish Priests* (1450), "All that falsen the popes lettres or billes or seales," quoted by *NED*.

⁶⁰ Cf. *Goe, lytyll byll, & doe me recommende*, ed. Brown, *Lyrics XVth Cent.*, pp. 75 f.

⁶¹ *TC.*, V. 1317-1421, 1590-1631. Cf. the English note, from an abbot to a nun, intercalated in an Anglo-Norman poem of the early fourteenth

century, Paul Meyer, "Mélanges anglo-normands," *Romania*, XXXVIII (1909), 437.

62 J. S. P. Tatlock, "The Epilog of Chaucer's Troilus," *MP*, XVIII (1920-21), 627.

63 See Carl Appel (ed.), *Provenzalische Chrestomathie* (6th ed.; Leipzig, 1930), pp. 63, 69, cited by Tatlock.

64 Thibaut de Champagne, *Chansons*, pp. 15, 19, 33, 47.

65 Leo Wiese (ed.), *Die Lieder des Blondel de Nesle* (Dresden, 1904), p. 142. Cf. No. 8.

66 Wright, *SLPoetry*, p. 64. Cf. "Einen brief ich sande einer vrowen gut," *Carm. Bur.*, No. 140a.

67 G. C. Macaulay (ed.), *The Complete Works of John Gower* (Oxford, 1899-1902), I, 339-41.

68 *Ibid.*, p. 339. Cf. two letters of Deschamps, *Oeuvres*, VII, 122-25; Cohen, *Ballade*, pp. 106-08. Miss Cohen, pp. 44 f., discusses the development of the ballade envoy in the *puys*.

69 Tatlock, pp. 629 f., found no author earlier than Boccaccio who used the envoy with longer works (e.g., *Teseide, Filostrato*). The Italian poet otherwise used the envoy conventionally in short lyrical poems.

70 *TC.*, V. 1786. Cf. the envoy to Hoccleve's *Regement of Princes*, EETSES, LXXII, 196, and J. Schick's notes to Lydgate's *Temple of Glas*, EETSES, LX, London, 1891, p. 122. Further, see Tatlock, p. 630.

71 Arthur Piaget, *Oton de Grandson: Sa vie et ses poésies* (Lausanne, 1941), pp. 132 f.; for the Valentine verse, see pp. 183, 226, 256, 309, 481.

72 See Haldeen Braddy, *Chaucer and the French Poet Graunson* (Baton Rouge, La., 1947), pp. 71 ff., for a discussion of the Valentine tradition.

73 *Encyl. Brit.*, 11th ed., *Valentine, q.v.*

74 Ewald Flügel (ed.), *Neuenglisches Lesebuch* (Halle, 1895), p. 39. Cf. examples collected by Bernhard Fehr, "Die Lieder des Fairfax MS.," *ASNS*, CVI (1901), 54; J. R. Kreuzer, "Some Earlier Examples of the Rhetorical Device in *Ralph Roister Doister* (III.iv.33 ff.)," *RES*, XIV (1938), 323; R. H. Robbins, "Punctuation Poems—A Further Note," *RES*, XV (1939), 206.

75 F. J. Furnivall (ed.), *Political, Religious, and Love Poems* (rev. ed.), EETS, XV, London, 1903, p. 260.

76 W. W. Skeat (ed.), *Chaucerian and Other Pieces* (Oxford, 1897), pp. 359 f.

77 Deschamps, *Oeuvres*, I, 81, 95.

78 Cohen, *Ballade*, pp. 51 f.

79 MacCracken, *PMLA*, XXVI, 179 f. See also two curious French poems, Seymour, *A-lLit.*, pp. 91 f.

80 The increasing popularity of octosyllables is evidenced by *fin de siècle* collections, notably MS. Rawlinson C. 813, edited by F. M. Padelford. *Anglia*, XXXI (1908), 309-97, and MS. Cambridge Univ. Ff.I.6.

81 *To My Lady Dear*, ed. Furnivall, EETS, XV, 69 f.

[82] *Now wold I fayne some myrthis make,* Wright-Halliwell, *Rel. Ant.,* I, 25.

[83] Also in Bodl. 6668. Chambers-Sidgwick, *EELyrics,* pp. 32 f., print a composite text.

[84] *Continuance / of remembraunce,* Wright-Halliwell, *Rel. Ant.,* I, 25 f., written in eighteen two-stress lines, is vaguely reminiscent of three lyrics of Charles d'Orléans, EETS, CCXV, 151 f.; the third poem, *My self walkyng all allone, Rel. Ant.,* I, 26, is without metrical distinction.

[85] Wright-Halliwell, *Rel. Ant.,* I, 169.

[86] Brown-Robbins, *Index,* p. 359.

[87] Cf. the following poems from Rawlinson C. 813: *Right best beloved & most in assurance* and *O resplendent floure! prynte this yn your mynde, Anglia,* XXXI, 395-97, 370 f.; and the Chaucer apocrypha, *Assembly of Ladies* and *The Flower and the Leaf,* both purporting to be the work of women.

[88] James Gairdner (ed.), *The Paston Letters* (Edinburgh, 1910), III, 170.

[89] *As I came by a bowre soo fayr, As I stode yn a parke streyght vpe by a tree,* and *Throughe a forest as I can ryde.* Padelford, *Anglia,* XXXI, Nos. 2, 20, 40.

[90] *Iesue, that ys most of myght, O my lady dere, bothe regarde & see,* and *O excelent suffereigne, most semely to see. Ibid.,* Nos. 4, 13, 32.

[91] *Anglia,* XXXI, 366. Cf. *With wooful hert & gret mornyng,* for another ludicrous portrait. Bernhard Fehr, "Weitere Beiträge zur englischen Lyrik des 15. und 16. Jahrhunderts," *ASNS,* CVII (1902), 53 f.

[92] W. T. Ritchie (ed.), *The Bannatyne Manuscript,* STSNS, XXIII, Edinburgh and London, 1928, p. 272.

[93] *Anglia,* XXXI, 372.

NOTES FOR CHAPTER SIX

THE DEBRIS OF THE TRANSITION

[1] Chambers, *Med. Stage,* I, 65 f.

[2] Chappell, *Pop. Music,* I, 47.

[3] *Satire on Edinburgh,* Dunbar, *Poems,* ii, 262.

[4] *Eneados,* Bk. 12, ed. John Small, *The Poetical Works of Gavin Douglas* (Edinburgh and London, 1874), IV, 86.

[5] *The New Chronicles of England and France,* reprinted from Pynson's edition of 1516 (London, 1811), p. 420.

[6] Virtually all of the carols written before 1550 are collected in Greene's *Early English Carols;* many of the 474 complete specimens survive in several versions. Among the earlier collections, the most useful for the study of secular carols are Chambers-Sidgwick, *Early English Lyrics;* Roman Dyboski (ed.), *Songs, Carols, and Other Miscellaneous Poems,* EETSES,

CI, London, 1908; M. R. James and G. C. Macaulay, "Fifteenth Century Carols and Other Pieces," *MLR*, VIII (1913), 68-87; Ewald Flügel, "Liedersammlungen des XVI. Jahrhunderts, besonders aus der Zeit Heinrich's VIII," *Anglia*, XII (1889), 225-72; Thomas Wright, *Songs and Carols*, Warton Club, IV, London, 1856, and *Songs and Carols of the Fifteenth Century*, Percy Soc., XXIII, London, 1847.

7 Greene, p. xxiii. Chambers, *Eng. Lit.*, p. 86, prefers the traditional designation *refrain*, since the term *burden* for the external repeated element did not come in until 1589.

8 Chambers, *Eng. Lit.*, p. 87, maintains that a third of the carols are associated with the Christmas season, though Greene's conclusion that the carol was not essentially a Yuletide form is not thereby disturbed.

9 Chambers, *Eng. Lit.*, p. 113. See Greene, *Carols*, p. xcv.

10 James Graves, "English and Norman Songs of the Fourteenth Century," *N&Q*, 1st Ser., II (1850), 385 f., seems to have been the first to call attention to these fragments.

11 Seymour, *A-ILit.*, pp. 73, 96-98, discusses the problem and prints the scraps.

12 STS, XXXIX, London and Edinburgh, 1897. See A. M. Mackenzie, *An Historical Survey of Scottish Literature to 1714* (London, 1933), p. 160.

13 Cf. the experiences of Sharp, *Folk Songs*, I, xxiii.

14 W. C. Hazlitt (ed.), *Remains of the Early Popular Poetry of England* (London, 1864-66), III, 2-22.

15 R. H. Robbins, "The Earliest Carols and the Franciscans," *MLN*, LIII (1938), 245.

16 See Hazlitt, I, 159 f.

17 Thomas Wright (ed.), *The Latin Poems Commonly Attributed to Walter Mapes*, Camden Soc., XVI, London, 1841, p. 223.

18 *Ibid.*, pp. 355 f. Cf. *Carm. Bur.*, pp. 43-45.

19 Wright, pp. 357-59.

20 Annie Abram, *Social England in the Fifteenth Century* (London and New York, 1909), p. 222.

21 W. E. Mead, *The English Medieval Feast* (London, 1931), pp. 38 f.

22 Hazlitt, *Remains*, I, 161-67.

23 *Versus de Nummo*, ed. Wright, p. 355; cf. *De Cruce Denarii*, p. 223.

24 *Ibid.*, p. 361.

25 *Ibid.*, p. 362.

26 Percy Soc., XXIII, 35 f.

27 E. P. Hammond, "London Lickpenny," *Anglia*, XX (1898), 409, argues that the characteristic features of Lydgate's style are entirely wanting.

28 *Ibid.*, p. 408.

29 F. Holthausen, "London Lickpenny," *Anglia*, XLIII (1919), 61-68.

30 W. W. Skeat (ed.), *Specimens of English Literature* (6th ed.; Oxford, 1892), pp. 373-76, explains the topical allusions.

31 Greene, *Carols*, p. 439.

32 *Ibid.*, p. 440. Cf. Wright, *Pol. Poems*, II, 141-48.

33 Child, *Ballads,* Nos. 1, 3.

34 Warton Club, IV, 33 f. Cf. the *Four Sisters, ibid.,* pp. 109-15; the *Ballad of Lord Roslin's Daughter,* Child, *Ballads,* No. 46 B.

35 Sharp, *Folk Songs,* II, 190 f.

36 Cf. the jocular account of the killing of a boar for Christmas. Percy Soc., XXIII, 25 f.

37 Thomas Wright (ed.), *Specimens of Old Christmas Carols,* Percy Soc., IV, London, 1841, p. 50.

38 Greene, *Carols,* p. ci.

39 Chambers, *Med. Stage,* I, 251, remarks, "Obviously amongst other evergreens the holly and the ivy, with their clustering pseudo-blossoms of coral and of jet, are the more adequate representatives of the fertilization spirit . . ."

40 Staminate and pistillate flowers are thought to occur seldom, if ever, on the same plant. Hence, fruiting is contingent upon the proximity of plants of opposite sex. The gender of Old English *holen* "holly" is masculine, but *ifig* "ivy" is neuter.

41 Hilderic Friend, *Flowers and Flower Lore* (2d ed.; London, 1884), p. 253, observes, "On Shrove Tuesday, Ash Wednesday, or some other early day in Lent, it used to be customary in France and England to carry round garlands of flowers, and dress effigies called the Holly-boy and Ivy-girl, which they burnt."

42 Many varieties are known. A gray-mottled type with yellow margin may correspond to "variegated."

43 Thomas Ratcliffe, "Evergreens at Christmas," *N&Q,* 11th Ser., VI (1912), 486.

44 Greene, p. c.

45 George Gascoigne, *The Complete Works,* ed. J. W. Cunliffe (Cambridge, 1907-10), II, 126 f.

46 Friend, p. 263.

47 G. L. Kittredge, "Note on a Lying Song," *JAF,* XXXIX (1926), 195-99, discusses this type, citing examples from America and Europe.

48 See Utley's discussions and full bibliography, *Crooked Rib,* pp. 45 f., 133 f. *et seq.*

49 J. A. H. Murray (ed.), *The Romance and Prophecies of Thomas of Erceldoune,* EETS, LXI, London, 1875, p. xviii.

50 On port receipts, see Mead, p. 125.

51 See Fred Brittain (ed.), *Medieval Latin and Romance Lyric to A.D. 1300* (Cambridge, 1937), pp. 144 f. Also preserved in MS. Reg. 16. E.viii, is a parody of the *Sequence Laetabundas,* which is another disguised begging song. See Wright-Halliwell, *Rel. Ant.,* II, 168 f., for the text; and Greene's comments, p. xxvi. See also the macaronic drinking song of MS. Bodleian 3340—*Fetys bele chere,* ed. F. M. Padelford, "English Songs in Manuscript Selden B. 26," *Anglia,* XXXVI (1912), 109.

52 Warton Club, IV, 92.

[53] See the *Latin Poems Commonly Attributed to Walter Mapes*, Camden Soc., XVI, London, 1841, p. 73.

[54] *Carm. Bur.*, pp. 240 f.

[55] Intercalated in *Gammer Gurton's Needle* (III, i, 1), though doubtless older than the comedy. Chambers-Sidgwick, *EELyrics*, pp. 229-31, prints a superior version. See A. C. Baugh, "A Fraternity of Drinkers," *Philologica: The Malone Anniversary Studies* (Baltimore, 1949), pp. 200-07.

[56] The works of Marbod and Hildebert may be consulted in Migne, *Patrologia Latina*, CLXXI; and those of Bernard and Neckham in the *Anglo-Latin Satirical Poets and Epigrammatists of the Twelfth Century*, Rolls Series, LIX, ii. The prose and poetry attributed to and associated with Mapes have been edited by Thomas Wright for the Camden Soc. (XVI, L).

[57] Utley, *Crooked Rib*, pp. 3-5. This book indexes all of the Middle English and early Renaissance writings bearing directly on the subject; many of the discussions of individual poems and types are very full.

[58] See Jean de Meun and Guillaume de Lorris, *Le Roman de la Rose*, ed. Ernest Langlois, SATF, Paris, 1914-24, ll. 8281-9360, 13265-14006.

[59] Langlois, *Origines et sources du Roman de la Rose* (Paris, 1891), pp. 101 ff.

[60] B. H. Dow, *The Varying Attitude Toward Women in French Literature of the Fifteenth Century* (New York, 1936), pp. 145-52.

[61] Brown, *Lyrics XIIIth Cent.*, pp. 101-07.

[62] F. Holthausen, "Die Quelle des mittelenglischen Gedichtes 'Lob der Frauen'," *ASNS*, CVIII (1902), 288-301, prints the original and the translation.

[63] See my articles, "Alysoun's Other Tonne," *MLN*, LIX (1944), 481-83; "The Pardoner's Interruption of the *Wife of Bath's Prologue*," *MLQ*, X (1949), 49-57.

[64] Henry Bergen (ed.), *Troy Book*, EETSES, XCVII, London, 1906, pp. 73-75; CIII, 1908, pp. 517-22.

[65] Bergen, *Fall of Princes*, EETSES, CXXI, London, 1924, pp. 132 f., 184-89.

[66] Lydgate, *Minor Poems* II, pp. 456-60. This volume contains numerous other brief satires of women.

[67] A scurrilous lyric of Harley 2253—*Lord that lenest vs lyf ant lokest vch an lede*—is probably the earliest English satire of feminine apparel.

[68] Utley, p. 64, puts the number of satires and defenses written between 1500 and 1568 at 250.

[69] See the *Bannatyne Manuscript*, ed. W. T. Ritchie, STSNS, XXII, 1928; XXIII, 1928; XXVI, 1930; 3d Ser., V, 1933, Edinburgh and London.

[70] J. O. Halliwell-[Phillipps] (ed.), *Nugae Poeticae* (London, 1844), pp. 37-39.

[71] STSNS, XXVI, 34-36.

[72] *Ibid.*, pp. 64-70.

[73] Chalmers, *Eng. Poets*, I, 563 f.

[74] *Ibid.*, p. 560.

[75] Joseph Bédier, *Les Fabliaux* (5th ed.; Paris, 1925), p. 321.

[76] See Utley, pp. 157 f., and a detailed history of the device by Irving Linn, "If All the Sky Were Parchment," *PMLA*, LIII (1938), 951-70.

[77] Greene, p. 433.

[78] Wright-Halliwell, *Rel. Ant.*, I, 24.

[79] *Ibid.*, I, 202.

[80] The burden, "Up son and mery wethir, / somer drawith nere," is irrelevant and may have been detached from a more popular song.

[81] Greene, p. 452.

[82] Bernhard Fehr, "Weitere Beiträge zur englischen Lyrik des 15. und 16. Jahrhunderts," *ASNS*, CVII (1901), 57.

[83] Wright-Halliwell, I, 1.

[84] Greene, p. 448. Strict prohibitions against well-wakes are preserved even from Anglo-Saxon times. See C. R. Baskervill, "Dramatic Aspects of Medieval Folk Festivals in England," *SP*, XVII (1920), 23 f.

[85] Frazer, *Golden Bough*, V, 246.

[86] *Ibid.*, II, 272.

[87] Baskervill, pp. 51-53, discusses the various activities of the occasion.

[88] Warton Club, IV, 35.

[89] Greene, p. 279.

[90] EETSES, CI, 111.

[91] The book is perhaps better known as Arnold's *Chronicle;* it may have been published in 1503. See *Camb. Biblio. of Eng. Lit.*, I, 823.

[92] W. W. Skeat (ed.), *Specimens of English Literature* (6th ed.; Oxford, 1892), p. 407, rejects Douce's contention that the source was a German translation of a Latin poem, *Vulgaris Cantio.* For analogues and discussions, see Hazlitt, *Remains*, II, 271 f.; Chambers-Sidgwick, *EELyrics*, p. 335; and Utley, *Crooked Rib*, pp. 114 f.

[93] See J. W. Hales and F. J. Furnivall (eds.), *Bishop Percy's Folio Manuscript* (London, 1868), III, 174 ff.

[94] F. B. Gummere, "Ballads," *CHEL*, II, 463.

[95] J. M. Berdan, *Early Tudor Poetry* (New York, 1920), p. 153.

[96] *Ibid.*, p. 149.

[97] *Ibid.*, p. 156. On the preceding page, Berdan surmises that the poet was "familiar with the Medieval Latin treatises."

[98] Jakob Schipper, *Englische Metrik* (Bonn, 1881-88), I, 365-67.

[99] Saintsbury, *Prosody*, I, 257.

[100] *Carm. Bur.*, p. 1. Here and elsewhere the couplets are printed in a single line to facilitate comparison. Schipper, p. 366, cites examples from Provençal and French also.

[101] Hazlitt, *Remains*, II, 272 f. Skeat, pp. 97 ff., prints each stanza as six septenaries, which clearly suggest the origin of the pattern.

[102] G. G. Perry (ed.), *Religious Pieces in Prose and Verse* (rev. ed.), EETS, XXVI, London, 1889, pp. 80-83.

[103] Saintsbury, *Prosody*, I, 257.

[104] *Anelida and Arcite*, ll. 272-80, 333-41.

[105] Greene, *Carols*, p. 193, dates the carol *ca.* 1372.

[106] Cf. Nos. 45, 93, 112, 146, 150, 151, 261, 270, 271, 462 in Greene's collection.

[107] Dunbar, *Poems*, ii, 168 f.

[108] W. W. Skeat (ed.), *The Romans of Partenay* (rev. ed.), EETS, XXII, London, 1899, p. vi.

[109] Child, *Ballads*, III, 4.

[110] *Ibid.*, IV, 390. Anapestic rhythm has here, as in many modern ballads, practically replaced the iambic.

[111] B. A. Botkin (ed.), *A Treasury of American Folklore* (New York, 1944), p. 108.

[112] Chambers, *Eng. Lit.*, p. 121.

[113] Berdan, p. 155.

[114] Jeanroy, *Origines*, p. 48.

[115] See Wells, *Manual*, pp. 411 ff.

[116] Brown, *Lyrics XIIIth Cent.*, pp. 101-07.

[117] J. O. Halliwell-[Phillipps] (ed.), *Nugae Poeticae* (London, 1844), pp. 37-39.

[118] This subject has been thoroughly explored in the *Crooked Rib, supra.*

[119] "The Scottish Chaucerians," *CHEL*, II, 283.

[120] Though surely intended in a general sense, *translated* is an unfortunate word in this context.

[121] H. J. C. Grierson and J. C. Smith, *A Critical History of English Poetry* (New York, 1946), p. 61.

[122] Thus defined by H. H. Wood (ed.), *The Poems and Fables of Robert Henryson* (Edinburgh and London, 1933), p. 266.

[123] A dramatized *pastourelle.* Adan's indebtedness to older *pastourelles* has been documented by Ernest Langlois (ed.), *Le Jeu de Robin et Marion* (Paris, 1924), pp. 58-68. This little drama in 780 lines bears no real resemblance to *Robene and Makyne.*

[124] G. G. Smith (ed.), *The Poems of Robert Henryson*, STS, LXIV, Edinburgh and London, 1914, I, lvi.

[125] W. P. Jones, "A Source for Henryson's Robene and Makyne?" *MLN*, XLVI (1931), 457 f. In the *Pastourelle* (Cambridge, Mass., 1931), p. 168, Jones does not press the case for indebtedness. Wood, p. 266, though unconvinced by Jones, nevertheless declares that the poem is "considerably indebted, in form and spirit, to the old French and Provençal *pastourelles* . . ."

[126] The Robin of the French poem rejects the love of one shepherdess and flies to another. Repulsed by the second, he returns to the first, only to be told, "mais or changie m'ai," Bartsch, *Rom. u. Past.*, pp. 303-05.

[127] Robin is also a common ballad name. Cf. Child, *Ballads*, Nos. 57, 80, 97, among others, exclusive of the Robin Hood ballads.

[128] Jeanroy, *Origines*, pp. 2-5.

129 Here as elsewhere the edition of the poem used is STS, LVIII, iii, 90-94.

130 Child, *Ballads*, II, 182.

131 Chaucer uses the formula in *An ABC.* Cf. *Quy à la dame de parays,* ed. Wright, *SLPoetry,* pp. 1-13, and the translation in the Auchinleck MS., compared with the original, F. Holthausen, "Die Quelle des mittelenglischen Gedichtes 'Lob der Frauen'," *ASNS,* CVIII (1902), 288-301.

132 "We alle desiren . . . / To han housbondes hardy, wise, and free, / And secree, and no nygard, ne no fool, / Ne hym that is agast of every tool, / Ne noon avauntour . . ." *CT.,* B². 2913-17.

133 Smith, I, lvi.

134 Child, *Ballads,* II, 488. Cf. Versions B, C, E. The proverb occurs in Thomas Preston's *Cambyses King of Persia* (1569-70), "Ye are vnwise if ye take not time while ye may: / If ye wil not now when ye would ye shall haue nay," quoted from B. J. Whiting, *Proverbs in the Earlier English Drama* (Cambridge, Mass., 1938), p. 290.

135 Smith, I, 59-61.

NOTES FOR CHAPTER SEVEN

WILLIAM DUNBAR

1 The standard edition of Dunbar's poetry is that of the Scottish Text Society.

2 This is not to minimize the relative excellence of the poems in the *Rose* tradition. See A. M. Mackenzie, *An Historical Survey of Scottish Literature to 1714* (London, 1933), pp. 92 f.

3 "The Scottish Chaucerians," *CHEL,* II, 291. In the *Transition Period* (New York, 1900), p. 53, Smith detected a "certain lyrical tendency" in Dunbar, at the same time remarking, "It is certainly absurd to discover any very distinct lyrical strain . . ."

4 See Smith, *Transition Period,* p. 58.

5 W. M. Mackenzie (ed.), *The Poems of William Dunbar* (Edinburgh, 1932), pp. xviii-xxiv.

6 Jakob Schipper, *William Dunbar: Sein Leben und seine Gedichte* (Berlin, 1884), pp. 77-81, conjectured that the poet went to France in 1491 with a diplomatic mission, sailing on the *Katherine,* as Kennedy declared in the *Flyting;* he may have remained there until 1497 as plenipotentiary of the king.

7 Toward the end of the fourteenth century Gower composed in French his undistinguished *Cinkante Balades,* ed. G. C. Macaulay, *The Complete Works of John Gower* (Oxford, 1899-1902), I, 335-78.

8 Though fully aware that Dunbar "raised lyrics on to a higher stage," Ten Brink, *Hist. Eng. Lit.,* II (Pt. II), 79, praises the poet's lyric talent

uncritically, examining neither the sources nor the conspicuous exemplars of his excellence.

⁹ W. W. Skeat (ed.), *Chaucerian and Other Pieces* (Oxford, 1897), pp. 347-58.

¹⁰ Saintsbury, *Prosody*, I, 291.

¹¹ Dunbar himself seems not to have been a great coiner, although the *NED* gives him credit for *mellifluate* "mellifluous" and *hodiern* "next," among others; and he may have preceded Douglas in using *sugurit* and *firmance* and Kennedy in introducing *umbrakle* "shade." Another Dunbar form, *lucyferat* "light-bearing," seems not to be entered in the *NED*. In general, Dunbar's most striking aureate forms were used earlier, for example, *batalrus, celsitude, matutyne, permansible, beriall, emerant, habitakle, mansuetude, precelling, sempitern,* and *vilipentioun*. P. H. Nichols, "William Dunbar As a Scottish Lydgatian," *PMLA*, XLVI (1931), 223, "Lydgate's Influence on the Aureate Terms of the Scottish Chaucerians," *PMLA*, XLVII (1932), 522, finds Dunbar far more heavily indebted to Lydgate than to Chaucer for his aureate diction.

¹² Mendenhall, *Aureate Terms*, p. 9.

¹³ *CHEL*, II, 291.

¹⁴ See W. M. Mackenzie, pp. xxvii f. Douglas has left some realistic descriptions of wild nature, though he expresses no enthusiasm for the winter scene which he delineates so vividly in the prologue to the seventh book of the *Eneados*, ed. John Small, *The Poetical Works of Gavin Douglas* (Edinburgh and London, 1874), III, 78.

¹⁵ See Dunbar, *Poems*, I, xxix; J. M. Smith, *The French Background of Middle Scots Literature* (London and Edinburgh, 1934), p. 77. Nichols, *PMLA*, XLVI, 214, would refer only the *Testament of Mr. Andro Kennedy* to contemporary French influence, having found that Dunbar resembles Deschamps in his management of themes and that he owes more to Lydgate than to any other single source.

¹⁶ Cf. the *Office for the Dead*, Lydgate's *So as I lay this othir nyght, Minor Poems* II, p. 828; *As I went in a mery mornyng*, Greene, *Carols*, p. 248.

¹⁷ Dunbar, *Poems*, III, 295.

¹⁸ See W. M. Mackenzie, pp. xvii f.

¹⁹ Dunbar, *Poems*, I, xxxii f.

²⁰ The *Petition* is dated before 1510 by the editors of the STS, I, clxvi. If born in 1460 or thereabouts, the poet would have been approaching fifty. The dating of Dunbar's poems is uncertain, however. Schipper set up hypothetical intervals in the poet's career, assigning the individual poems on internal evidence. Mackay generally follows Schipper, STS, I-II, clvii ff. (App. II).

²¹ G. G. Smith, *Scottish Literature: Character and Influence* (London, 1919), p. 5.

²² W. P. Ker, *Form and Style in Poetry*, ed. R. W. Chambers (London, 1928), p. 89. Ker's criticism is gracious by comparison with the pompous

judgment passed by James Russell Lowell in his essay, *Spenser* (1875):
". . . and whoso is national enough to like thistles may browse there
[in Dunbar's verse] to his heart's content. I am inclined for other pasture,
having long ago satisfied myself by a good deal of dogged reading that
every generation is sure of its own share of bores without borrowing from
the past."

INDEX

I

(Titles and first lines of Middle English lyrics)

INDEX

II

Reading and Interpreting the Works of

ALICE WALKER

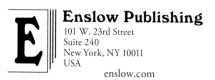

Enslow Publishing
101 W. 23rd Street
Suite 240
New York, NY 10011
USA
enslow.com

Reading and Interpreting the Works of

ALICE WALKER

Lisa A. Crayton

Published in 2017 by Enslow Publishing, LLC
101 W. 23rd Street, Suite 240, New York, NY 10011

Copyright © 2017 by Enslow Publishing, LLC

Library of Congress Cataloging-in-Publication Data

Names: Crayton, Lisa A., author.
Title: Reading and interpreting the works of Alice Walker / Lisa A. Crayton.
Description: New York, NY : Enslow Publishing, 2017. | Series: Lit crit guides | Includes bibliographical references and index.
Identifiers: LCCN 2016026260 | ISBN 9780766083592 (library bound)
Subjects: LCSH: Walker, Alice, 1944-—Criticism and interpretation—Juvenile literature.
Classification: LCC PS3573.A425 Z59 2016 | DDC 813/.54—dc23
LC record available at https://lccn.loc.gov/2016026260

Printed in Malaysia

To Our Readers: We have done our best to make sure all website addresses in this book were active and appropriate when we went to press. However, the author and the publisher have no control over and assume no liability for the material available on those websites or on any websites they may link to. Any comments or suggestions can be sent by email to customerservice@enslow.com.

Photo Credits: Cover, p. 3 Peter Kramer/Getty Images; pp. 6, 33, 49, 94 © AP Images; p. 17 Anthony Barboza/Archive Photos/Getty Images; p. 21 John D. Kisch/Separate Cinema Archive/Archive Photos/Getty Images; p. 24 MPI/Archive Photos/Getty Images; p. 30 Library of Congress Prints and Photographs Division; pp. 35, 40, 42, 80 Bettmann/Getty Images; p. 46 Images Press/Archive Photos/Getty Images; p. 51 Archive Photos/Moviepix/Getty Images; p. 56 Mondadori Portfolio/Getty Images; pp. 59, 62, 66 Michael Ochs Archives/Moviepix/Getty Images; p. 68 Walter McBride/WireImage/Getty Images; p. 71 Per-Anders Pettersson/Hulton Archive/Getty Images; p. 84 Michael Ochs Archives/Getty Images; p. 87 AF archive/Alamy Stock Photo; p. 91 Stefan Zaklin/Getty Images; p. 92 Jamie McCarthy/Getty Images.

CONTENTS

Alice Walker

UNVEILING SECRETS: BACKGROUND OF ALICE WALKER

"Did This Happen to Your Mother? Did Your Sister Throw up a Lot?"

These intriguing questions form the title of a poem by Alice Walker, a renowned African American author. Walker's work includes poems, short stories, novels, and nonfiction essays. She started writing as a child and had her first collection of poems published a few years after she graduated from college. She went on to become a Pulitzer Prize–winning author as well as a fervent activist for human rights.

Walker's collection of poems, *Good Night, Willie Lee, I'll See You in the Morning*, was first published in 1975. "Did This Happen to Your Mother? Did Your Sister Throw up a Lot?" is part of that collection and is a good example of the type of vivid poetry for which Walker is known. The title raises questions, none of which can be answered by baffled readers who try to find meaning simply from the title. These stumped readers, however, may find help in the poem's first lines:

I love a man who is not worth
my love.[1]

Readers are enlightened. The questions refer to love. Indeed, "Did This Happen to Your Mother? Did Your Sister

Throw up a Lot?" is a love poem. In it, Walker wonders whether other women have experienced similar conflicting emotional and physical effects of love. Admittedly, love can be exciting, fun, scary, or a combination of these and other emotions. Or worse. "Love has made me sick," writes Walker.[2] How sick?

> . . . My stomach sits jumpy in my chest.
> My chest is the Grand Canyon
> sprawled empty
> over the world.[3]

This emotive writing explores the depth of feelings associated with being "lovesick." Drawing to the close of the poem, she admits she will never tell the loved one that he is unworthy of her affection. Its conclusion invites a rereading. Why? The anguish described in the poem is relatable for many readers. It is also a good example of how Walker weaves universal topics into her writing.

emotive
Emotional, sensitive; able to engage readers' senses.

Sharing Rainbows

In Walker's many years of writing, she has tackled various genres. Plainly, her achievements as a writer are characterized by an astonishing versatility. She is equally at home with poetry and fiction—it is worth remembering that she was first published as a poet, not as a novelist or fiction writer. Indeed, as an essayist alone she would be a noteworthy presence in America letters.[4]

Collectively, Walker's work examines life in all its beauty—and ugliness. Critic Barbara Christian notes, "Alice Walker's works are quilts—bit and pieces of used material rescued from oblivion for everyday use. She takes seemingly ragged edges and arranges them into works of function though terrifying beauty."[5] This quilt analogy is especially apt, given Walker's memories of her own mother making quilts when Walker was a child.

QUILTS

In Walker's short story "Everyday Use," quilts are a symbol of heritage. Questions arise regarding the purpose of those quilts. Should they be hung for decoration or enjoyed for "everyday use"? Ultimately, Walker reveals that celebrating one's heritage includes the daily enjoyment of family heirlooms—even if they aren't priceless.

Quilting is a tradition that dates back to the early years of America. English and Dutch settlers brought their own traditions of quilting when they first came to the New World. And as soon as slavery was established, African Americans also made quilts. Some slaves made them because they were forced to perform the task. Others did so to add extra warmth to cold sleeping quarters. At times, slaves were even able to sell quilts for money.

Quilts are made by piecing together squares of material. These can be cut from old clothing, blankets, or anything else from which material can be reused. The squares are then stitched together by hand or machine. Some quilts are simple; others are quite elaborate. Many quilts have themes associated with them. Patriotism, family life, seasons, and holidays are common quilt themes. Religion and spirituality are also popular themes. Quilts made for special occasions like baby showers, birthdays, and weddings all focus on those key topics. Quilts can reflect every area of life, and the themes available for use are nearly limitless.

In her writing, Walker explains that she is personally acquainted with the quilt-like quality of life. In the preface to the poetry collection *Hard Times Require Furious Dancing*, she notes:

> Once a person of periodic deep depressions, a sign of mental suffering in my family that affected each sibling differently, I have matured into someone I never dreamed I would become: an unbridled optimist who sees the glass as always full of something. It may be half full of water, precious in itself, but in the other half there's a rainbow that could exist only in the vacant space.[6]

Writing from a deep well of personal experiences, Walker takes on roles of writer and activist. Thus, readers can expect to read about topics such as interracial relationships and political activism. She also writes about issues she believes need to be exposed and addressed. In *Once*, a poetry collection, she includes poems about suicide. (She once considered taking her own life.) Her novel *The Color Purple* includes central themes of rape and incest. In *Possessing the Secret of Joy*, Walker exposes the practice of female circumcision and its physical and psychological effects.

analogy

A comparison between two like things.

Whether writing fiction or nonfiction, Walker grabs readers' hearts and minds. However, it is her novels that seem to stand out most to many readers. They boast gritty themes, colorful characters, and vivid prose. Moreover, they have cemented Walker's reputation as one of the finest African American writers of all time. Indeed, in 1983, she received the

Pulitzer Prize for Fiction for her fifth novel, *The Color Purple*. The work also won a National Book Award.

Genres

Like the many topics she explores, Walker is not limited to one genre. Rather, her impressive body of work proves she is adept at multiple forms of writing. Walker's published work includes novels, fictional short stories, personal essays, and poetry. She has also written children's books. Few authors can pen such diverse material with such remarkable skill and ease.

Walker's first published work was a poetry collection called *Once*. It came out of a difficult time she experienced and celebrates the joy of living. She has written many novels, with *The Color Purple* being the most well-known. Walker's early essay collection *In Search of Our Mothers' Gardens* celebrates women's creativity and other topics. Her more recent collections focus on political issues and other social concerns, including 9/11, global warming, war, and US elections.

Characters

Women are key characters in Walker's prose. In whatever capacity one investigates the work of Alice Walker—as a poet, novelist, short-story writer, critic, essayist, and apologist of black women—it is clear that the special identifying mark of her writing is her concern for the lives of black women.[7]

Walker's prose shows particular concern for black women's struggles. She captures their pain and despair. She writes about the violence they endure. She reveals the beauty in lives marred by hardship, neglect, and oppression. Notes critic Helen Washington, "The true empathy Alice Walker has for the oppressed woman comes through in all her writings—stories, essays, poems, novels."[8]

When all of her characters are considered, it is clear that Walker's fictional people mirror those in a typical community. Boys, girls, women, and men abound in her work, whether they are young or old, kind or mean, neighborly or reclusive. Some are religious, while others have no interest in spiritual matters. Walker portrays characters who are poor and those with few financial concerns. Some are streetwise, while others are book smart. Some are hailed as heroes, while others are villains. Few of her characters are stereotypical. Yet, her characters interact much as one would expect in a real community where similarities and differences converge daily.

Sometimes Walker's characterizations cast an admirable light on her subjects, as in her short story "To Hell with Dying." In it, a family helps restore an elderly friend's spirits when he is depressed. Part of the story's charm lies in the fact that the children are the saviors. They help bring Mr. Sweet back from the brink of death by tickling him until he revives while their father utters, "To Hell with dying." This ritual occurs often over a couple decades. Each time, Mr. Sweet recovers, except at the story's end. It is a story that celebrates life while reminding readers of the importance of community—of taking care of each other, even into old age.

On the other hand, as pointed out by author Louis H. Pratt, "His story is one of stunted ambition and thwarted romance, both of which cause Mr. Sweet to retreat from the real world of accelerated stress, high tension, and crass materialism and turn to his homemade alcohol and elaborate playacting for relief and satisfaction."[9] Even in this generally uplifting story, Walker does not try to hide life's harsh realities.

Across Walker's body of work, men are generally cast in an unfavorable light compared to women. Pratt explains, ". . . several questions concerning Walker's art have continued to haunt her. One of the most significant (and current) of these is why she has chosen to create a super-abundance of kind, loving women who triumph in spite of the odds, played off against weak, self-centered, violent men."[10] He also notes, "Many never speak; they are presented to the reader through the eyes of another person—usually a woman."[11] The result is often unflattering. The men come across as cold, unfeeling, and abusive. Pratt contends, "The men in Walker's fiction are so miserable because there is an absence of love in their lives which leads them to abuse their wives and children."[12]

One thing is certain: few, if any, of Walker's characters are perfect or have perfect lives. Indeed, as in real life, many of the characters struggle with at least one personal issue. Moreover, some of the characters never overcome their flaws or failings.

Character-Driven Dialogue

Walker uses language that enhances her characterization. A character's speech, diction, dialect, or vocabulary can naturally reflect his or her age, intellect, upbringing, or nationality. For example, Celie, the narrator in *The Color Purple*, is illiterate. Her vocabulary is very limited. She uses slang, misspells words, and sometimes uses the wrong word or term. This is shown in the letters she writes to God and later to her sister, Nettie. When writing about Christopher Columbus's trip to America, for example, she notes her young sister's attempt to help her recall details through name association. Still she botches the names of the ships used in the voyage.

On the other hand, the character of Pierre in *Possessing the Secret of Joy* is well-educated, smart, and sophisticated, as demonstrated by his proper, eloquent speech. And in "Everyday Use," language is used to show a character's uppity attitude and disdain for others. The character of Dee is ambitious and considers herself more progressive than her mother and sister. When she speaks to them, it is in a condescending fashion.

Slang and profanity also play a role in Walker's use of language, as they reveal some aspect of a character—for better or worse. For example, *The Color Purple* opens with Celie using slang terms to describe her body parts as she is raped by her stepfather, although at this point in the novel she believes he is her father. Her crass language paints a graphic picture in readers' minds. At the same time, it reveals her level of maturity and hints at her educational level. Readers are left with the impression of a vulnerable, helpless young girl. Walker's use of language is effective: Celie is all of those at the onset of the novel.

Walker's language choices receive mixed reviews from readers. On one hand, some contend the language is necessary to fully depict the range of characters, themes, and issues reflected in the author's works. Opponents, however, contend the language is too raw, especially for younger readers studying the novel in school. In fact, the language in *The Color Purple* is a major reason some parents, educators, and other adults oppose its use in curriculums across the country.

Themes

All of Alice Walker's novels are highly critical in their opposition to "racism, sexism, classism and colorism" and their plea for universal equality.[13].

Sometimes the themes tackled in her work can be gleaned simply by reading their titles, such as: "Suicide" (poem), "To Hell with Dying" (short story), *You Can't Keep a Good Woman Down* (essays), and *Hard Times Require Furious Dancing* (poems). Other titles are a bit more subtle, giving just a hint of their themes. Those include *The Third Life of Grange Copeland* (novel), *Possessing the Secret of Joy* (novel), "Everyday Use" (short story), and "I Know My Duty to Life" (poem).

If there is anything common to these themes, it is the fact that Walker is trying to raise readers' consciousness about issues she believes are worthy of exploration in fiction, poetry, and nonfiction essays—as well as in the real world.

Walker's prose resonates with readers because of the many topics covered. Indeed, she is a courageous author who pens fiction and nonfiction about easy and tough topics, light and dark issues. Within her key themes, she writes about the resilience of the human spirit and individuals' ability to triumph over adversity. On the other hand, she openly exposes secrets, taboos, and societal ills many people wished were kept hidden away. Those include rape, incest, physical abuse, and mental illness. She helps readers see the root causes of these but does not provide fairy-tale solutions that miraculously wipe away characters' pain and suffering.

> **diction**
>
> The style or choice of words in speech or writing.

> **dialect**
>
> A specific variety of a language often distinctive to a certain region.

Walker explores everything from interpersonal relationships to African American life to women's issues to spirituality. She examines topics that are of local, national, and international importance. At times, Walker meshes a myriad of these in one work. *Possessing the Secret of Joy*, for example, boasts themes related to women's sexuality, mental health, tribal customs, and romantic relationships. It also explores how childhood trauma impacts individuals as they age. The work's focus is national as well as international, as it begins in Africa and then shifts when the characters move to America.

Literary Devices

As with Walker's multitude of themes, literary devices vary as well. Common literary devices throughout her work include hyperbole, irony, imagery, personification, and symbolism. Walker employs more than one device in each work. This use of multiple devices in her poetry and essays enhances readers' enjoyment and comprehension of current events, political issues, biographical references, and other aspects of those works. The literary devices in her novels and short stories help readers better understand themes, characterization, and plots.

The Color Purple is one of Walker's novels that incorporates various literary devices. Her description of the day Celie meets Shug involves both hyperbole and irony. When Celie sees Shug's fashionable attire for the first time, she notes, "And she dress to kill."[14]. Here we have hyperbole, which is an exaggeration, as well as irony, as Shug will actually end up saving Celie in many ways.

The Color Purple is full of powerful imagery, engaging readers' senses and drawing them into the work with its vivid pictures. Celie's first impression of Shug is captured in the following imagery:

> She got on a red wool dress and chestful of black beads.
> A shiny black hat with what look like chickinhawk
> feathers curve down side one cheek, and she carrying a
> little snakeskin bag, match her shoes.[15]

Yet another literary device, personification, comes into play when Celie describes Shug's attire: "She looks so stylish it like the trees all round the house draw themself up tall for a better look."[16]

The Color Purple abounds with symbolism. The novel's title hints that purple is one such symbol. Another is flowers.

In the novel, the two symbols are connected. Shug Avery mentions the color while explaining to Celie how God places things in nature for people's delight. Celie admits that her life is so difficult that she has never noticed the startling color

Walker's writing focuses on the struggles of African American women, embracing their strengths as well as their vulnerabilities.

in a field. Later, as Celie's life dramatically improves, she incorporates a purple flower theme in the home she inherits. This further reinforces the turnaround she has experienced. Previously worked to the bone, she now has time to enjoy life, including purple flowers.

Later in the novel, the wearing of pants serves as a symbol of Celie's role reversal from a meek, downtrodden wife to an empowered businesswoman. Additionally, quilts and quilt-making are symbols of life and unity. The women in the novel unite to make quilts, just as the various pieces of the quilt come together.

Meanwhile, in *Possessing the Secret of Joy*, scarification serves as a visual symbol of Tashi's commitment to cultural tradition. Scarification is the process of permanently marking the skin with patterns or designs. It is performed on the face, torso, or other body parts. The skin is cut using various tools, such as knives or stones. The resulting design is more than decoration, often having a specific tribal or cultural meaning.

hyperbole

A literary device that uses exaggeration to emphasize an action, fact, idea, or feeling.

irony

The use of a words to convey the opposite of their literal meaning.

First, Tashi gets her face cut in order to feel a connection to her culture. Then she undergoes the traditional vaginal cutting that scars her physically, mentally, and emotionally. The devastating impact to her body and psyche underscores why the African ritual sparks controversy.

Walker learned about genital mutilation while in Kenya as a student. At that time she did not completely understand the process or its impact on women and children. It took her twenty years before she began penning her novel addressing the issue. She explains,

> . . . in writing a book like *Possessing the Secret of Joy* I see myself very much in the role of a witness. That if nothing else, I say that I know that this is happening. I know that these children are suffering, I know that these women are in pain. And I think that there is power in that because if you have ever been hurt in privacy by anyone, and you have a sense that no one knows this, and this is something that is yours alone to bear, you know how hard that is, it's a double oppression. But if you have just one person, a teacher, or a friend, or whoever, who at least stands beside you in this role as someone who just knows, then whatever the hurt is shared. [17]

personification

Giving human characteristics to animals or inanimate objects.

Critical Reviews

Walker has garnered a mixed bag of responses to her prose. On one hand, she is praised for her creativity, realistic themes, and versatility. On the other, she is criticized for exposing issues that have long been kept secret. The duality of the acceptance of her work is best seen with *The Color Purple.* The novel won a Pulitzer Prize and is regularly taught in high schools and universities. Yet it is often slammed for its subject matter, which many parents and other concerned adults consider inappropriate for students.

WALKER'S WORKS: MAJOR THEMES

When it was published in 1982, *The Color Purple* drew widespread praise—as well as sharp criticism. This is true of the novel and the film:

> In 1985 just before the opening of the film *The Color Purple*, based on Alice Walker's novel, with an all-star cast including Oprah Winfrey and Whoopi Goldberg, a coalition was formed to boycott the film across the country. Beginning with its premiere in Los Angeles, theaters showing the film were met with picket lines and general protests as African American men walked back and forth in front of theaters carrying signs objecting to both the film and the novel.[1]

Why do people feel so strongly about this particular novel compared to Walker's other works? Perhaps one reason is that Walker did not shy away from themes considered taboo topics. Another reason may be her open criticism of black masculinity in her portrayal of African American men. A third may be that she exposes a falsehood that it is OK for a man to treat a woman poorly simply because she is his wife, daughter, or stepdaughter.

Nearly all of the male characters in *The Color Purple*, with the exception of Samuel, treat women like dirt. Arguably, they cause as much—if not more—harm than the white towns-people. Yet those male characters do not see how they oppress the women in their lives:

Walker in 1982, the year *The Color Purple* came out. She was surprised by the strong backlash the novel received, particularly in regard to her negative portrayal of black men.

In Walker's novel the oppressed become the oppressors. One supposition is that because black men are unable to retaliate against the whites who cause their suffering, they, like many other men, take their fury out on those whom they can control—in this case, black women.[2]

For example, Harpo regularly fights Sofia. He initially wants to just whip her, but she resists. He attempts to break her spirit and make her obey, as if she was a stubborn mule. He especially wants to curb her habit of talking back to him. He gains weight in hopes of being able to whip her one day. That day never comes.

When Sofia slaps the mayor's wife, she is jailed and beaten. Celie writes her sister Nettie about the situation and Sofia's condition:

> When I see Sofia I don't know why she still alive. They crack her skull, they crack her ribs. They tear her nose loose on one side. They blind her in one eye. She swole from head to foot. Her tongue the size of my arm, it stick out tween her teef like a piece of rubber. She can't talk. And she just about the color of an eggplant.[3]

Harpo is as upset as everybody else concerning the brutality directed at Sofia. However, he does not admit that he has treated his wife equally brutally.

Many of the themes in *The Color Purple* are ones Walker returns to in her other novels, as well as in her poetry, essays, and short stories. Six recurring themes in Walker's work are: the South; the quest for self/identity; African American women; relationships and sexuality; spirituality; and cultural issues.

The South

Born in Georgia during a time of segregation in America, Walker knows a lot about this region of the country. She returns to it often as the setting or topic of her prose. *The Color Purple* is set in the South. Another novel, *Meridian*, takes place in the southern states of Alabama, Mississippi, and Georgia. Her short story "Roselily" boasts a protagonist from the South. "South: The Name of Home" is a poem included in the collection *Once*. Walker writes:

> i
>
> all that night
> I prayed for eyes to see again
> whose last sight
> had been
> a broken bottle
> held negligently
> in a racist
> fist
> God give us trees to plan
> And hands and eyes to
> Love them.[4]

For Walker, writing about the South is a way for her to both celebrate her roots while shining a light on the conflicts inherent in that area of the country. Setting her work in the South immediately adds racial and social conflict and provides a means of revealing true-to-life characters who either conform to or defy stereotypes. Further, Walker uses the backdrop of the South to reveal the resilience of the human spirit, especially African Americans' ability to rise about the trauma of living in such conflict-driven situations.

On the subject of "The Black Writer and the Southern Experience," Walker notes:

In large measure, black Southern Writers owe their clarity of vision to parents who refused to diminish themselves as human beings by succumbing to racism. Our parents seemed to know that an extreme negative emotion held against other human beings for reasons they do not control can be blinding. Blindness about other human beings, especially for a writer, is equivalent to death.[5]

A family stands outside their home in North Carolina in 1935. Walker's stories are often set in the rural South, serving to celebrate her own background while illuminating the African American experience.

Quest for Self and Identity

The quest for self and identity is a recurring theme in Walker's fiction and nonfiction. One of the best examples of this can be seen in the character of Tashi in *Possessing the Secret of Joy.*
Tashi is an African member of the Olinka tribe. However, because she has not undergone vaginal circumcision, she feels like an outcast. Her community shuns her. She does not see herself as truly African. She marries an American man and moves to the United States.

> **protagonist**
>
> The main character in a work of fiction.

Still struggling to solidify her identity, Tashi returns to Africa in order to embrace the cultural rites of scarification and circumcision. When her husband Adam returns to Africa to find her, he finds Tashi emotionally and physically devastated. She recalls: "My eyes see him but they do not register his being. Nothing runs out of my eyes to greet him. It is as if my self is hiding behind an iron door. I am like a chicken bound for the market."[6] The experiences sparks Tashi's "life-long tendency to escape from reality into the realm of fantasy and storytelling."[7]

Men play an important role in shaping women's identity in Walker's work. However, their influence is often negative. This is especially true in *The Color Purple.* Author Henry O. Dixon explains: "the male characters play crucial and significant roles in the development of Celie's character and in her final transformation . . . Through their brutal behavior the men [Mr.___ and Albert] ironically contribute to Celie's growth and development, permitting her to define her own womanhood."[8]

25

African American Women

Walker's works are filled with African American women. This includes her poetry, essays, short stories, and novels. Story collections *In Love & Trouble* and *You Can't Keep a Good Woman Down* demonstrate Walker's versatility in capturing the essence of African American women. The collections cover many different women. Some of these face similar situations and may come from similar backgrounds, but none are exactly the same. In these portrayals, Walker successfully shows the uniqueness of individual women based on their individual lives.

Many of the women Walker writes about are victims who have suffered various types of trauma, including rape, incest, and verbal and physical abuse. Also, Walker's work shows that the issues African American women face are not necessarily unique to America. *Possessing the Secret of Joy*, for example, is set in Africa and America as well as Switzerland. Tashi's African homeland has scarred her, while in America she feels displaced. Thus, it is almost a natural conclusion that neither of those countries is able to provide the healing she needs.

Relationships and Sexuality

In the course of her writings, Walker covers nearly every aspect of relationships imaginable. Her focus is on family bonds, both conventional and unconventional. Readers see some traditional home settings, while others would be considered nontraditional. For example, not all couples are married and not all families have a mother and a father. The main character in the short story "How Did I Get Away with Killing One of the Biggest Lawyers in the State? It Was Easy" points out: "My mother and father were not married. I never knew him. My mother must have loved him, though; she never talked against him when I was little. It was like he never existed."[9] Walker also includes interracial relationships, as with Adam and Lisette in *Possessing the Secret of Joy.*

People of all ages appear in Walker's work. They help to shed light on the many facets of family and community life. Writing about the reasons she often includes African American women and the aged in her works, Walker noted: "For me, black women are the most fascinating creatures in the world. Next to them, I place the old people—male and female—who persist in their beauty in spite of everything. How do they do this, knowing what they do? Having lived what they have lived? It is a mystery, and so it lures me into their lives."[10]

Her fictional relationships reflect the truism that no relationship is perfect. Walker highlights marriage and divorce. She shows the good, bad, and ugly things that happen when people are united in various relationships by blood, marriage, or community. It is no wonder domestic abuse—verbal and physical—crops up in her work.

Similarly, Walker's focus on sexuality is expansive. She includes the joy of sexual relationships, as with Adam and Tashi's youthful encounters in *Possessing the Secret of Joy.* Shug Avery and Albert's adulterous relationship also falls into this aspect of sexuality. On the other hand, Walker also uncovers the horror of forced sex, as in the rape and incest Celie endures in *The Color Purple.* She shows how trauma impacts sexuality. She illustrates the consequences of sexual contact, including unwanted pregnancies and abortion. Further, Walker boldly includes such subthemes as adultery, lesbianism, and bisexuality (Pierre in *Possessing the Secret of Joy,* for example).

Finally, Walker bravely explores habits or issues that impact sexuality, such as pornography. Pornography is the theme of several of her short stories in *You Can't Keep a Good Woman*

Down, for example. Those stories cast the issue in a negative light, as demonstrated by the impact that pornography has on the characters. In "Porn," a couple's relationship declines after the man shares his magazine collection with his partner. She tries to forget what she has seen, but cannot.

One interesting way Walker links the themes of identity, relationships, and sexuality is through Shug Avery's character in *The Color Purple*. Because she enjoys sex and is involved with a married man, the community looks down on her. Yet the community seems not to cast the same bad reputation onto Albert. Walker highlights the contradiction in society's norms for women and men and its impact on people's identity and relationships.

In *Possessing the Secret of Joy*, Pierre talks about this hypocrisy. Speaking of the woman he once loved, he shares intimate issues about her. Shocked, Adam tries to find a word to describe the woman.

> The word you are looking for, says Pierre, is *wantonly.*
> *Loosely.* A woman who is sexually "unrestrained"
> according to the dictionary, is by definition "lasciv-
> ious, wanton and loose." By why is that? A man who is
> sexually unrestrained is simply a man. [11]

Finally, Walker examines yet another angle of relationships and sexuality when she adds violence to the mix. Such is the case in "How Did I Get Away with Killing One of the Biggest Lawyers in the State? It Was Easy." The young protagonist of the story is raped by her mother's boss, but then the waters are muddied when a sort of consensual relationship occurs between the two. The girl recalls: ". . . he raped me. But afterward he told me he hadn't forced me, that I had felt something for him, and he gave me some money. I was crying, going down the stairs. I wanted to kill him."[12] She eventually does kill him.

Spirituality

Christianity, folklore, and Buddhism are all addressed in Walker's prose, alternately portrayed positively or negatively. Her characters embrace their individual spirituality as they choose, with the result being that spirituality comes across differently as it appears in different works. For example, in *The Color Purple*, Celie pens letters to God as a way of expressing the painful things she endures. She has been silenced by her stepfather from telling anyone else, so naturally—for her—she turns to God. But even as she writes these letters, she doubts whether God is interested in someone like her.

Celie's faith goes through stages. This is seen later in the novel when she questions why God has not changed her condition. After her life improves, her faith is restored. Yet now she has moved from a place of traditional religion to a place of spirituality where she sees God in many things. In her last letter she writes, "Dear God. Dear Stars, dear trees, dear sky, dear peoples, Dear Everything. Dear God."[13]

In *Possessing the Secret of Joy*, a Christian missionary couple travels to Africa to share their religion, but they have a difficult time getting the Olinka tribe to convert. The challenge is great because the tribe's religious practices and concept of deity are radically different from those of Christianity. As Adam's sister Olivia tries to talk Tashi out of her plan to get her face scarred, Tashi says, ". . . the nerve of you to bring us a God someone else chose for you! He is the same as those two stupid braids you wear, and that long dress with its stupid high collar."[14] Ultimately, Tashi is unable to reconcile the two religions, and her struggle to find her place in either culture drives her mad.

Cultural Issues

Cultural issues in Walker's work incorporate many of her other themes, such as finding one's own identity and race relations. Walker's writing portrays segregation, discrimination, and the American civil rights movement. In *The Color Purple*, she highlights the horrors of lynching, a common practice for many years in the United States, particularly in the South.

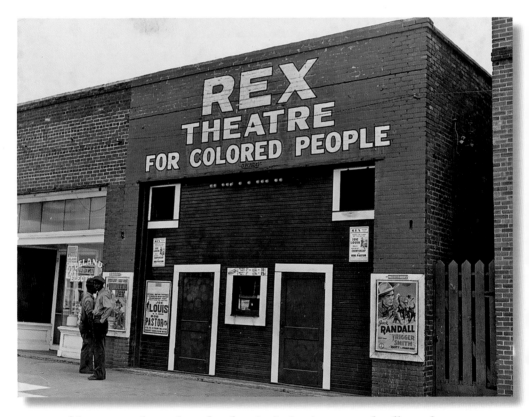

African Americans in Leland, Mississippi, were only allowed to view movies at this theater "for colored people." Segregation is one of the many injustices faced by Walker's characters.

Celie learns that her father had been lynched by a mob of white men. Lynching has long been a sensitive topic because of the many African Americans killed in this horrific manner by whites, but Walker sees the value of shedding light on even these most painful of subjects.

Walker also tackles the subject of interracial romantic relationships in her writing. In *Possessing the Secret of Joy,* Lisette, a white woman, has a sexual relationship with Adam, a black man. As a result of their affair, they have a biracial son, Pierre. Pierre's maternal grandparents are initially unhappy that Lisette is having a biracial child. She recalls, "My father and mother, after overcoming, to a remarkable degree, their normal outrage, racism and shock, showered me with advice and affection. It was recognized in almost a formal way—"Alors, nothing can be done!" said my mother . . .".[15] After he is born they develop a strong bond with Pierre, whom they love deeply. His heritage does not seem to be an issue with others in France. Tashi recalls a conversation with Pierre in which he contends, "No one is surprised he is biracial . . .".[16] Walker also highlights interracial social relationships in *The Color Purple*, in her portrayal of Sophia and the white mayor's wife for whom she works. Meanwhile, Walker's short story "Nineteen Fifty-Five" shows the negative economic impact of interracial relationships.

Cultural differences between nations play an important role in *Possessing the Secret of Joy.* Among other things, the way different cultures worship, dress, braid their hair, and define women's roles are seen in the novel. The scarification practices also underscore these differences. Olivia cannot understand the cultural importance of the rites of passage and is unable to comprehend why anyone would willingly undergone pain to connect to community and culture.

HARD TIMES, GOOD TIMES: ABOUT ALICE WALKER

Alice Walker writes about people's trials and triumphs. She pens prose about overcoming adversity and realizing dreams. Death and love, community discord and unity, self-hate and self-love are all captured in her work. Indeed, in poetry, short stories, essays, and novels, Walker captures life's roller-coaster moments filled with sorrow and joy.

All of these dichotomies mirror the dual aspects of Walker's own life. Indeed, hers has been filled with great lows and highs. Some defining moments include a childhood disfigurement, her involvement in civil rights demonstrations as a college student, an unplanned pregnancy, and the publication of her first book at age twenty-three.

Throughout the course of her career, it has become clear that Walker is passionate about social justice issues that impact individuals, communities, and nations. She not only writes to expose those issues, but she also gets personally involved in addressing some of them. As author Valerie Schloredt aptly notes, "She is a prominent activist who has worked, marched, traveled, and spoken out to support the causes of justice, peace, and the welfare of the earth."[1]

Roots in the South

Alice Malsenior Walker was born at home on February 9, 1944, in the town of Ward Chapel, a neighboring community of Eatonton, Georgia.[2] Her parents were Minnie Lou Talulah

Looking back: In 2009 Walker stands in front of a picture of herself as a college student. The photo is part of Walker's literary archives housed at Emory University.

Grant Walker and Willie Lee Walker. They had eight children all together: sons Curtis, Fred, James, Robert, and William, and daughters Molly, Ruth, and Alice (the baby of the family).

Alice's parents raised their children during a time when sharecropping was common in the South. Following the Civil War, newly freed slaves worked on farms that belonged to wealthy landowners, in exchange for wages in the form of money or crops. Those wages were grossly unfair. Sharecropping greatly benefited the white landowners but deprived the workers of decent wages and living conditions. For example, the system did not account for the many hours each person worked. Plus, landowners often took out fees for such things as the use of farm equipment and other things sharecroppers needed to live and work on the farm. As a result, sharecroppers were poor and lived in barely habitable dwellings owned by the landowners. By all accounts, the economic system did little to improve the lives of African Americans following slavery.

Recalling her childhood in Georgia, Walker wrote:

> We knew, I suppose, that we were poor. Somebody knew;
> perhaps the landowner who grudgingly paid my father
> three hundred dollars a year for twelve months' labor.
> But we never considered ourselves to be poor, unless of
> course, we were deliberately humiliated. And because we
> never believed we were poor, and therefore worthless, we
> could depend on one another without shame.[3]

Asked in an interview whether she visited her childhood home, Walker noted the shacks she once lived in no longer exist. She added:

> . . . And there were many of them . . . Each year the
> people who owned the land (that they had stolen from
> the Indians), after they had taken the labor for the year,
> forced us to another shack. How could people do that, to

people that they recognized as people? They did this to babies, they did this to small children, they could look at the people they were exploiting and actually see that they were working them into ill health and early death. It didn't stop them.[4]

Growing up in a segregated town shaped Walker's views of race relations:

. . . on hot Saturday afternoons of my childhood I gazed longingly through the window of the corner drugstore where white youngsters sat on stools in air-conditioned comfort and drank Cokes and nibbled ice-cream cones.

A sharecropper's cabin located on a plantation in Mississippi. As the daughter of sharecroppers in Georgia, Walker learned early on the importance of family when faced with difficult times.

Black people could come in and buy, but what they
bought they couldn't eat inside. When the first motel was
built in Eatonton in the late fifties the general under-
standing of *place* was so clear that the owners didn't even
bother to put up a "Whites Only" sign.

I was an exile in my own town, and grew to despise its
white citizens almost as much as I loved the Georgia
countryside where I fished and swam and walked
through fields of black-eyed Susans. . . .[5]

In spite of the back-breaking work and crowded living
quarters, Minnie Lou and Willie Lee Walker found joy through
storytelling, singing in church, and other family activities.[6]
Minnie Lou's handmade quilts added beauty and warmth
to the household. Meanwhile, her gardens beautified every
shabby place they lived. Neighbors took note. Walker recalls:

Whatever she planted grew as if by magic, and her
fame as a grower of flowers spread over three counties.
Because of her creativity with flowers, even my memories
of poverty are seen through a screen of blooms—
sunflowers, petunias, roses, dahlias, forsythia, spirea,
delphiniums, verbena . . . A garden so brilliant with
colors, so original in its design, so magnificent with life
and creativity...."[7]

Minnie Lou's creativity, as expressed through quilt-making
and gardening, had a profound impact on Walker. She found
her own creative outlook in writing, sometimes even incorpo-
rating the gardens and quilts of her childhood into her prose.

Scarred for Life

Walker's sense of well-being was shattered when she was eight
years old. One day in 1952, she was outside playing a game

modeled after western movies. Two of her brothers pretended to be cowboys, while she played the Indian. They wielded BB guns, toys that shoot small pellets. The game took a terrible turn when one of the pellets struck Walker in the right eye. The last thing she remembered seeing in that eye was a tree in the front yard.

Her parents tried nursing young Alice back to full health. It did not work. A week later they took her to the doctor. The bad news? Her eye would never be the same. It was permanently blinded. The injury greatly impacted Alice's view of herself, which was already shaky due to attending a new school where she had yet to make friends. Struggling with falling self-esteem, she retreated into herself. She spent time in the woods. She even considered suicide.

Walker recalled, "For a long time I thought I was very ugly and disfigured. This made me shy and timid, and I often reacted to insults and slights that were not intended. I discovered the cruelty (legendary) of children, and of relatives, and could not recognize it as the curiosity it was."[8] She added, "I believe, though, that it was from this period—from my solitary, lonely position, the position of an outcast—that I began to really see people and things, really to notice relationships and to learn to be patient enough to care about how they turned out.[9] Another benefit of the horrific accident? Walker started writing poetry. This newfound creative outlet would become part of her life's work.

School Years

Alice's feelings about herself changed during a 1958 visit to her brother Bill in Boston. Amazed that she still struggled with the psychological effects of the scarring, he arranged for his sister to have eye surgery. The doctor successfully removed the offending white "glob." However, a bluish ring remained around her blind right eye.

Nonetheless, the surgery succeeded in improving Alice's self-image. Her days of feeling ugly, shy, and timid were short-lived. Prior to the surgery, she used to walk around with her head down. It was her way of hiding the injury and withdrawing within herself. After the surgery, Alice looked up when she spoke. She looked people in the eye. She became more social. Her grades improved as her self-confidence soared.

Alice thrived in high school. In fact, she graduated as vale-dictorian from Butler-Baker High School in 1961. She was also the prom queen. Being prom queen made her realize that people no longer saw her as scarred. As graduation neared, she readied for new challenges. For her, that meant college.

Walker received a scholarship to attend Spelman College in Atlanta, Georgia. It boasted a reputation as a prestigious learning institution for African American women. Walker was excited about attending the school in the city known as the hub of the civil rights movement. Before graduating from high school, Walker had learned about the movement and its importance to the African American community. An added bonus to living in Atlanta? Dr. Martin Luther King Jr. lived there. He was Walker's hero! With excitement for her future, Walker enrolled in Spelman.

As she had hoped, Walker became engaged in activism while in Atlanta. She joined protests staged by the Student Nonviolent Coordinating Committee. These events offered opportunities to work for social change alongside both whites and blacks. Then, in 1962, Walker had the chance to attend the World Youth Peace Festival in Helsinki, Finland, as a delegate. This was an honor. Before she departed, she had the honor of meeting with Coretta Scott King, wife of Dr. Martin Luther King Jr. Walker was thrilled to be in Dr. King's home, meeting with his wife. Of the life-changing experience, she wrote:

> I recalled vividly our few minutes in the King home, a modest, almost bare-looking home with exceedingly nondescript furniture. I was delighted that the furniture was so plain, because it was the same kind of stuff most black people had. . . . I felt quite comfortable on the sofa.[10]

The following year, she had a chance to see Dr. King up close. In 1963, she attended the March on Washington for Jobs and Freedom in Washington, DC. From a distance, sitting in a tree, she heard Dr. King deliver his famous "I Have a Dream" speech.

While her extracurricular activities met Walker's expectations, Spelman College did not. The curriculum was too rigid. She felt that many of her classmates focused too much on outer appearance. Worse, her writing was not as well received as Walker would have liked. Thus, she transferred from there to Sarah Lawrence College in Bronxville, New York. Again she had received a scholarship to pay for her studies. Unlike at Spelman, Walker thrived at Sarah Lawrence. There, biographer Evelyn C. White writes, "Unlike the stodgy, regimented approach to learning Alice has endured in most of her classes at Spelman, she was encouraged to write as she pleased and to develop her own voice."[11]

While at Sarah Lawrence, Walker participated in voter registration drives, encouraging young people to become involved in the election process. She also traveled to Africa before her senior year in college. She recalled, ". . . I had been to Africa during the summer, and returned to school healthy and brown, and loaded down with sculptures and orange fabric—and pregnant."[12] She was traumatized.

Walker did not want a baby. She did not have money for an abortion, the only option that seemed viable to her. Plus, she did not know where to find a doctor who performed the procedure. Despondent, Walker decided to end her life. "I felt there was no way out," she recalled, ". . . I planned to kill myself, or—as I thought of it then—to 'give myself a little rest.'"[13] Sleeping with a razor under her pillow for three days, Walker faced death unafraid. In the end, friends of Walker gave her the information and money she needed to have the abortion she desired.

Dr. Martin Luther King Jr. gives his famous "I Have a Dream" speech. Like many young people of her time, Walker was inspired by King's vision of a more peaceful and just nation.

She emerged from the ordeal more hopeful for the future. To express her feelings, Walker poured out her heart in poetry. She wrote about Africa, suicide, love, and life in the South—familiar topics she continually returns to in her prose. She wrote about suicide, ". . . because I felt I understood the part played in suicide by circumstances and fatigue. I also began to understand how alone woman is, because of her body."[14]

Walker shared those poems with Muriel Rukeyser, one of her literature professors. She remembered, "I didn't care what she did with the poems. I only knew I wanted someone to read them as if they were new leaves from an old tree. The same energy that impelled me to write them carried them to her door."[15]

Rukeyser was impressed by Walker's writing. She, in turn, shared them with her literary agent. The result? Walker's heart-wrenching poems born out of despair and hope were published in 1968 as a collection dubbed *Once*. The collection was released three years after Walker graduated from Sarah Lawrence College. Out of her experience with the pregnancy and abortion, Walker also had her first short story published: "To Hell with Dying" was published in *The Best Short Stories by Negro Writers: An Anthology from 1899 to Present* in 1967. The anthology was edited by Langston Hughes, a famous black writer known for his poetry, novels, and plays. Her career as a professional writer had officially begun.

Family Life

After graduating from college, Walker moved to New York City and took a job working in the city's welfare office, working on behalf of the poor people of the area. From there she moved on to Mississippi, where she met another civil rights worker, a white attorney named Melvyn ("Mel") Leventhal. The couple

Walker and her husband, Mel Leventhal, spend time with their daughter, Rebecca, in 1970.

were married in 1966 and settled in New York City, later relocating to Mississippi. Their daughter, Rebecca Grant, was born on November 17, 1969. The couple later divorced in 1976.

Prolific Author

During the first years of her marriage, Walker continued to write in different genres. Her first published novel, *The Third Life of Grange Copeland*, debuted in 1970. Then in 1973, she released two projects: a poetry collection dubbed *Revolutionary Petunias and Other Poems* and a collection of short stories entitled *In Love & Trouble: Stories of Black Women*.

Walker's novel *Meridian* was published in 1976. She followed that up with the 1979 publication of a poetry collection called *Goodnight, Willie Lee, I'll See You in the Morning*. The title is said to be the last words that Walker's mother said to her father, Willie Lee, before he died. *You Can't Keep a Good Woman Down* was a short story collection released in 1981.

Walker's next project is considered by many to be her best work. *The Color Purple*, published in 1982, was awarded the Pulitzer Prize for Fiction and also won the National Book Award for Fiction.

In 1983, Walker's essay collection *In Search of Our Mothers' Gardens* debuted. In it, she explores the topics of living in the South, women's creativity, feminism, and other topics. The many personal issues discussed provide a glimpse into the author's life and the events shaping her writing career. Other published works during that time period include *Horses Make a Landscape Look More Beautiful* (poetry, 1984), *Living by the Word* (essays, 1985), *To Hell with Dying* (children's book, 1988), and *The Temple of My Familiar* (novel, 1989).

During the 1990s, Walker continued to prove herself a prolific, versatile writer. A key project from this time was

FROM PAGE TO STAGE

The film version of *The Color Purple* was released in 1985. It was directed by Steven Spielberg and featured comedian Whoopi Goldberg in the role of Celie. The cast also included veteran actor Danny Glover as Albert and, in her film debut, Oprah Winfrey as Sofia. At the film's release, Winfrey was still hosting her widely popular talk show.

The Color Purple was nominated for numerous Academy Awards and received generally positive reviews. While it did not win an Oscar, the film helped attract additional attention to Walker's novel.

Possessing the Secret of Joy, released in 1991. Then in 1993 her book and documentary collaborations with filmmaker Pratibha Parmar were released. They were dubbed *Warrior Marks: Female Genital Mutilation and the Sexual Blinding of Women*. These three projects were significant in first raising, then keeping, the issue of female genital mutilation before readers and viewers. Indeed, the practice continues to raise controversy around the world. In June 2016, for example, twin seventeen-year-old sisters underwent the procedure in a private hospital in Egypt. It was an illegal operation, as the country banned the practice in 2008. One of the twins died. Her death sparked outrage and once again raised awareness about the practice and its potential dangers.

Additional published works in the 1990s were two essay collections, followed by a variety of other material in the following decade. Since 2000, Walker has published a variety of material. One of these was *Sent by Earth: A Message from the Grandmother Spirit After the Attacks of the World Trade Center and Pentagon.*

Walker's poetry collection *Hard Times Require Furious Dancing* debuted in 2010. This was followed by the release of her memoir in 2011. It is dubbed *The Chicken Chronicles: Sitting with the Angels Who Have Returned with My Memories.* In 2013, Walker saw the publication of a poetry collection as well as an essay collection. These later works highlight Walker's shifting emphasis on writing poetry and essays, rather than novels. They were written while Walker experienced physical ailments and deaths in her family, situations that are reflected in some of the work.

Other Jobs

Walker taught at various schools even as she continued to prove herself a prolific writer. Those schools include Tougaloo College and Jackson State University in Mississippi, Wellesley College, and the University of Massachusetts. She also served in 1974 as an editor of *Ms.* magazine. At *Ms.*, Walker worked alongside Gloria Steinem, an outspoken feminist and one of the magazine's cofounders. The two activists had a lot in common.

Key Influences

Many of the early influences on Walker's prose include writers that she studied in college. Among those were Russian writers, including Leo Tolstoy. Zora Neale Hurston, Langston Hughes, and Jean Toomer were other African American writers who influenced Walker's work. She has also been influenced by haiku, a form of Japanese poetry. Further, she has cited numerous poets who influenced her creativity. These include Emily Dickinson, e. e. cummings, and Robert Graves.

Walker's work was strongly inspired by African American women writers, particularly poet Gwendolyn Brooks and Hurston, who wrote short stories, folk tales, and novels. Her work greatly influenced Walker's creativity. Hurston died in poverty and was buried in an unmarked grave. A very personal achievement in 1973 for Walker was locating and placing a marker on Hurston's grave. Another way Walker honored Hurston's memory and work was by editing *I Love Myself When I Am Laughing . . . and Then Again When I Am Looking Mean and Impressive*. The book was released in 1979 and featured a compilation of Hurston's work.

When asked about those that have had a significant impact on her writing, Walker concedes: "It is impossible to list all of

Gloria Steinem was a leading force in the feminist movement of the sixties and seventies. Walker worked briefly as an editor on Steinem's *Ms.* magazine.

the influences on one's work . . ." [16] She does, however, readily admit that music, travel, and other authors play an important role in shaping her work. And, of course, Walker's mother was an early and lasting influence on her life, so much so that a year after her mother died in 1993, Walker changed her name to Alice Tallulah-Kate Walker.

Recognition for Prose

More than fifteen million copies of Walker's books have been sold.[17] In addition to the outstanding sales and continued popularity, Walker has received acclaim for her writing over the years. In 1967, she was given an Ingram Merrill Foundation fellowship, a monetary award given to promising writers and artists. The following year, she received the National Institute of Arts and Letters' Rosenthal Award.

Other recognition for Walker's work includes the Guggenheim Fellowship, Radcliffe Institute Fellowship, and the Merrill Fellowship. In 1974, she received the National Endowment for the Arts' Lillian Smith Award. Arguably her most prestigious award came in the form of the Pulitzer Prize for *The Color Purple*. The prize brought Walker increased recognition as well as intense scrutiny of her work.

In Living Color: Examining *The Color Purple*

"I think it pisses God off if you walk by the color purple in a field somewhere and don't notice it."[1]

Shug Avery speaks these words that are the source of the title of Walker's most famous novel. *The Color Purple*, published in 1982, was her third full-length fiction project. Shug is a raunchy singer with a bad reputation, and she is sharing her views on religion and spirituality with her friend Celie, the story's protagonist. The remarks were sparked by comments Celie had uttered concerning her discontent with her life and displeasure with God for not improving her situation.

Shug attempts to help Celie see her life not as one of hardship and disappointment, but one with purpose despite its limitations. In doing so, she offers a very different viewpoint than Celie is used to. Shug believes God wants people to experience life in its fullness. Shug also believes God loves people without strings attached.

Celie is shocked. "You telling me God love you, and you ain't never done nothing for him? I mean, not go to church, sing in the choir, feed the preacher and all the like?"[2] Shug's reply? "But if God love me, Celie, I don't have to do all that. Unless I want to. There's a lot of other things I can do that I speck God likes."[3]

In 1983, Walker became the first African American woman to be awarded the Pulitzer Prize for Fiction.

While Celie grapples with this new image of God, Shug tries to enlighten her friend by pointing out ordinary things God gets pleasure from—including people's awareness and enjoyment of flowers in a field. Shug argues that Celie's thinking has kept her from viewing God in a positive light. Particularly, she has long considered God an "old white man." About her view, Celie says: "Trying to chase that old man out of my head, I been so busy thinking bout him I never truly notice nothing God make. Not a blade of corn (how it do that?) not the color of purple (where it come from?). Not the little wildflowers. Nothing."[4]

The conversation between Shug and Celie occurs near the end of the novel, but questions surrounding God and faith are present throughout the entire story. Indeed, spirituality is one of the key themes of *The Color Purple*. In a new preface to the book, Walker felt many readers missed that point. She noted:

> Whatever *The Color Purple* has been taken for during the years since its publication, it remains for me the theological work examining the journey from the religious back to the spiritual that I spent much of my adult life, prior to writing it, to avoid . . .
>
> I would have thought that a book that begins "Dear God" would immediately been identified as a book about the desire to encounter, to hear from, the Ultimate Ancestor. Perhaps it is a sign of our times that this was infrequently the case.[5]

Setting

The Color Purple is set in Georgia, with events spanning from the early 1900s to the 1940s. The novel's timeline spans many significant events in US history that impacted African Americans and other citizens. In 1909, for example, the National Association for the Advancement of Colored People (NAACP) was founded. One of its goals was to end segregation, such as that faced by the characters in *The Color Purple*. During the time of the novel, sharecropping had replaced the economic system of slavery, but blacks were still experiencing significant hardships. They faced racism, were victims of hate crimes, and worked in low-paying jobs. In the novel, this is reflected in the lives of Celie, Sophia, and Celie's father, among other characters.

A scene from the 1985 film version of *The Color Purple* depicts a plantation in Georgia in the 1930s. The novel's location and time period are key elements that shape who the characters become.

Contrasts in rural and city life are prominent in the novel's setting. Celie's life is significantly different when she moves in with Shug. She has more freedom and more opportunities. This shift in Celie's life mirrors what was happening in the country at the time. Many African Americans were migrating north in hopes of better economic opportunities and living conditions. That migration contributed to the Harlem Renaissance, a cultural celebration of African American creativity in the 1920s centered in the Harlem area of New York City. The era sparked the invention of jazz, as well as the release of increased numbers of literary works by African Americans. Shug's career as a singer and her increased popularity reflects how events in the North also impacted the South.

Finally, while the novel takes place primarily in the South, the reader is also exposed to events in Africa through Nettie's letters. This correspondence serves to place events in a different light and give Celie a broader view of the world. We also see how racial conflict exists in both countries.

Themes

Is it possible to overcome a trauma and recover one's self-esteem? Based on the characters in *The Color Purple*, the answer is a resounding yes. Overcoming adversity, particularly oppression, is a key theme in the novel. Walker admits to enduring her own difficult times as she was bringing the story to life:

> I don't always know where the germ of a story comes
> from, but with *The Color Purple* I knew right away. I was
> hiking through the woods with my sister, Ruth, talking
> about a lovers' triangle of which we both knew. She said:
> "And you know, one day The Wife asked The Other
> Woman for a pair of drawers." Instantly the missing piece

BANNED BOOK

The Color Purple continues to spark interest and controversy. People who believe a book is not suitable for inclusion in academic settings often lobby to have the book banned from a particular school or school system. Opponents of the literature contend it is the only way to assure their children are not reading material adults deem unsuitable for a specific age group. Proponents of inclusive curricula, on the other hand, say that banning a book is not the answer. Controversial topics won't go away simply by removing a book from a school's library or curriculum.

In some cases, efforts to ban books succeed. In other cases, they do not. On each side of the debate, people argue the virtues and disadvantages of book banning. Sometimes, explaining why a certain book is included in a child's reading list helps adults better appreciate its inclusion. Other times, nothing will sway adults' opinions. They adamantly advocate for the removal of certain books. That has been the case with *The Color Purple*.

of the story I was mentally writing—about two women who felt married to the same man—fell into place. And for months—through illnesses, divorce, several moves, travel abroad, all kinds of heartaches and revelations—I carried my sister's comment delicately balanced in the center of the novel's construction I was building in my head.[6]

The love triangle is just one of the themes in *The Color Purple* that continues to spark controversy years after its release. The novel also deals with rape and incest, opening with Celie's letter to God:

Dear God,

I am fourteen years old. I am I have always been a good
girl. Maybe you can give me a sign letting me know what
is happening to me.[7]

She then details events leading up to the man she believes
is her father repeatedly raping her. It is a heart-wrenching
opening to a novel that leaves readers stunned. Walker goes on
to tackle other challenging themes such as domestic abuse and
lesbianism. In doing so, she does not provide pat answers or
create a fairy-tale novel that satisfies every reader. Instead, she
raises questions, while probing into issues some people would
rather she left alone.

Walker also examines the role of race as it pertains to her
characters. As an adult, Celie learns from her sister that the
man they called "Pa" and believed was their father is actually
their stepfather. Their father had been lynched by a white mob.
Celie, shocked, writes: "My daddy lynch. My mama crazy. All
my little half-brothers and sisters no kin to me. My children
not my sister and brother. Pa not pa."[8] Notes English professor
and writer Lauren Berlant:

For Celie and Nettie's biological father, race functions
much as gender functions for the sisters: not as a site of
positive identification for the victim, but as an excuse for
the oppressor's intricate *style* of cultural persecution.[9]

By the novel's end, however, the sisters have overcome the
adversities that could have kept them as victims for life. Celie
is a businesswoman who is free from the husband that abused
her. She is happy and successful and reunited with her chil-
dren. Nettie is married and reunited with the sister she had
to leave because of Mr.___'s inappropriate attention. They

are enjoying lives that completely contrast with the ones they faced when the novel opened.

Style

The Color Purple's narrative style is epistolary, or in the form of letters. Primarily, the protagonist Celie writes letters to God. She also receives letters from her sister, Nettie, as she travels. Why did Walker choose to have the story unfold through letters?

For Celie, letter writing is rooted in the childhood trauma she endured. Her stepfather repeatedly raped her, beginning when she

> **epistolary**
>
> Having to do with letters.

was fourteen years old. He warned her back then: "You better not tell nobody but God. It'd kill your mammy."[10] The novel opens with that ominous warning, and from that point on the story unfolds through Celie's letters. Contends author Diane Garbielsen Scholl:

> To call *The Color Purple* a radical novel is not to make a surprising charge, considering the alarming number of critics who have protested the novel's raw language, its frank depiction of sexual expression, particularly lesbianism, and its bitter castigation of male and female roles. Its somewhat avant-garde epistolary narration also might earn the novel my designation of "radical" since the major portion of the letters are penned by a semi-literate black woman.[11]

In other words, Scholl argues, it is not the "shocking" subject matter that should take readers aback, but the fact that the story is told in letters written by an uneducated black woman. Walker's choice of narrative style is crucial to the reader's understanding of Celie and her development throughout the story.

Point of View

The epistolary form of the novel allows for a first-person perspective of those characters writing letters. The reader gains a strong understanding of Celie through her letters to God that would not be possible with, for example, an omni-

The character of Celie (portrayed in the film by Whoopi Goldberg) holds a letter from her sister, Nettie. It is primarily through these letters that we develop an understanding of the relationship between the two sisters.

scient narrator. We also learn secondhand about what other characters are feeling by the events and dialogue the letter writer pens. Celie, for example, conveys conversations she has had with other people or those between other characters. Of course, we do not gain the same level of intimacy with those characters, as we are seeing them only through Celie's eyes.

Language

Walker uses vivid language and imagery throughout the novel. For example, although Celie has difficulty grasping schoolwork, she conveys her thoughts about her life and the situations she encounters in a way that is emotionally stirring. Her words are simple, yet descriptive.

Nettie also engages readers' emotions in the letters she writes to Celie. Trying to convey how hot Africa is, she writes: "It's hot here, Celie . . . Hotter than July. Hotter than August and July. Hot like cooking dinner on a big stove in a little kitchen in August and July. Hot."[12] Any reader who has experienced the heat from cooking on a summer day can easily relate to this description.

Walker's unique style also extends to her use of dialogue. In the novel, there are no actual conversations between characters as traditionally seen in novels. Instead, Celie writes about what other people have said. She records their words and actions. Unlike traditional use of quotations, punctuation is not used to show a character is speaking or has spoken. We only "hear" the other characters through Celie.

Characters

Celie

Celie is the novel's protagonist. The story centers around her traumatic life and her ability to triumph over life's adversities.

The novel begins when Celie is a teenager. Her life is marked by years of abuse. First, she is raped by her stepfather when she is just fourteen years old. He continues molesting her for years. As a result, she has children from the incestuous relationship. Her stepfather gives—or, more likely, sells—the children to a pastor and his wife.

Celie is physically unattractive. She struggles to learn how to read and has trouble keeping up with schoolwork. She is eventually pulled out of school when she becomes pregnant with her first child. It is a ploy on the part of her stepfather to stop the townspeople from learning about her condition.

Celie is also abused by her husband, Albert, whom she thinks of simply as Mr.___. He regularly beats her because he does not love her and feels as if he was forced to marry her. The abuse lasts for years until Shug makes him stop. Talking to Shug about her return to town after a long absence, Celie notes: "He ain't beat me much since you made him quit . . . Just a slap now and then when he ain't got nothing else to do."[13]

Celie soon falls in love with Shug, igniting a love triangle with Celie, Shug, and Albert. While Celie and Shug do engage in a romantic relationship, eventually Shug moves on to another woman. Celie is devastated, but eventually she moves on and begins to heal emotionally from her past wounds. She starts a successful business selling pants and begins to gain confidence along with her independence. She remains hopelessly in love with Shug, but when Shug starts up with a nineteen-year-old, Celie finally realizes that she will never be her only love interest.

Celie's life takes another turn for the better when she learns her stepfather did not own her childhood home and that instead, she and her sister inherited it when their mother died. Celie moves back there, establishing her business from the place that once was the site of her devastation. Her complete and successful trek to wholeness is revealed when Shug plans a trip to see her and Celie is not fazed. She has learned to love herself, embrace her creativity, and enjoy a life she never dreamed she could have.

Pa/Alphonso

Celie's stepfather rapes her while pretending to be her father, thus inflicting lasting scars. He acts like he hates her, calls her names, and takes the children he fathered away. She reveals

Young Celie (played here by Desreta Jackson) struggles with finding her own self-worth because of the abuse she suffers at the hands of her stepfather and later her husband.

PRETTY UGLY

"Beauty is skin deep, but ugly is to the bone." This saying contrasts outer beauty with inner ugliness, contending that true beauty is an inward, not outward, quality. Many people struggle with feelings of unattractiveness at some point, even those who are considered attractive by conventional standards. Alice Walker captures some of those feelings and insecurities in *The Color Purple*. Specifically, she shows that outer attractiveness is not as important as a beautiful heart.

Many characters in the novel see Celie as ugly. Her stepfather admits that she's ugly when he tries to get Mr.___ to marry her. Shug meanwhile seems to have heard about Celie's unattractiveness. Soon after the women meet, Celie writes: "She look me over from head to foot. Then she cackle. Sound like a death rattle. You sure *is* ugly, she say, like she ain't believed it."[14] Yet her kindness, faithfulness, and dedication allow readers to forget her outer appearance and applaud her inner loveliness.

this in her letter to God: "He act like he can't stand me no more. Say I'm evil an always up to no good. He took my other little baby, a boy this time . . . I keep hoping he fine somebody to marry. I see him looking at my little sister. She scared. But I say I'll take care of you. With God's help."[15] Celie is brave for her sister, but does not stand up to Pa, who acts like a jealous husband: "He beat me today cause he say I winked at a boy in church. I may have got something in my eye but I didn't wink. I don't even like mens."[16]

Albert/Mr.___

Celie thinks of, and writes about, her "husband" without referring to his first or last name. Celie's refusal to name her husband, whose real name is Albert, may stem from her fear of men or the lack of any real attachment between the two.

After the death of his wife, Mr.___ finds himself attracted to Nettie, but when her father refuses to allow the marriage, he settles for Celie instead, mainly to help with his children. This is, in fact, the second time he marries a woman he does not love. His one true love is Shug Avery, but his father would not allow him to marry her.

Early on, Albert is a discontented father and unwilling husband to Celie. He beats her. He belittles her when speaking to her privately or in front others. He cheats on her with Shug. As the novel continues, Albert starts to change. He stops beating Celie at Shug's insistence. He is shocked when Celie moves out to live with Shug. That event, however, marks a change in their relationship. He accepts he no longer has any hold over her as a husband. As Celie becomes more successful selling her clothing, Albert starts seeing her as a person worthy of respect. In time, the two began to accept each other, which is marked by Albert's more gentle treatment of Celie.

Shug Avery

Shug Avery is the woman Albert wanted to marry when they both were young. Celie hears Shug's name for the first time when Mr.___ comes to the house to ask to marry Nettie, which Pa refuses because of rumors he heard about Mr.___ and Shug. Intrigued, Celie later asks her new stepmother about Shug. Her stepmother does not tell her much about Shug but does bring Celie a picture to see what she looks like. Celie is mesmerized by Shug, who she describes as "[t]he most beautiful woman I ever saw. She more pretty than my mama. She bout ten thousand times more prettier than me. I see her there in furs. Her face rouge. Her hair like somethin tail. She grinning with her foot up on somebody motorcar."[17] The picture captures Shug's carefree attitude to life.

Shug is Albert's one true love, but he is forbidden to marry her. Shug resents Albert's inability to stand up to his father and walks away, but the two maintain a sporadic relationship even after Albert marries his first wife. Eventually she leaves town, only to return years later. When she becomes ill, no one in the town will help her because of her questionable reputation, which is based on the fact she continued to have sex

Shug Avery is glamorous and confident—everything that Celie is not. The nature of the relationship between the two women changes over time and finally develops into a lasting friendship.

with Albert even after he married his first wife. Because of that, women did not trust her around their husbands. Albert finds her and brings her home, to the secret delight of Celie. As Celie tends to Shug, the two become close friends. This does not, however, stop Shug from continuing her affair with Albert once she has recovered. When she prepares to leave, Shug learns that Albert beats Celie. She is dumbstruck. She confronts Albert and convinces him to stop beating Celie.

Shug later returns to town with her husband, much to Celie and Albert's dismay. In a letter to God, Celie tells Shug that Albert is upset about the marriage, but Celie does not mention her own feelings. Shug's reaction:

> Aw, she say. That old stuff finally over with. You and Albert feel just like family now. Anyhow, once you told me he beat you, and won't work, I felt different about him.[18]

Shug continues to treat them as family. She helps Celie get away from Albert and encourages Celie's business ideas. She becomes a mentor and advisor who is important to Celie's improved self-esteem. As Celie nursed Shug to physical health many years before, Shug now becomes the healer, leading Celie to physical and emotional well-being.

Harpo

Harpo is Albert's son from his first wife, the woman Albert marries when he is unable to marry Shug. His father browbeats him as much as he does Celie. When Harpo decides to marry Sofia, Albert forbids the marriage. It appears as if history will repeat itself in the family until Harpo finds the courage to stand up to his father and marries Sofia. Unfortunately, Harpo does adopt some of his father's oppressive, sexist attitudes about women and their place in society. He even attempts to beat Sofia to prove he is the man of the house whom she must obey. This backfires as Sofia is bigger and stronger than he is. Ultimately, Harpo learns that love—not domestic abuse—is the key to a woman's heart and marital bliss.

Sofia

Harpo's wife, Sofia, is a fearless woman who has the courage to stand up to men and to fight them if necessary. Through much of the story, her strength stands in sharp contrast to Celie's timidity, and Celie comes to admire Sofia's bravery and independence. But Sofia's mouth and defiance cause her problems with the white people in town, including the mayor's wife. Sofia is jailed for slapping her and spends years in prison for doing so. The experience challenges her attitude: she is changed from a strong, independent woman to a meek person who barely speaks. By the novel's end, she recovers some of her spunk. Her spirit, not oppression, wins.

Nettie

Nettie is Celie's younger sister and her antithesis in many ways. Where Celie is homely and passive, Nettie is smart, shapely, and pretty. Despite their differences, the sisters have a strong bond, and Celie believes Nettie is the only person who ever truly loved her.

Nettie lives with Celie for a short time, before Celie's husband demands she leave. He is attracted to her, but neither she nor Celie will allow him to touch Nettie. Albert catches up to Nettie on the road and tries but fails to seduce her. Angry, he warns her that Celie will never be in touch with her again.

After leaving home, Nettie works with a family in town. The couple are Christians: the husband is a pastor, and both he and his wife are missionaries. In fact, they are the same people who took in Celie's children when her stepfather made her give them up. Nettie ends up moving to Africa with the couple to serve as missionaries to the Olinka people, a fictional group of people living in Africa. For years, Celie worries about her sister, convinced that she is dead because there have been no letters. Only with Shug's assistance does Celie discover that Albert had hidden every letter Nettie wrote.

Nettie's letters are well written, reflecting the intelligence she displayed even as a young girl. In them, she shares information about Africa, showing Celie a new part of the world that is hard for Celie to imagine. Once Celie begins reading the letters, an entire new world opens up to her. She basks in the love and acceptance Nettie pours outs in them. She learns the startling truth that oppression and racism are universal, found in the United States, Africa, and other places around the world. From the letters, Celie gains confidence and courage to write Nettie and push back against the oppression she faces at home. She is truly free by the time the two sisters reunite many years after Nettie first left for Africa.

Nettie ends up marrying Samuel, the pastor she works with. The two eventually return to America and Nettie's childhood home. They bring along Celie's adult children, whom they have raised. The family is reunited at last, and the sisters are able to look to the future with hope.

Samuel

Samuel is the American pastor who raises Celie's children in Africa. He is married to Corrine when Nettie accompanies him and his family to Africa, but Corrine dies of a fever while they are there. Witnessing the tender love he has for his wife endears him to Nettie. She writes to Celie about Samuel's compassion, spirituality, and tenderness. Samuel and Nettie are married after Corrine's death. In a letter to Celie, Nettie writes,

"From a skinny, hard little something I've become quite plump. And some of my hair is gray!

But Samuel tells me he loves me plump and graying. Does this surprise you?

Celie (*right*) and Nettie support one another through their difficult childhood, so when the two are separated, the loss is devastating for both sisters.

We were married last Fall in England where we tried to get relief for the Olinka from the churches and the Missionary Society."[19]

Later in the letter she adds, "You may have guessed that I loved him all along, but I did not know it. Oh, I loved him as a brother and respected him as a friend, but Celie, I love him bodily, *as a man!*"[20]

Reviews

Upon its release in 1982, *The Color Purple* drew widespread praise as well as sharp criticism. Professor Maria Lauret notes:

> Scores of articles have been written about [*The Color Purple*], every critical anthology of feminist literary scholarship contains multiple references to it, and the release of [producer and director] Steven Spielberg's film yielded a whole new crop of journalistic and academic responses, as well as protest marches and public debates. *The Color Purple* seemed a most unlikely text to be adopted by the mainstream, given the controversial nature of its political and sexual context.[21]

While many readers and literary critics applauded the sensitive subjects covered in the book, others criticized its use of seemingly vulgar language and its explicit sexual content. It soon gained a reputation as a book that people either loved or hated. Despite this mixed-bag reception, *The Color Purple* won Walker literary acclaim. It cemented Walker's standing in literary circles, winning the Pulitzer Prize and the National Book Award.

The book's popularity has not waned since its publishing debut more than thirty years ago. It continues to be read in high schools and colleges across America despite continual efforts at banning from schools. On another front, stage adaptations are performed in schools, community theaters, and other venue.

The Color Purple began its run as a Broadway revival in 2015 (it originally played on Broadway from 2005 to 2008, in addition to several national tours). Critics and viewers have applauded the production, which was nominated for several awards, perhaps most notably four Tony Award nominations. The production won in two of the categories, including Best Revival of a Musical.

Walker receives applause at the 2015 Broadway opening night for *The Color Purple*. The play has had many revivals over the years, as well as several national tours.

Joy Lost...and Found: Examining *Possessing the Secret of Joy*

> "I married him because he was loyal, gentle and familiar. Because he came for me. And because I found I could not fight with the wound tradition had given me. I could hardly walk."[1]

The speaker of these lines is Tashi "Evelyn" Johnson, the protagonist in Walker's fifth novel, *Possessing the Secret of Joy*. She utters these words while explaining to her psychiatrist why she married her husband, Adam. She uses the word "wound" to describe the physical and mental trauma she suffers after undergoing a traditional rite of passage performed on African females. The procedure left her irreparably scarred.

Adam rescues Tashi, marries her, and brings her to the United States, but ultimately he cannot save her. The novel catalogues Tashi's descent into madness, her long fight to salvage and reconstruct a self, her return to Africa, her final, costly liberation, and her discovery that "resistance is the secret of joy."[2]

The Problem with Tradition

Possessing the Secret of Joy centers around the "telling" of suffering and the breaking of taboos[3], both of which are closely linked to tradition keeping. The novel reveals how traditions can be beautiful or ugly. They can unite people or divide them. They can lead followers on a path to empowerment or destruction. Related activities can bond individuals, families, or nations—or destroy them over time. For example, the Olinka did not openly talk about the process of cutting or its lasting impact. The women did not share about it either, fearing disapproval from tribal leaders. About preserving traditions, Walker noted in an interview, "Ninety-nine and ninety-nine one-hundredths percent of traditions should be done away with because women did not make them."[4]

In *Possessing the Secret of Joy*, Walker explores how people who adhere to destructive traditions can influence the past as well as the present. The novel examines the idea of the rite of passage, a tradition embraced by a family, community, culture, or nation. It is usually a joyous time of celebration marking a young person's transition from childhood to adulthood. In this story, Walker sheds light on a specific rite of passage for African girls. In the novel, the Olinka (the same fictitious tribe visited by Nettie in *The Color Purple*) call it a "bath." In real life, the tradition is dubbed "female circumcision" by many who practice it. Opponents—contending the term is a euphemism—call it female genital mutilation.

As in real life, the rite of passage in the novel is performed on girls when they are very young, not long after they are born, or when they are five or six years old, but some older girls, teenagers, and women also undergo it. Essentially, it is a process that involves cutting a female's vagina. There are several ways of performing the procedure, with the methods varying in intensity of the cut. Walker's novel reveals that a female's overall well-being is impacted regardless of which cut is made. Nations that hold to the tradition claim it is vital in ensuring a female's virginity at marriage. They also contend it ensures a future husband's sexual pleasure.

Despite these proclaimed benefits, the tradition sparks controversy. Most females are too young to consent to it, and it is painful to endure, causing long-term pain and/or other medical problems. In addition, it hinders a female's basic body functions, such as urination. Further sparking the controversy is the fact the procedure is often performed by nonmedical professionals in nonmedical environments, greatly increasing the inherent health risks. Walker uses fiction to shed light on this real-life controversial procedure that has long existed in many nations.

Young girls in Ethiopia, where female circumcision is still a common practice. Many people, including the villagers where these girls live, have begun protesting the tradition.

Caught in a clash of cultures, Tashi succumbs to "tradition" as a young woman and undergoes the procedure voluntarily. She then descends into madness.[5] The novel raises numerous questions: What happens when the quest to fulfill tradition results in tremendous personal loss, rather than the anticipated fulfillment a person expects? How does keeping related secrets impact a person, family, or entire nation? What happens when a tradition keeper decides to right past wrongs? Is there ever a point when tradition needs to be tossed aside or modified? Another troubling question centers on whether or not a person who willingly keeps tradition is a victim.

Clearly, this controversial practice is a sensitive topic for a novel. Indeed, Walker is credited with being among the first authors to address the subject at the time the novel was released. What sparked her to write about the subject? In an interview she noted:

> . . . I could not continue going on blithely, as if this weren't happening. As if this was not a part of what's wrong with Africa. Of what's wrong with us. I firmly believe that the reason AIDS spreads faster in Africa is because of these genital mutilations. And I think that if it continues, it will depopulate the continent—maybe not in my lifetime, or even in my child's lifetime, but it will happen.[6]

Walker was criticized by some people who felt an American—or Westerner—could never truly understand the cultural significance and meaning behind genital cutting. Thus, they contended, she was out of her league in trying to write about the practice and its practitioners. Acknowledging criticism of the novel, Walker wrote, "I have done the best that I could with a challenging subject; perhaps my writer's shortcomings might be viewed against the magnitude of the calamity."[7] That "calamity" is at the heart of the novel's themes, characterization, and plot development.

Themes

Clearly, the relevance of tradition is a key theme of the novel. Other major themes are the search for identity or self and resisting oppression. Walker incorporates these themes through her characters, the act of naming, and cultural differences between American and African citizens. Where is the link between joy and resistance? Walker explained the meaning of the phrase "resistance is the secret of joy" as used in the novel, noting in an interview:

WAGING EMPATHY

Walker's focus on female genital mutilation (FGM) continues to spark debate as well as activism. One recent project is the essay collection *Waging Empathy: Alice Walker, Possessing the Secret of Joy, and the Global Movement to Ban FGM*. It is edited by Tobe Levin, who has actively worked to ban FGM since she first heard about the practice. The essays are written by a variety of writers.

Of the books, Alice Walker writes on her website:

Each essay on the novel, no matter the country, is rich, deep, thoughtful, engaging. I like it that this international bouquet of insights will reach students, or any reader, in ways that make FGM and its victims and perpetrators easier to understand. After all, it is comprehension not punishment we seek, since we realize everyone in a culture loses when the cries of a deliberately wounded child fall on ears too wounded to hear.[8]

... It means that the joy is in the struggle against whatever is keeping you from being your true self. You have to fight it. You cannot expect to have happiness in an intolerable situation where you are thoroughly oppressed and violated. There is no greater joy than being who you are, and what you are, and truly that. And to have someone come and say to you: "Well, you know, your body would be okay if you didn't have a vulva. Let me cut that off." It's not acceptable. You really have to fight it.[9]

Character Development

Tashi

Tashi is the protagonist in *Possessing the Secret of Joy*. In the novel she is known as Evelyn—and four other names! Her African birth name is Tashi. She was born in Africa as a member of the Olinka people. Her other four monikers are: Evelyn-Tashi, Tashi-Evelyn, Tashi-Evelyn-Mrs. Johnson, and Tashi Evelyn Johnson Soul. Why so many names?

Walker uses naming as a literary device to reflect changes in the protagonist's life. These changes encompass the character's nationality, marital status, and self-perception. The names also mirror shifts in her mental condition. As her mind declines, her name also is fragmented by her use of a hyphen. A name is also used to show the protagonist's evolution into someone whose mind and heart are whole. At the book's end she is known as Tashi Evelyn Mrs. Johnson Soul. There are no hyphens in the name, reflecting her journey to wholeness is complete. The addition of the name "Soul" is also significant. Despite dying for the murder she committed, she is at peace. Her soul is at rest. In the *Southern Literary Journal*, Geneva Cobb Moore explains:

... And, finally, there is Tashi Evelyn Johnson Soul, who achieves the Self upon her reconciliation of opposites, resistance to lies, and acceptance of death for her "crime" of alerting other women to her conviction that resistance to lies (imposed through silence upon suffering women in a patriarchal social order) is the real secret of joy.[10]

Dura

Dura, Tashi's older sister, bled to death following a traditional rite of passage for village girls. Her death becomes a defining moment in Tashi's life. It sparks Tashi's deep-rooted fear of blood. It also sparks a recurring dream whose significance she only realizes many years later as an adult. Tashi represses her memories of Dura for years. As Olivia recalls,

> Years later, in the United States, she [Tashi] would begin to remember some of the things she'd told me over the years of our growing up. That Dura had been her favorite sister. That she had been headstrong and boisterous and liked honey in her porridge so much she'd sometimes stolen a portion of Tashi's share. That she had been excited during the period leading up to her death. Suddenly, she had become the center of everyone's attention . . .[11]

Adam Johnson

Adam, Tashi's childhood friend, is American. His adopted family traveled to Africa to share Christianity with the Olinka people. Adam and Tashi begin dating when they are teenagers and have a passionate relationship. After Tashi's "bath," Adam rescues her from a militant camp. He loves Tashi deeply. He marries her and takes her back to America, but their relationship is crippled by Tashi's physical wounds and declining mental health. Despite his love for Tashi, Adam begins a long-term sexual relationship with a friend who lives in France. He had met Lisette when her church youth group came to Africa.

Olivia

Olivia is Adam's sister and a close friend of Tashi's. In fact, they are as close as sisters. Olivia does not understand Tashi's motivation for participating in the scarring rites. Nonetheless, she remains supportive throughout the novel.

Lisette

Lisette is the white feminist with whom Adam has an affair. As a result of the affair, the two have a son named Pierre.

Benny Johnson

Benny is Tashi and Adam's son. Because of Tashi's vaginal cutting, she has difficulty giving birth to him. As a result, he suffers brain damage and some mental retardation. Tashi blames herself for his birth defects. She treats him harshly because of her guilt and depression.

Pierre

The biracial son of Lisette and Adam, Pierre tries to befriend Tashi but she resents him. Over time, the two bond as Pierre works to help Tashi become emotionally whole.

M'Lissa

M'Lissa holds the position of *Tsunga* among the Olinkas. She is the person responsible for performing the circumcisions on the Olinka girls, including Dura, who died as a result of the procedure. Over time, Tashi views M'Lissa as a murderer who was never punished for the deaths she caused. Tashi decides that she will seek revenge for those deaths.

Mzee

Lisette's cousin Mzee is Tashi's psychiatrist. Walker patterned his character after Carl Jung, a famous psychiatrist.

Narrative Style

Possessing the Secret of Joy is unique in that it is a story told from the viewpoint of multiple characters. Key to the novel are the first-person narratives the protagonist Tashi shares at different stages of her life before and after undergoing the traditional cutting ceremony. Complicating her narratives is the fact that they are shared under different names. Readers soon realize this technique is used to underscore how fragmented Tashi is becoming emotionally and mentally.

In addition, all of the other key characters in Tashi's life provide first-person points of view about some aspect of their interaction with the protagonist. These accounts help flesh out Tashi's character and motivations.

Structure

Walker makes navigating the novel easy for readers by dividing it into twenty-one "Parts," or chapters. Each Part is further divided into subsections labeled with a character's name. Readers understand that the named character is the person sharing his or her viewpoint about the events that unfold. In the case of Mzee, the psychiatrist, Walker uses letter writing as a means of sharing the doctor's point of view.

Reviews

Possessing the Secret of Joy received cheers and jeers. It was a *New York Times* best seller, with readers and critics applauding Walker's willingness to expose a practice that had long harmed women. On the other hand, some contended Walker's view was biased and that she did not fully understand the cultural significance and importance of female circumcision. When an interviewer asked how she would respond to the question, "What gives this Westerner a right to intervene in our affairs?"[12] Walker replied:

> Slavery intervened. As far as I'm concerned, I am speaking for my great-great-great-great-grandmother who came here with all this pain in her body. Think about it. In addition to having been captured, put in the hull of a ship, packed like sardines, put on the auction block, in addition to her children being sold, she being raped, in addition to all of this, she might have been genitally mutilated. I can't stand it! I would go nuts if this part of her story weren't factored in.[13]

Reflecting on her goals for the novel, Walker said: "I have one requirement: that, because of this books, one little girl, somewhere, won't be mutilated. And that's plenty. That'll keep me laughing. I'll go home. I'll kick up my heels, and I'll feel that on this issue I've saved one child. That's enough."[14]

WOMANIST PROSE: EXAMINING *YOU CAN'T KEEP A GOOD WOMAN DOWN*

Published in 1981, *You Can't Keep a Good Woman Down* is a collection of short stories. The title hints at the main theme of the entire collection: the resilience of women. They are, as Evelyn C. White describes them, "...fourteen provocative tales about women struggling, but not defeated."[1] She adds:

> Women like the protagonist who, in the story "How Did I Get Away with Killing One of the Biggest Lawyers in the State? It Was Easy," finds herself sitting in bed savoring fried chicken prepared by the wife of the man who had stolen her youth. Or Elethia, a "salad girl" at a café (segregated) who liberates a waxen replica of a docile black man that has been placed, by the restaurant's white owners, in a window display to attract customers. And then there was Gracie Mae Still, a talented songwriter who watched in disgust, but not despair, as a swivel-hipped white boy (read: Elvis Presley) made hit records off of her artistry.[2]

Women in these stories face trauma, heartbreak, disappointment, and other challenges. Rather than breaking from the pressure, the featured women rise above life's struggles. Writing about her focus on women in her prose, Walker notes, "I am committed to exploring the oppressions, the insanities, the loyalties, and the triumphs of black women . . . For me, black women are the most fascinating creations in the world."[3]

Themes

The collection covers a wide array of themes other than the strength of women. These include the South, love and romance, sexual relations, race relations, home and family, and fame.

Musician Tom Waits presents Walker with the Purple Globe award for artistic talent in 1986.

Each theme offers Walker's unique characterization, realistic language, and descriptive detail. Each is depicted in various subthemes, including abortion, death and dying, and rape.

The theme of love and romance comes into play in many of Walker's stories, and not always in a favorable light. One twist on this theme is seen in the negative impact pornography has on relationships. That theme is central to "Porn" and "Coming Apart," two of the stories in the collection that deal with men forcing their sexual fantasies upon their wives and girlfriends. Among other things, they reveal the oppression of women stemming from the use of pornography. The stories also reveal how men and women think differently about the subject of pornography. Those differences shape their behavior, self-concept, and ability to relate to their lover or spouse.

In her introduction to "Coming Apart," Walker shares why she chose to address this particular topic in print. She notes, "I believe it is only by writing stories in which pornography is confronted openly and explicitly that writers can make a contribution, in their own medium, to a necessary fight."[4]

The subject of race relations comes into play in different ways in the stories of this collection. Segregation is a key theme of "Elethia," which is about the title character's attempt to fight against society's stereotypes of happy slaves or African Americans who are content with their lot in life. The short story centers on Albert Porter, a feisty former slave whom whites could not control. He is the exact opposite of a brown dummy, intended to be his likeness, that is displayed in the window of a segregated restaurant, Old Uncle Albert's. The smiling dummy is dressed like a waiter and holding a tray. One day Elethia and her friends steal the dummy, burning it and its offensive image. She carries the ashes around with her as a reminder not to be that docile dummy, although she meets real-life "Uncle Alberts" over the years. The story concludes, "And she was careful that, no matter how compelling the hype, Uncle Alberts, in her own mind, were not permitted to exist." [5]

Issues of race also form the backdrop for "A Sudden Trip Home in the Spring," this time coupled with the topics of family and death and dying. Sarah Davis is a college student who suddenly returns home after her father's death. Louis H. Pratt, writing in *Studies in Popular Culture,* explains:

> "A Sudden Trip Home in the Spring" is a short story, narrated by Sarah Davis, which focuses on the death of her father and the new, brief insight which she gains into the significance of her nameless grandfather's life . . . What impressed Sarah, most . . . was his determination to allow his Blackness to be defined by this family, rather than by whites. This produced in the old man a unique kind of toughness, a hardness that defied Sarah's efforts to capture him on canvas. Instead, Walker allows the old man one solitary line which summarizes his durability: "if you want to make me, make me up in stone."[6]

Overcoming Injustice

The collection begins with "Nineteen Fifty-Five," a short story that gives readers a taste of life in the South during segregation. The story depicts the inequalities African Americans faced during this turbulent period in the United States. In large part, it uses music to illustrate this truth. Protagonist Gracie Mae is a singer who was once famous for her legendary voice. However, she has fallen on hard times and her singing days are over. One day, as she is sitting at home, she notices a peculiar sight:

> The car is a brand new red Thunderbird convertible, and it's passed the house more than once. It slows down real slow now, and stops at the curb. An older gentleman dressed like a Baptist deacon gets out on the side near the house, and a young fellow who looks about sixteen gets out on the driver's side. They are white, and I wonder what in the world they doing in this neighborhood.[7]

Readers wonder the same thing as they read this introduction—if they know anything about the South in 1955, they are probably also wondering if this is a story about racial strife. Indeed, Walker does a good job of building tension from the beginning of this short story, which is told from Gracie Mae's point of view.

As the plot quickly unfolds, Gracie Mae discovers that her older visitor—whom she only refers to as "the deacon"— is interested in her music. He contends the younger man, Traynor, loves her songs: "The boy learned to sing and dance livin' round you people out in the country. Practically cut his teeth on you," he tells Gracie Mae.[8]

In short order, the deacon explains the reason for their visit. He wants Gracie Mae to allow Traynor to record one of her songs. Some readers believe that Traynor is a fictional character modeled after the singer Elvis Presley because of his physical appearance and his ability to emulate an African American singing style, and because Presley had been accused of stealing the music of African Americans.

The deacon offers Gracie Mae five hundred dollars, a large amount of money at that time, to seal the deal. But there's one catch: Gracie Mae must destroy all copies of the original record. Gracie is not so easily hoodwinked. She realizes something is fishy about the deal:

Well, love it or not, I'm not so stupid to let them do that without making 'em pay. So I says, Well, that's gonna cost you. Because really, that song never did sell all that good, so I was glad they was going to buy it up. But on the other hand, them two listening to my song for themselves and nobody else getting to hear me sing it, give me a pause.[9]

All told, she receives one thousand dollars in exchange for the rights to the song. Unfortunately, Traynor makes a lot more than that off her music after he records and performs it as if it were his song. Gracie Mae receives credit on the album as the writer, but that fact is soon lost. The deacon and Traynor go on to buy other songs from Gracie Mae, and soon Traynor becomes famous and rich for "his" songs.

The character of Traynor in "Nineteen Fifty-Five" is modeled after rock 'n' roll legend Elvis Presley.

Over time, Gracie Mae also becomes wealthy from their arrangement, both from the money she earns and expensive gifts from the deacon. That does not make her any happier concerning the way her music is basically stolen by a white person for his greater economic gain. Ironically, Traynor admits he does not even understand the underlying meaning of the songs he sings.

Many years later Gracie Mae provides some answers. Her songs are rich in culture, she explains. They are born out of adversity and they bind African Americans in the unified struggle for independence. These are themes Traynor, a white man, can never truly understand or appreciate. Neither can his fans. Proof of this comes when Gracie Mae sings her song on television with Traynor but the audience does not appreciate how she sings it.

The story ends with Traynor dying in 1977 and his devastated fans mourning his passing. According to Gracie, "They were crying and crying and didn't even know what they was crying for. One day this is going to be a pitiful country, I thought."[10]

The fact that Gracie Mae does not already think that it is "pitiful" reveals her triumph over adversity. She is not bitter because of what has been done to her. Themes in "Nineteen Fifty-Five" include oppression, women's resilience, love, and race relationships. Those recur throughout *You Can't Keep a Good Woman Down*.

Reviews

You Can't Keep a Good Woman Down was published after Walker's short story collection *In Love & Trouble*. The collection was met with mixed reviews, in part because people compared the two books. Some reviewers praised *You Can't Keep a Good Woman Down*, while others argued that it lacked the substance, style, or cohesiveness of *In Love & Trouble*.

Calling Walker "exceptionally brave," writer Alice Adams states: "She takes on subjects at which most writers would flinch and quail, and probably fail. She shrinks from no moral or emotional complexity and she writes consummately skillful short stories."[11] Meanwhile, Katha Pollitt of the *New York Times* says, "I give Alice Walker . . . much credit for daring to engage in fiction terms (well, quasi-fictional terms . . .) some of the major racial-sexual-political issues of our times."[12] After criticizing aspects of the collection, however, Pollitt concludes the review with, "As a storyteller, she [Walker] is impassioned, sprawling, emotional, lushly evocative, steeped in place, in memory, in the compelling power of narrative itself. A lavishly gifted writer, in other words—but not of this sort of book."[13]

WHOSE ART IS IT?

"Nineteen Fifty-Five" is one of Walker's works of fiction that is steeped in truth, depicting the reality for many African American singers and songwriters in the 1950s. Unlike Gracie Mae, however, many were never even asked permission to use their songs. Others never became rich from their art that was rerecorded by white singers.

Numerous movies and stage plays have brought this disparity to life. One of these is the 2006 movie *Dreamgirls*. It was based on an award-winning Broadway play of the same name. It also mirrored true life. In 1955, a gospel music group performed at the famous Apollo Theater. It was a historic event, as no such religious group had ever performed in that setting. Their success led to road tours playing in other nonreligious venues, similar to the scenes in *Dreamgirls*.

The movie featured a cast of well-known African American actors and performers, including Jamie Foxx, Eddie Murphy, and Beyoncé. Jennifer Hudson made her movie debut in the movie, winning a 2006 Academy Award for her performance.

English professor and author Alice Hall Petry was equally unimpressed with the collection. She contends, for example, that "The Lover" is just one example of how the collection fails to live up to reader expectations. The heroine, she believes, comes across as foolish because of the lover she chooses. Petry contends:

> And that points to a major problem with *You Can't Keep a Good Woman Down*: whereas the stories of *In Love & Trouble* move the reader to tears, to shock, to thought, those of the latter volume too often move him to guffaws. Too bad they weren't meant to be humorous.

A scene from the 2006 film *Dreamgirls* (starring, left to right: Anika Noni Rose, Beyoncé Knowles, and Jennifer Hudson). The movie shines a light on the unfair treatment of black performers in the mid-1900s.

> One would think that a writer of Alice Walker's stature and experience would be aware that, since time began, the reduction of love to fornication has been the basis of jokes, from the ridiculous to the sublime. And whether they come across as comic . . . examples of bathroom humor, or zany parodies, the characters, subject matter and writing style of most of the stories in *You Can't keep a Good Woman Down* leave the reader with a she's-gotta-be-kidding attitude that effectively undercuts its very serious intentions.[14]

Petry further argued: "What Alice Walker needs is to take a step backward: to return to the folk tale formats, the painful exploration of interpersonal relationships, the naturally graceful style that made her earlier collection of short stories, the durable *In Love & Trouble,* so very fine."[15]

Despite negative reviews, individual stories in *You Can't Keep a Good Woman Down* were well received. For example, in 1981, "The Abortion" won the prestigious O. Henry Prize. "Elethia" was republished in the 2003 anthology *Imagining America: Stories from the Promised Land.* Additionally, the film version of "How Did I Get Away with Killing One of the Biggest Lawyers in the State? It Was Easy" was released in 1989, titled *Behind God's Back.*

"Everyday Use": Alice Walker Today

Hearing a poet, novelist, or essayist read his or her own work can offer a reader insights into what parts of the writing should be emphasized. Today, some writers conduct this type of reading during videotaped interviews, while others offer short video clips on their websites or social media. In some of these, authors answers questions posed by readers. This is an aspect of reading and interpreting literature that was not available to early readers of Alice Walker's work. But it is now.

Quite a number of videos exist in which the prolific author reads her work and/or shares her views about the themes, characters, and/or plots in the works. In one such example, she reads the essay she wrote to President Barack Obama before he was elected. His historic run for president had a profound impact on Walker, a child of the segregated South. She includes a number of essays in her memoir on the subject.

As in her writing, Walker's discussions of her work make it clear that resistance is a hallmark of her life and legacy. And if resistance is truly the road to possessing the secret of joy, then Alice Walker has discovered that joy. She has written novels, poetry, short stories, and essays on resistance themes. She has marched against injustice. She has spoken out against issues she believes need to be at the forefront of people's consciousness.

"'Color Purple' author, 26 others arrested at peace rally" was the headline of a CNN.com article on March 9, 2003.[1]

Walker and thousands of other protestors marched in Washington against the possibility of America embarking on a war with Iraq. That Walker was in the throes of the rally was no surprise to anyone who has read her prose. Nor would it surprise anyone if Walker showed up at a protest event today.

Not only is Walker well known for her resistance efforts, but she has also been honored for her activism. For example, in 2010, she received an award that typifies her life and work: the Lennon Ono Grant for Peace. The award was created to honor the legacy of John Lennon, a member of the Beatles and an activist who was murdered in 1980. Walker was one of four recipients "selected based on their courage and commitment to peace, truth and human rights."[2] Walker donated the funds to an African orphanage that helps children of AIDS victims, an act of resistance against the deadly disease that has ravaged Africa for years. It also underscores her commitment to helping Africa.

Recent Projects

Winning the Pulitzer Prize for *The Color Purple* was a high point of Walker's career. Evelyn C. White notes, "The prestige of the Pulitzer Prize sparked new interest in a novel that many had overlooked upon its initial release, winning reviews notwithstanding."[3] Despite that fact, chances are Alice Walker never imagined the book would remain in print as long as it has.

Few writers experience such longevity for a work of fiction or nonfiction. The new stage adaptation that debuted on Broadway in 2015 served as further proof that people are still enamored with the characters and themes Walker created more than thirty years ago.

This 2003 rally in Washington, DC, was organized to protest the imminent war in Iraq. Walker attended this protest and was arrested for her involvement.

Walker's many other projects since then have provided new material for readers and critics to love (or hate). Regardless of people's acceptance of any individual project, Walker continues to write what is important to her. Lately, she has focused on essays and poetry more than novels. There is a reason for that.

> ... [I]t seems to me that all of my poems—and I write groups of poems rather than singles—are written when I have successfully pulled myself out of a completely numbing despair, and stand again in the sunlight. Writing poems is my way of celebrating with the world that I have not committed suicide the night before.[4]

Walker discusses her work at the New School in New York City in 2015. Now in her seventies, she continues to publish a wide range of writing while remaining politically and socially active.

Walker's difficult early years, as well as the death of her parents and several siblings, have undoubtedly contributed to this "numbing despair," and her poetry has served as a crucial outlet in overcoming difficult periods.

Walker's most recent novel, *Now Is the Time to Open Your Heart*, was released in 2004. Her latest short story collection is *The Way Forward Is with a Broken Heart*, which debuted in 2000. Those types of writing have taken a backseat to writing poetry and essays.

Walker's two most recent poetry collections are *Hard Times Require Furious Dancing: New Poems* (2010) and *The World Will Follow Joy: Turning Madness into Flowers* (2013). Since 2010, Walker has also published four nonfiction books. They are: *Overcoming Speechlessness: A Poet Encounters the Horror in Rwanda, Eastern Congo and Palestine/Israel* (2010), *The World Has Changed: Conversations with Alice Walker* (2010), *The Chicken Chronicles: Sitting with the Angels Who Have Returned with My Memories, a Memoir* (2011), and *The Cushion in the Road: Meditation and Wandering as the Whole World Awakens to Being in Harm's Way* (2013).

Lasting Change

From her very first published poetry collection in 1968, Alice Walker has been a pioneering author who shatters perceptions about what is appropriate for inclusion in African American literature. As professor of African American studies Barbara Christian explains:

> . . . Walker was one of the first contemporary black women writers to insist that sexism existed in the black community and was not only an issue for white women. She did this at a time when most black leaders focused only on racism and considered her position to be

practically heresy. At the same time, she also dramatized in her works the nature of racism and the relationship between sexism and racism as modes of oppression that restricted the lives of all women and men in the country . . .[5]

Each year, students are introduced—or reintroduced—to Walker's pioneering writing. In fact, in 2016, *Time* magazine included her on a list of the "100 Most-Read Female Writers in College Classes."[6] Walker was number thirteen. Her works most read were the short story "Everyday Use" and the novels *The Color Purple* and *Possessing the Secret of Joy.*

Christian provides a clue as to why Walker's work remains popular:

Walker meets with Palestinian women in the Gaza Strip in 2009. She is vocal in her condemnation of Israeli attacks on the area.

Walker has, more than any contemporary writer in America, exposed the "twin afflictions" that best black women, the sexism and racism that historically and presently restrict their lives. Walker develops literary forms (for example her concept of quilting, her use of folk language) that are based on the creative legacy left her by her ancestors.[7]

What's Next?

In her memoir *The Cushion in the Road,* Walker noted that poetry will be a main focus in the coming years. She explains:

> I am embracing poetry as a priority, which is what, in my opinion, current movements for liberation and justice desperately need. Poetry is the lifeblood of rebellion, revolution, and the raising of consciousness. And it is the raising of consciousness that is the most effective way to ensure lasting change.[8]

For an activist writer like Walker, effecting long-term change is a dream come true.

CHRONOLOGY

1944– Alice Walker is born on February 9 in Eatonville, Georgia.

1952– Suffers blindness in right eye after being shot by BB gun.

1958– Undergoes surgery to remove scar tissue from eye.

1961– Graduates as valedictorian from Butler-Baker High School.

1961– Receives scholarship to attend Spelman College in Atlanta, Georgia.

1962– Meets with Coretta Scott King, wife of Dr. Martin Luther King Jr.; attends World Youth Peace Festival in Helsinki, Finland, as delegate.

1963– Hears Dr. King's famous "I Have a Dream" speech while attending the March on Washington for Jobs and Freedom in Washington, DC; transfers to Sarah Lawrence College in Bronxville, New York, after receiving scholarship.

1964– Travels to Africa.

1965– Graduates from Sarah Lawrence College with a Bachelor of Arts degree; moves to New York City, taking job in a city agency; moves to Mississippi; writes her first short story, "To Hell with Dying."

1966– Marries Melvyn ("Mel") Leventhal.

1967– Awarded a fellowship from the Ingram Merrill Foundation; receives the National Institute of Arts and Letters' Rosenthal Award.

1968– Publishes *Once*, a collection of poems mostly written years earlier while at Sarah Lawrence College. Begins teaching at Jackson State University.

1969– Gives birth on November 17 to daughter, Rebecca Grant.

1970– Publishes first novel, *The Third Life of Grange Copeland*; receives Radcliffe Institute Fellowship; teaches at Tougaloo College.

1972– Accepts positions to lecture at Wellesley College and the University of Massachusetts.

1973– Publishes *Revolutionary Petunias and Other Poems*; publishes *In Love & Trouble: Stories of Black Women*; father dies; locates and places a marker on novelist Zora Neale Hurston's grave.

1974– Begins working as editor of *Ms.* magazine; children's book *Langton Hughes: American Poet* is released; *Revolutionary Petunias* receives nomination for a National Book Award.

1976– Publishes novel *Meridian*; marriage ends in divorce.

1978– Receives the National Endowment for the Arts' Lillian Smith Award.

1979– Publishes poetry collection, *Goodnight, Willie Lee, I'll See You in the Morning; I Love Myself When I am Laughing . . . and Then Again When I Am Looking Mean and Impressive* is published.

1981– Releases *You Can't Keep a Good Woman Down,* a short story collection.

1982– Publishes novel *The Color Purple.*

1983– Awarded Pulitzer Prize for Fiction for *The Color Purple.*

1983– Wins National Book Award for Fiction for *The Color Purple*; releases essay collection, *In Search of Our Mothers' Gardens.*

1984– Publishes poetry collection *Horses Make a Landscape Look More Beautiful.*

1985–1986– *The Color Purple* film, directed by Steven Spielberg, is released; film is nominated for eleven Oscars, but does not win any.

1988– Publishes essays *Living by the Word* and children's book version of *To Hell with Dying*.

1989– Releases novel *The Temple of My Familiar*.

1991– Publishes *Her Blue Body Everything We Know: Earthling Poems*, and *Finding the Green Stone*, a children's book.

1992– Novel *Possessing the Secret of Joy* is released.

1993– *Warrior Marks: Female Genital Mutilation and the Sexual Blinding of Women* book and documentary released; filmmaker Pratibha Parmar collaborates on both; mother dies.

1994– Changes name to Alice Tallulah-Kate Walker.

1996– Releases *The Same River Twice, Honoring the Difficult* essay collection; William Walker, her brother, dies.

1997– Publishes essays *Anything We Love Can Be Saved: A Writer's Activism*; named "Humanist of the Year" by the American Humanist Association.

1998– Novel *By the Light of My Father's Smile* is published.

2000– Releases short stories *The Way Forward Is with a Broken Heart*.

2001– *Sent by Earth: A Message from the Grandmother Spirit After the Attacks on the World Trade Center and Pentagon* is released; is honored as one of the first inductees into the Georgia Writers Hall of Fame.

2002– James Walker, her brother, dies.

2003– *Absolute Truth in the Goodness of the Earth: New Poems* and *A Poem Traveled Down My Arm* are published; arrested while protesting against the war.

2004– *Now Is the Time to Open Your Heart* is released; *The Color Purple* musical production debuts in Atlanta; Curtis Walker, her brother, dies.

2006– Publishes *We Are the Ones We Have Been Waiting For: Light in a Time of Darkness* essay collection; and *There Is a Flower at the Tip of My Nose Smelling Me* children's book; is inducted into the California Hall of

Fame at the California Museum for History, Woman, and the Arts.

2007– Emory University in Atlanta opens Walker's archives to the public; *Why War Is Never a Good Idea*, a children's book, is published.

2010– Receives Lennon Ono Grant for Peace and donates monetary award to East African orphanage serving children of AIDS victims; publishes *Overcoming Speechlessness: A Poet Encounters the Horror in Rwanda, Eastern Congo, and Palestine/Israel*; *Hard Times Require Furious Dancing*; *The World Has Changed: Conversations with Alice Walker* is released.

2011– Publishes memoir *The Chicken Chronicles: Sitting with the Angels Who Have Returned with My Memories.*

2013– Publishes poetry collection *The World Will Follow Joy: Turning Madness into Flowers*; releases essays *The Cushion in the Road: Meditation and Wandering as the Whole World Awakens to Being in Harm's Way.*

2015– *The Color Purple* musical debuts on Broadway in December.

2016– *The Color Purple* musical is nominated for five Audience Choice Awards and six Drama Desk Awards.

CHAPTER NOTES

Chapter 1. Unveiling Secrets

1. Alice Walker, *Good Night, Willie Lee, I'll See You in the Morning* (New York: The Dial Press, 1979), p. 2.
2. Ibid.
3. Ibid., p. 3.
4. Henry Louis Gates Jr., "Preface," *Critical Perspectives Past and Present*, ed. Henry Louis Gates Jr. and K. A. Appiah (New York: Amistad Press, 1993), x.
5. Barbara Christian, "Novels for Everyday Use," *Critical Perspectives Past and Present*, p. 50.
6. Alice Walker, *Hard Times Require Furious Dancing* (New York: New World Library, 2010), xv.
7. Mary Helen Washington, "An Essay on Alice Walker," *Critical Perspectives Past and Present*, p. 37.
8. Ibid., p. 39.
9. Louis H. Pratt, "Alice Walker's Men: Profiles in the Quest for Love and Personal Values," *Alice Walker: Bloom's Modern Critical Views*, ed. Harold Bloom (New York: Infobase Publishing, 2007), pp. 8–9.
10. Ibid., p. 5.
11. Ibid., p. 7.
12. Ibid., p. 10.
13. Bonnie Braendlin, "Alice Walker's *The Temple of My Familiar* as Pastiche," *Alice Walker: Bloom's Modern Critical Views*, p. 116.
14. Alice Walker, *The Color Purple* (New York, NY: Houghton Mifflin Harcourt, 1982), p. 45.
15. Ibid.
16. Ibid.
17. Alice Walker, Jean Shinoda Bolen, and Isabel Allende, "Giving Birth, Finding Form: Where Our Books Come From," *The World Has Changed: Conversations with Alice Walker*, ed. Rudolph P. Byrd (New York: The New Press, 2011), p. 115.

Chapter 2. Walker's Works

1. Claudia Durst Johnson, *Women's Issues in Alice Walker's* The Color Purple (Farmington Hills, MI: Greenhaven Press, 2011), p. 9.
2. Ibid., p. 10.
3. Alice Walker, *The Color Purple* (New York: Houghton Mifflin Harcourt, 1982), p. 86.
4. Alice Walker, *Once: Poems* (New York: Harcourt Brace Jovanovich, 1968), p. 39.
5. Alice Walker, *In Search of Our Mothers' Gardens: Womanist Prose* (Orlando, FL: Harcourt, 1983), p. 19.
6. Alice Walker, *Possessing the Secret of Joy* (New York: The New Press, 2008), p. 45.
7. Ibid., p. 130.
8. Johnson, p. 98.
9. Alice Walker, "How Did I Get Away with Killing One of the Biggest Lawyers in the State? It Was Easy," *You Can't Keep a Good Woman Down* (Orlando, FL: Harcourt, 1981), p. 21.
10. Walker, "From an Interview," *In Search of Our Mothers' Gardens*, p. 251.
11. Walker, *Possessing the Secret of Joy*, p. 175.
12. Walker, "How Did I Get Away with Killing One of the Biggest Lawyers in the State? It Was Easy," p. 23.
13. Walker, *The Color Purple*, p. 285.
14. Walker, *Possessing the Secret of Joy*, p. 23.
15. Ibid., p. 98.
16. Ibid., p. 171.

Chapter 3. Hard Times, Good Times

1. Valerie Schloredt, "Alice Walker: 'Go to Places That Scare You,'" *Yes,* October 2, 2012, http://www.yesmagazine.org/issues/its-your-body/alice-walker-go-to-the-places-that-scare-you.
2. Alice Walker Literary Society, "Alice Walker," Emory University, accessed April 17, 2016, http://www.emory.edu/alicewalker/sub-about.htm.

3. Alice Walker, "The Black Writer and the Southern Experience," *In Search of Our Mothers' Gardens: Womanist Prose* (Orlando, FL: Harcourt, 1983), p. 17.

4. Schloredt.

5. Walker, "Choosing to Stay at Home," *In Search of Our Mothers' Gardens*, pp. 161–162.

6. Caroline Lazo, *Alice Walker: Freedom Writer* (Minneapolis: Lerner, 2000), p. 14.

7. Walker, "From an Interview," *In Search of Our Mothers' Gardens*, p. 241.

8. Ibid, p. 244.

9. Ibid.

10. Walker, "Coretta Scott: Revisited," *In Search of Our Mothers' Gardens*, p. 146.

11. Evelyn C. White, *Alice Walker* (New York: W.W. Norton & Company, 2004), p. 100.

12. Walker, "From an Interview," *In Search of Our Mothers' Gardens*, p. 245.

13. Ibid.

14. Ibid., p. 248.

15. Ibid., pp. 248–249.

16. Ibid., p. 259.

17. "Alice Walker: Official Biography," *Alice Walker: The Official Website*, accessed June 11, 2016, http://alicewalkersgarden.com/about-2/.

Chapter 4. In Living Color

1. Alice Walker, *The Color Purple* (New York: Houghton Mifflin Harcourt, 1982), p. 196.

2. Ibid., p. 193.

3. Ibid.

4. Ibid., p. 197.

5. Ibid., preface.

6. Alice Walker, "Writing the Color Purple," *In Search of Our Mothers' Gardens: Womanist Prose* (Orlando, FL: Harcourt, 1983), p. 355.
7. Walker, *The Color Purple*, p. 1.
8. Ibid., p. 177.
9. Lauren Berlant, "Race, Gender and Nation in *The Color Purple*," *Modern Critical Interpretations: Alice Walker's* The Color Purple, ed. Harold Bloom (Philadelphia: Chelsea House, 2000), p. 9.
10. Walker, *The Color Purple*, p. 1.
11. Diane Gabrielsen Scholl, "With Ears to Hear and Eyes to See: Alice Walker's Parable *The Color Purple*," *Modern Critical Interpretations: Alice Walker's* The Color Purple, p. 107.
12. Walker, *The Color Purple*, p. 148.
13. Ibid., p. 109.
14. Ibid., p. 46.
15. Ibid., p. 3.
16. Ibid., p. 5.
17. Ibid., p. 6.
18. Ibid., p. 109.
19. Ibid., p. 226.
20. Ibid., p. 238.
21. Maria Lauret, "Feeling Like an Outsider," *Women's Issues in Alice Walker's* The Color Purple (Farmington, MI: Greenhaven Press, 2011), p. 32.

Chapter 5. Joy Lost . . . and Found

1. Alice Walker, *Possessing the Secret of Joy* (New York: The New Press, 2008), p. 121.
2. Janette Turner Hospital, "What They Did to Tashi," *New York Times*, June 28, 1992, https://www.nytimes.com/books/98/10/04/specials/walker-secret.html.
3. Ibid.

4. Paula Giddings, "Alice Walker's Appeal," *Essence*, 1992, in *The World Has Changed: Conversations with Alice Walker*, ed. Rudolph P. Byrd (New York: The New Press, 2010), p. 90.

5. Evelyn C. White, *Alice Walker* (New York: W.W. Norton & Co., 2004), p. 458.

6. Giddings, p. 86.

7. Walker, *Possessing the Secret of Joy*, ix.

8. Alice Walker, "Waging Empathy: Alice Walker, *Possessing the Secret of Joy*, and the Global Movement to Ban FGM," accessed April 17, 2016, http://alicewalkersgarden.com/?s=waging+empathy.

9. Tami Simon, "My Life as Myself," Sounds True, 1995, in *The World Has Changed: Conversations with Alice Walker*, p. 144.

10. Geneva Cobb Moore, "Archetypal Symbolism in Alice Walker's *Possessing the Secret of Joy*," *Southern Literary Journal* 33, no. 1, Fall 2000, p. 114.

11. Walker, *Possessing the Secret of Joy*, p. 9.

12. Giddings, p. 87.

13. Ibid.

14. Ibid., p. 92.

Chapter 6. Womanist Prose

1. Evelyn C. White, *Alice Walker* (New York: W.W. Norton & Co., 2004), p. 327.

2. Ibid.

3. Alice Walker, "From an Interview," *In Search of Our Mothers' Gardens: Womanist Prose* (Orlando, FL: Harcourt, 1983), p. 250.

4. Alice Walker, "Coming Apart," *You Can't Keep a Good Woman Down* (New York: Harcourt, 1981), p. 42.

5. Ibid., 31.

6. Louis H. Pratt, "Alice Walker's Men: Profiles in the Quest for Love and Values," *Alice Walker: Bloom's Modern Critical Views*, ed. Harold Bloom (New York: Infobase Publishing, 2007), p. 8.

7. Alice Walker, "Nineteen Fifty-Five," *You Can't Keep a Good Woman Down*, p. 3.

8. Ibid., p. 4.
9. Ibid., p. 5.
10. Ibid., p. 20.
11. White, p. 329.
12. Katha Pollitt, "Stretching the Short Story," *New York Times,* May 24, 1981, http://partners.nytimes.com/books/98/10/04/specials/walker-woman.html.
13. Ibid.
14. Alice Hall Petry, "Alice Walker: The Achievement of the Short Fiction," *Alice Walker: Bloom's Modern Critical Views*, ed. Harold Bloom (New York: Infobase Publishing, 2007), p. 38.
15. Ibid., p. 49.

Chapter 7. "Everyday Use"

1. "'Color Purple' author, 26 others arrested at peace rally," *CNN. com*, March 9, 2003, http://www.cnn.com/2003/US/03/08/sprj.irq.war.rallies/.
2. "The Lennon Ono Grant for Peace 2010," Imagine Peace, October 12, 2010, http://imaginepeace.com/archives/13031.
3. Evelyn C. White, *Alice Walker* (New York: W.W. Norton & Co., 2004), p. 363.
4. Alice Walker, "From an Interview," *In Search of Our Mothers' Gardens* (Orlando, FL: Harcourt, 1983), p. 249.
5. Barbara Christian, "Walker's Childhood, Education, and Crusade for African American Women," *Women Issues in Alice Walker's The Color Purple* (Farmington Hills, MI: Greenhaven Press, 2011), p. 21.
6. David Johnson, "These Are the 100 Most-Read Female Writers in College Classes," *Time*, February 25, 2016, http://time.com/4234719/college-textbooks-female-writers/.
7. Christian, p. 17.
8. Alice Walker, *The Cushion in the Road: Meditation and Wandering as the Whole World Awakens to Being in Harm's Way* (New York: The New Press, 2013), p. 236.

LITERARY TERMS

analogy—A comparison between two like things.

dialect—A specific variety of a language, often distinctive to a certain region.

diction—The style or choice of words in speech or writing.

emotive—Emotional, sensitive; able to engage readers' senses.

epistolary—Having to do with letters.

hyperbole—A literary device that uses exaggeration to emphasize an action, fact, idea, or feeling.

irony—The use of words to convey the opposite of their literal meaning.

personification—Giving human characteristics to animals or inanimate objects.

protagonist—The main character in a work of fiction.

Major Works by
Alice Walker

Novels

The Third Life of Grange Copeland (1970)
Meridian (1976)
The Color Purple (1982)
The Temple of My Familiar (1989)
Possessing the Secret of Joy (1992)
By The Light of My Father's Smile (1998)
Now Is the Time to Open Your Heart (2004)

Short Story Collections

In Love & Trouble: Stories of Black Women (1973)
You Can't Keep a Good Woman Down (1981)
The Complete Stories (2000, 1994)
The Way Forward Is with a Broken Heart (2000)

Nonfiction/Essays

In Search of Our Mothers' Gardens: Womanist Prose (1983)
Living by the Word (1988)
*The Same River Twice: Honoring the Difficult; A Meditation of Life,
Spirit, Art and the Making of* The Color Purple *(1996)*
Anything We Love Can Be Saved: A Writer's Activism (1997)
The Way Forward Is with a Broken Heart (2000)
*Sent by Earth: A Message from the Grandmother Spirit After the
Attacks on the World Trade Center and Pentagon (2001)*
We Are the Ones We Have Been Waiting For (2006)
*Overcoming Speechlessness: A Poet Encounters the Horror in
Rwanda, Eastern Congo, and Palestine/Israel (2010)*
*Chicken Chronicles: Sitting with the Angels Who Have Returned
with My Memories (2011)*

The Cushion in the Road: Meditation and Wandering as the Whole World Awakens to Being in Harm's Way (2013)

Poetry

Her Blue Body Everything We Know: Earthling Poems 1965–1990 (1965, 1991)
Once (1968)
Revolutionary Petunias and Other Poems (1973)
Good Night, Willie Lee, I'll See You in the Morning (1979)
Horses Make a Landscape Look More Beautiful (1984)
Absolute Trust in the Goodness of the Earth (2003)
A Poem Traveled Down My Arm: Poems and Drawings (2003)
Hard Times Require Furious Dancing: New Poems (2010)
The World Will Follow Joy: Turning Madness into Flowers (2013)

Children's Books

Langston Hughes, American Poet (1974, 2002)
To Hell with Dying (1988)
Finding the Green Stone (1991)
There Is a Flower at the Tip of My Nose Smelling Me (2006)
Why War Is Never a Good Idea (2007)

Other Projects

I Love Myself When I'm Laughing… and Then Again When I Am Looking Mean and Impressive: A Zora Neale Hurston Reader (editor) (1979)
Warrior Marks: Female Genital Mutilation and the Sexual Blinding of Women (1993) (coauthored with Pratibha Parmar)
The World Has Changed: Conversations with Alice Walker (2010) (interviews)

FURTHER READING

Books

Kerr, Christine. *Bloom's How to Write About Alice Walker*. New York, NY: Chelsea House, 2008.

Lauret, Maria. *Alice Walker*. New York, NY: Palgrave Macmillan, 2011.

Lazo, Caroline. *Alice Walker: Freedom Writer*. Minneapolis, MN: Lerner, 2000.

Walker, Alice. *The Cushion in the Road: Meditation and Wandering as the Whole World Awakens to Being in Harm's Way*. New York, NY: The New Press, 2013.

White, Evelyn C. *Alice Walker*. New York, NY: W.W. Norton & Co., 2004.

Websites

Alice Walker, Talks at Google
youtube/MGYCTUTXdKE
Video of author's visit to Google, with readings.

Alice Walker Literary Society
www.emory.edu/alicewalker
Includes information about AWLS, videos, events, and other information.

Alice Walker Reads Her Letter to President-Elect Barack Obama on Democracy Now!
youtube/x9spSzk3NS0
Video of Alice Walker reading her letter to President-Elect Barack Obama.

Alice Walker's Garden
alicewalkersgarden.com
Author's personal website, including information on books, projects, and other resources.

INDEX